DAY *by* DAY
with BHAGAVAN

From the Diary of

A. DEVARAJA MUDALIAR

SRI RAMANASRAMAM
TIRUVANNAMALAI
INDIA

DAY BY DAY WITH BHAGAVAN (English):
From the Diary of A. Devaraja Mudaliar

First Combined Reprint in	*1968 (3000 copies)*
Second Reprint	*1977 (5000)*
Third Reprint	*1989 (3000)*
Fourth Reprint	*1995 (3000)*
Fifth Reprint	*2002 (3000)*
Sixth Reprint	*2006 (3000)*
Seventh Reprint (Hardbound)	*2011 (1000)*
Eighth Reprint	2014

1000 copies

CC No: 1013

ISBN: 978-81-88018-82-6

Price: ₹ 200

Published by:
V.S. Ramanan
President
SRI RAMANASRAMAM
Tiruvannamalai 606 603
Tamil Nadu, INDIA
Email : ashram@sriramanamaharshi.org
Web : www.sriramanamaharshi.org

Printed by:
Saibonds Print Systems Pvt. Ltd.,
Chennai 600 106, INDIA
email: saiprints@gmail.com

PREFACE

A word as to the origin of this work may not be out of place. It was my great good fortune to live for more than four years, from August 1942 till the end of 1946, at Sri Ramanasramam and to have the inestimable benefit of daily contact with our Bhagavan. After I had been there for some months various people who visited the Asramam began to suggest that it would be a good thing if I recorded Bhagavan's utterances on spiritual topics, either in answer to questions from visitors or in any other context. For a long time, however, I was too lazy to make the effort. Nevertheless, whenever I read the 'Gospel of Sri Ramakrishna Paramahamsa', as I used to now and then, I felt how desirable it was that a similar book should be compiled in the case of our Bhagavan. When I had drifted on like this for some years, on the morning of January 1st, 1945, within the space of about an hour, three different persons — a lawyer's clerk, son of Sankara Ammal doing service in the Asramam, a businessman of Madras by name M.V.P. Sastri, whom I had known since his boyhood at Chittoor, and O.P. Ramaswami Reddi, who later became Chief Minister of Madras — all urged me to undertake the task as, in their kind opinion, I was best fitted for it besides having the necessary facility of constant close contact with Bhagavan.

The appeal coming from such widely different persons on the first day of the year and all of them approaching me in such quick succession and without any previous consultation amongst themselves made such a deep impression on me that I took it as a call really from Bhagavan. So, that very day I started keeping an Asramam Diary. My idea was to preserve for Bhagavan's devotees all that took place in the Asramam that might be of interest or importance from one point of view or another, and mainly Bhagavan's answers to questions addressed to him by visitors from all quarters of the globe, for many of whom I acted as a sort of official translator in Bhagavan's Court.

I told Bhagavan of the circumstances under which I started the work, thus asking for his blessing on it. Then I obtained permission from the *Sarvadhikari*. Also, for the first few days I read out to Bhagavan whatever I had recorded so that he could correct me anywhere where I had gone wrong. Even when I was interpreting Bhagavan to visitors, if I made the slightest mistake Bhagavan would pull me up. Whenever I myself was in doubt as to what Bhagavan meant I used to ask for further clarification and Bhagavan willingly explained things again for my benefit. After the first two or three days I gave up reading my entries to Bhagavan daily, but on any day when I was in doubt whether I had accurately recorded what Bhagavan had said, I used to read out my entry for the day and correct it wherever he indicated that it was necessary.

Only a part of these records of mine seems to be available to the Asramam authorities for publication just now. I am glad that at least so much is to be published by them immediately. I believe they came into existence because Bhagavan willed it and I believe it is his will that at least a part of them should now appear in print. I hope and pray to Bhagavan that the publication may prove not merely of interest but of great use to those who read it and that he may bestow his grace on all who go through it in earnestness and faith.

1st January 1952 A. DEVARAJA MUDALIAR

Day by Day with Bhagavan

16-3-45 Morning

A visitor: Should I give up my business and take to reading books on Vedanta?

Bhagavan: If the objects have an independent existence, *i.e.*, if they exist anywhere apart from you, then it may be possible for you to go away from them. But they don't exist apart from you; they owe their existence to you, your thought. So, where can you go, to escape them? As for reading books on Vedanta, you may go on reading any number of them. They can only tell you, 'Realise the Self within you'. The Self cannot be found in books. You have to find it out for yourself, in yourself.

Evening

Almost the same question was put by another visitor in the afternoon and Bhagavan said, "Where can you go, fleeing from the world or objects? They are like the shadow of a man, which the man cannot flee from. There is a funny story of a man who wanted to bury his shadow. He dug a deep pit and, seeing his shadow at the bottom, was glad he could bury it so deep. He went on filling the pit and when he had completely filled it up he was surprised and disappointed to find the shadow on top. Even so, the objects or thoughts of them will be with you always, till you realise the Self."

17-3-45 Afternoon

Mr. T.P. Ramachandra Aiyar asked Bhagavan about the meaning of ஆர் ஒளி in the stanza of 'உள்ளது நாற்பது' (*Reality in Forty Verses*).

B: ஆர் ஒளி means நிறைந்த ஒளி. It refers to that light of *manas* in which we see all the world, both the known and the unknown of the world. There is first the white light, so to call it, of the Self, which transcends both light and darkness. In it no object can be seen. There is neither seer nor seen. Then there is total darkness or *avidya* in which also no objects are seen. But from the Self proceeds a reflected light, the light of pure *manas*, and it is this light which gives room for the existence of all the film of the world which is seen neither in total light nor in total darkness, but only in the subdued or reflected light. It is this light which is referred to in the stanza.

18-3-45

On or about 15-3-45 Bhagavan had asked someone in the hall to read aloud *Bhakta Vijayam*, to illustrate from the story of Tulasi Das, how one totally immersed in sensual life, suddenly recoils and goes to the other extreme of a highly religious life. In the story, Tulasi Das runs away from wife and home and is mad after Hari at Banaras. The wife and mother go and entreat him to come back, reminding him of his great love for them all. He takes no notice of them at all, but asks them, "Has my Hari come? Yes. He is coming there!" etc. He was mad after Hari alone and took interest in nothing else. When this portion was being read out, Bhagavan said, "I was somewhat like this at Madura. Going to school, books in hand, I would be eagerly desiring and expecting that God would suddenly appear before me in the sky; and so I would be looking up at the sky. What sort of progress could such a one make in his studies at school!"

[This was apparently shortly before he left Madura. I have never heard before, either from Bhagavan or from others, that he was so God-mad at Madura. So I record it here.]

19-3-45 Morning

A visitor from Sind, very probably Kundanlal A. Mahatani of Hyderabad, Sind, (now Pakistan) asked: "It is said the world and the objects that we see are all unreal, like the snake in the rope. It is also stated in other places that the seer and the seen are the same. If the seer and the seen are same, then how can we say that the seen is unreal?"

B.: All that is meant is that the seen regarded as an independent entity, independent of the Self, is unreal. The seen is not different from the seer. What exists is the one Self, not a seer and a seen. The seen regarded as the Self is real.

V.: It is said the world is like a dream. But there is this difference between dream and the waking state. In dream I see my friends or relations and go through some experiences with them. When I wake up and ask those friends or relations whom I met in the dream about the dream, they know nothing about it. But in the waking state what I see and hear is corroborated by so many others.

B.: You should not mix up the dream and the waking states. Just as you seek corroboration about the waking state experiences from those whom you see in the waking state, you must ask for corroboration about the dream experiences from those whom you saw in the dream state, *i.e.*, when you were in the dream. Then in the dream, those friends or relations whom you saw in the dream would corroborate you.

The main point is, are you prepared when awake to affirm the reality of any of your dream experiences? Similarly, one who has awakened into *jnana* cannot affirm the reality of the waking experience. From his viewpoint, the waking state is dream.

V.: It is said only some are chosen for Self-realisation and those alone could get it. It is rather discouraging.

B.: All that is meant is, we cannot by our own *buddhi*, unaided by God's grace, achieve realisation of Self.

I added, "Bhagavan also says that even that grace does not come arbitrarily, but because one deserves it by one's own efforts either in this or in previous lives."

V.: Human effort is declared to be useless. What incentive can any man then have to better himself?

I asked, "Where is it said you should make no effort or that your effort is useless?"

The visitor thereupon showed the portion in *Who am I?* where it is said, "When there is one great Force looking after all the world, why should we bother what we shall do?" I pointed out that what is deprecated there is not human effort, but the feeling that "I am the doer". Bhagavan approved of my explanation, when I asked him if it was not so.

Afternoon

Bhagavan said he once had a dream that he went to Palni and that he then devoured the Palni God (Lord Subramanya); and that he had at another time a dream that he visited Tiruchendur temple (where also the deity is Lord Subramanya). The details of this dream Bhagavan does not remember.

I remembered that some people once wanted to know if a *jivanmukta* can have dreams. The doubt is natural, because we believe *jnanis* have no sleep like ordinary men. So they may not have dreams. I therefore asked Bhagavan about this matter, and he said, "If the *jnani* can have a waking state, what is the difficulty about his having a dream state? But of course as his waking state is different from the ordinary man's waking state, so his dream state also will be different from the ordinary man's dream state. Whether in waking or in dream he will not slip from his real state which is sometimes called the fourth or *turiya* state."

24-3-45 Afternoon

I was reading *Vichara Sangraha* (*Self Enquiry*). I came across the statement that something in the heart நான் நான் என்று ஸ்புரித்துக் கொண்டிருக்கிறது, *i.e.*, something is shining or sounding as 'I-I' in the heart. I have always had doubt what exactly the word *sphurana* means. So I asked Bhagavan and he said, "It means 'விளங்குவது or விளக்குவது' *i.e.*, which shines or illuminates." I asked, "Is it not a sound we hear?" Bhagavan said, "Yes, we may say it is a sound we *feel* or *become* aware *of*". He also referred to the dictionary and said, "The word means 'throbbing', 'springing on the memory', 'flashing across the mind'. Thus both sound and light may be implied in the word *sphurana*. Everything has come from light and sound."

I asked Bhagavan what it is that 'shines', whether it is the ego or the Self. He said it was neither the one, nor the other, but something in between the two, that it is something which is a combination of the 'I' (Self) and the 'I-thought' (ego), and that the Self is without even this *sphurana*.

Explaining how the Self is mere light and how it is both the word or sound and also that out of which word or sound originally came, Bhagavan said, "Man has three bodies, the gross one made of the five elements, the *sukshma* or subtle one made of *manas* and *prana*, and the *jiva*. Similarly even *Iswara* has three bodies. All the manifested universe is His gross body, light and sound are His *sukshma* body, and the Self His *jiva*."

25-3-45 Afternoon

One P. Sri Krishniah of Peddapalayam, near Tenali, came to the Asramam on the 22nd and started reading with Bhagavan's permission a small work on the life of Dhanurdasa (பிள்ளை உறங்கா வில்லி சரித்திரம்), composed by him in Telugu verse and dedicated to Bhagavan. The dedication is both humorous and touching, the poem being regarded as a virgin offered to Bhagavan for marriage, as *kanyadana* is considered the best gift. He seems to have written the dedication first and later composed the work. Thus he chose his son-in-law before he begot his daughter and in the end of his dedication he says, "You have already wedded *mukti*. Please take this girl of mine also and treat her kindly and well, correcting her faults and ignoring her weaknesses. I cannot ask you to go over to our house, though you have become my son-in-law, as so many Rajahs and others are always coming to you here for your *darshan*." He also says, "By this marriage of my *vaishnava* daughter to Bhagavan, *advaita* and *visishtadvaita* have become wedded."

He read the dedication once again on the 25th afternoon and also read out his parting or farewell song of which the following is a free translation: "For men like us, various desires often occur. Some get fulfilled, others not. Here all my desires got their satisfaction. One of my desires was to compose a life of Dhanurdasa in verse, another was to come here in company with my friends and relations and to offer the hand of my girl (the poem) to you, a third was to eat to my satisfaction in your company at the above marriage feast, a fourth was to stay here a few days and feast my eyes on a sight of you. All these together I got, by virtue of your grace. Please give me leave to depart. Oh, one of pure life! What magic have you stored in this form of yours, that those who have seen it become entranced? What power have you instilled in this air, that it is able to ward off all distress? What drug have you mixed in the water of this place that it is able to subdue all ailments? What powder of enchantment have you spread over these premises that those who come here feel reluctant to depart? You alone can know your greatness. However long we may remain, the feet will not move to depart from here. What can I do? Please grant me leave to depart, *purushottama* (best among men)."

31-3-45

One night, a few days ago, after supper, when Bhagavan was resting on his cot in the verandah, east of his hall, something funny took place. He was facing south. Chadwick was sitting behind Bhagavan's back. Soon after Bhagavan took his seat and leaned on the cushions, Chadwick from behind stealthily and unnoticed fanned Bhagavan. When Bhagavan turned and looked, Chadwick withdrew the fan and remained still. When Bhagavan turned his face south, Chadwick resumed fanning again. Bhagavan turned round and Chadwick stopped. Bhagavan was left wondering how he got the breeze. Chadwick then laughed out and Bhagavan joined in the laughter. This shows how even with such an eminent Master a devotee can play and both can enjoy the joke like children.

Afternoon

It seems a visitor, the Raja of Sivaghar in U.P., told Bhagavan that he had surrendered himself to Bhagavan and Bhagavan should give him *jnana*. Bhagavan referred to an article on Nama Dev's insistence on the importance of the Lord's name, in the September 1937 issue of *Vision*, where it is pointed out that only when the 'I', the ego, is surrendered the significance of the Lord's name will be realized. When I entered the hall the story of how *Ashtavakra Gita* came to be taught was being recounted in English, for the benefit of the above Raja and other visitors. After the story was read out, Bhagavan said, "Because *Brahma jnana* is not something external, which is somewhere far away where you can go and get it, you cannot say that it will take so long or so short a time to attain it. It is always with you. You are That! The story of *Ashtavakra Gita* is intended to teach that for getting *Brahma jnana* all that is necessary is to surrender yourself completely to the guru, to surrender your notion of 'I' and 'mine'. If these are surrendered, what remains is the Reality. Then, it becomes impossible to state what further time it would take to attain *Brahma jnana*. It would be wrong to state that it takes as much time as a man would require to put his other foot into the second stirrup after having placed one foot in the first stirrup. The moment when ego is completely surrendered, the Self shines."

Proceeding, Bhagavan quoted the last two lines of the following stanza from *Yoga Vasishta*: "நானெனும் பொருள்கா ணாதோர் ஞானவா காயங் காணார். நானெனும் பொருளைக் கண்டோர் ஞானவா காய மாவார்; நானெனு மகங்காரங்கள் ஞானவிண் மதியைமூடி னானெம் பரம வாம்ப னன்மலர் விரியாதன்றே." which state that unless the cloud of the 'I' or 'ego-sense' which covers the moon of the Divine consciousness (*chidakasa*) is removed, the lily of the heart which knows nothing of the sense of 'I' (*ahankara*) will not open out in full bloom.

Bhagavan also added, "We have to contend against age-long *samskaras*. They will all go. Only, they go comparatively soon in the case of those who have already made *sadhana* in the past, and late in the case of the others." In this connection I asked, "Do these *samskaras* go gradually or will they suddenly disappear one day? I ask this, because though I have remained fairly long here I do not perceive any gradual change in me." Bhagavan asked, "When the sun rises, does the darkness go gradually or all at once?"

Another visitor asked, "How to conquer passions?" Bhagavan said, "If the passions are something external to us we can take arms and ammunition and conquer them. They all come from within us. If, by looking into the source whence they issue, we see that they don't come out of us, we shall conquer them. It is the world and the objects in it that arouse our passions. But the world and these objects are only created by our mind. They don't exist during our sleep."

After all this talk Bhagavan drank a little water from his *kamandalam* and turning to his attendant enquired whether he had already drunk some water (*i.e.*, after he returned to the hall about 3-30 P.M.). The attendant said 'yes', and thereupon Bhagavan said he had forgotten it, and to make sure he drank some again. He further added, almost in an unguarded moment, as he rarely gives expression to such experiences of his, that sometimes he does not even know whether it is morning, mid-day or evening and has to look at the clock and try to remember before he knows what time of day it is. On one occasion, he has told me that he scratched his skin, where there was eczema once, as we scratch during sleep. And once when I was concerned over some physical pain of his, he told me he feels that pain 'கனுக்கண்டாற்போல்', *i.e.*, it was a passing and faint experience like that in a dream. These are clues to the sort of life Bhagavan leads in our midst, seeming to act and move and feel as we do, but really living in a world of his own where the things we experience don't exist.

5-6-45 Afternoon

Myself, Harindranath Chattopadhyaya, G.V. Subbaramayya and T. P. Ramachandra Aiyar were sitting in the front row just opposite Bhagavan in the hall and G.V.S. said to H.C. "I recently came across a typed copy of some of your verses made at Aurobindo Ashram, with Sri Aurobindo's notes on the margin highly commending some verses." Thereupon H.C. told Bhagavan, "I stayed at Aurobindo's Ashram for two years and I then made about 4000 sonnets and a poem of 50,000 lines plus other poetry." Apparently the fact that H.C. had been at Aurobindo's Ashram before for two years was news to Bhagavan, though it was not to some of us. This is the third visit of H.C. to Bhagavan. H.C. then gave us a recitation of two of his earliest poems and one out of those made at Pondicherry. They are given below. Bhagavan enjoyed the recitation.

THE EARTHEN GOBLET

(A conversation between the poet and the goblet)

"O silent goblet! red from head to heel,
    How did you feel
When you were being twirled
    Upon the Potter's wheel
Before the Potter gave you to the world?"
I felt a conscious impulse in my clay
    To break away
From the great Potter's hand
    That burned so warm.
I felt a vast
    Feeling of sorrow to be cast
Into my present form.
Before that fatal hour
    That saw me captive on the Potter's wheel
And cast into this crimson goblet-sleep,
    I used to feel
The fragrant friendship of a little flower
Whose root was in my bosom buried deep.
The Potter has drawn out the living breath of me,
And given me a form which is the death of me;
My past unshapely natural state was best,
With just one flower flaming through my breast.

PITCHERS OF CLAY

Outside the Potter's shop upon the way
In patient rows we stand, pitchers of clay —
Under a copper-clouded sky of gold
Expecting every moment to be sold.

Although we have no language, yet we feel
A bitterness towards the Potter's wheel

Which moulded us, what though without a flaw,
To shape, which is against our being's law.

Pitchers are beautiful and yet, indeed,
Even from beauty we would all be freed
And, slipping into Earth, secure escape
From the enchanted tyranny of shape.

Some of us pitchers, tired of being, drop
And break to pieces in the Potter's shop.
Pathetic things! What does the Potter care
For the pale weariness of Earthenware?

SHAPER SHAPED

In days gone by I used to be
A potter who would feel
His fingers mould the yielding clay
To patterns on his wheel;
But now, through wisdom lately won,
That pride has died away,
I have ceased to be the potter
And have learned to be the clay.

In other days I used to be
A poet through whose pen
Innumerable songs would come
To win the hearts of men;
But now, through new-got knowledge
Which I hadn't had so long,
I have ceased to be the poet
And have learned to be the song.

I was a fashioner of swords,
In days that now are gone,
Which on a hundred battle-fields
Glittered and gleamed and shone;

But now that I am brimming with
The silence of the Lord
I have ceased to be a sword-maker
And learned to be the sword.

In by-gone days I used to be
A dreamer who would hurl
On every side an insolence
Of emerald and pearl.
But now that I am kneeling
At the feet of the Supreme
I have ceased to be the dreamer
And have learned to be the dream.

After this I asked H.C. to recite before Bhagavan (or rather act as on the stage) a piece from a play of his in which a dock-labourer groaning under his work bursts out into a complaint. H.C. did so and all saw how moving a good recitation can be. After a while H.C. asked Bhagavan, "How is it, Bhagavan, we sometimes feel choked with tears in Bhagavan's Presence?" Bhagavan smiled and kept quiet. I said, "It is a good thing if one's tears gush forth like that and even of Bhagavan it is recorded that when he used to go and stand before the image in the temple at Madura, before he came here, tears used to flow involuntarily out of his eyes, not as the result of any joy or pain, but purely out of *bhakti*." Bhagavan was thereupon kind enough to add, "Even after coming here such a thing has happened. Even on reading or hearing touching passages from books such a thing has happened. Apparently a stock of emotional tears is latent in so many of us, so that at any opportune moment, or on the slightest provocation, they well out without any control on our part." Then Bhagavan narrated, very dramatically as is usual with him, an incident which occurred when he was about 22 and living in the Virupakshi Cave. It seems he was sitting on a rock near the cave and a boy of about 8 or 10 years came there, looked at Bhagavan and, not being able to bear the sight of such a young and bright person taking to such a hard life of penance, was so moved to compassion that he started to sob and sobbed violently for some time. Bhagavan said, "Who could say what was the reason for his sobbing and why tears flowed out of him merely at his seeing me?" Bhagavan continued in a reminiscent mood later in the day and added that another boy, also about 8 or 10 years old, met Bhagavan another day in his Virupakshi cave days and took such pity on Bhagavan that the following conversation took place between them. Bhagavan was sitting on a rock near the cave, all alone, and the boy came and met him there.

Boy: Why are you here, all alone, like this?

Bhagavan: I had some trouble at home and so have come away like this.

Boy: Then how about your food?

Bhagavan: I eat if anybody gives me anything to eat.

Boy: I have a good master. I shall take you to him. First, you may have to volunteer your services free. If he approves of your work, he will give you three pies a day and gradually he will increase it to six pies, and so on.

Bhagavan: Yes, please do so.

Bhagavan added, "There was no doubt that the boy was very much concerned over what he considered my sad plight and that he was moved by great and genuine pity."

Bhagavan also recalled the incident in which an old Harijan woman, one day about noon time, accosted Bhagavan on one of his rambles on the rough jungle path down the hill and remarked, "உன்னைப் பாடையிலே வைக்க! ஒரே இடத்திலே சிவனே யென்று இருக்கக்கூடாதா?". ("A curse on you! Why can't you stay quiet in a place?")

Bhagavan said, "Yes, this is very good advice," and also slapped his own cheeks, as if in punishment for not having known what the woman taught then.

Relating the above incident, Bhagavan said that, when first the old woman began abusing him, he could not understand how he deserved it and was dumbfounded as to what offence he could have given to the woman.

This made Mr. T.S. Rajagopal recall an article by one Miss Souris in a Telugu journal called *Bharati*. For the benefit of Harindranath Chattopadhyaya and some others who were new to it, Bhagavan again related the incident to the merriment of all of us.

Bhagavan said, "One day the Mauni brought the *tapals* (post) as usual. I left the papers and magazines on the couch and was looking at the letters. After showing the *tapals* to me, Mauni left the hall and took the *Bharati* number with him, saying he would read it and bring it back. After a little time he came back, left the magazine on my couch and was going out. While near the door, he suddenly said, 'What a thief is Bhagavan!' and before I could ask why he said so, he had gone. I was wondering what I could have done to have made the Mauni reproach me like that. It sort of rankled in my mind. And only after I read the article in the *Bharati* and came to the very last sentence in it, which was 'Oh, what a thief is Bhagavan!' I could understand the joke."

23-8-45 Morning 10 a.m.

Mr. Kundanlal Mahatani, of Karachi, who has been staying here for about eight months, asked Bhagavan for direct *upadesa*, urging that all the books emphasise that nothing can be achieved by anybody except with the help of *upadesa* from a guru and that though he has read all the directions given by Bhagavan for Self-enquiry and attaining stillness of mind where God can be realised as 'I', he still did not know what was the best method for him individually. This was not the first time he had made such a request. At least twice before, once in June and again in July, he had done so. Neither then nor now did Bhagavan make any reply. The gentleman was very much dejected and was worried whether he was not fit to receive any reply and whether he had committed any offence on account of which Bhagavan was not pleased to reply.

Later in the day, in the evening, Bhagavan in connection with some other matter, referred to a Tamil poem, and to look at a translation of it, Mr. Mahatani borrowed my note book on 24-8-45. As often happens to devotees, who indirectly receive necessary instructions, Mr. Mahatani found in the note book instructions which suited him. Further, on 25-8-45 about 2 p.m., when he was having a nap he had a vision in his dream in which Bhagavan appeared and quoted a Sanskrit *sloka* and interpreted it as meaning, 'There is no better karma or *bhakti* than enquiry into the Self'. He was greatly delighted and later in the same dream another devotee put the same question to Bhagavan and Mahatani repeated the above answer to him and laughed heartily. All this was reported to Bhagavan on the 25th by Mahatani.

8-9-45 Morning

Mr. Subba Rao of Bezwada asked Bhagavan, "What is the difference between imagination and vision?"

Bhagavan: One is voluntary and the other is not. But in the ultimate analysis, though not in the immediate present, even vision must have had its origin in the voluntary sphere.

Subba Rao: As dreams have their origin there?

B: Yes.

Another Visitor: It is said that our waking life is also a dream, similar to our dream during sleep. But in our dreams we make no conscious effort to get rid of the dream and to awake, but the dream itself comes to an end without any effort on our part and we become awake. Similarly why should not the waking state, which is in reality only another sort of dream, come to an end of its own accord, and without any effort on our part, and land us in *jnana* or real awakening?

B: Your thinking that you have to make an effort to get rid of this dream of the waking state and your making efforts to attain *jnana* or real awakening are all parts of the dream. When you attain *jnana* you will see there was neither the dream during sleep, nor the waking state, but only yourself and your real state.

I pressed Bhagavan, "But what is the answer to the question? Why should not the waking state also pass like our dreams without any effort on our part and land us in *jnana*, as a dream passes off and leaves us awake?"

B: Who can say that the dream passed off of its own accord? If the dream came on, as is generally supposed, as the result of our past thoughts or karma, probably the same karma also decides how long it should last and how after that time it should cease.

I was still unsatisfied and, as the result of further talk with Bhagavan, I feel that the waking state, though a sort of dream, is clearly distinct from the dream during sleep in this, namely that during dream it never occurs to us that it is a dream, whereas in the waking state we are able to argue and understand from books and gurus and from some phenomena that it may be only dream after all. Because of this, it may be our duty to make an effort to wake into *jnana*. Bhagavan says that we don't deem a dream, a dream till we wake up, that the dream looks quite real while it lasts; and that similarly this waking state will not appear a dream till we wake up into *jnana*. Still, it seems to me that, because of the above difference between the dream and the waking states, our effort is called for.

14-9-45

Three or four days ago Mr. Desai, Retired Sub-Judge, asked Bhagavan (with reference to what is said in *Ramana Gita*), "How to direct the *prana* or life-current into the *sushumna nadi*, so that as stated in *Ramana Gita* we could achieve the severance of the *chit-jada granthi*?" Bhagavan said, "By enquiring 'Who am I?' "

"The yogi may be definitely aiming at rousing the *kundalini* and sending it up the *sushumna*. The *jnani* may not be having this as his object. But both achieve the same result, that of sending the Life-force up the *sushumna* and severing the *chit-jada granthi*. *Kundalini* is only another name for *atma* or Self or *sakti*. We talk of it as being inside the body, because we conceive ourselves as limited by this body. But it is in reality both inside and outside, being no other than Self or the *sakti* of Self."

Desai: How to churn up the *nadis*, so that the *kundalini* may go up the *sushumna*?

Bhagavan: Though the *yogi* may have his methods of breath-control, *pranayama, mudras*, etc., for this object, the *jnani's* method is only that of enquiry. When by this method the mind is merged in the Self, the Self, its *sakti* or *kundalini*, rises automatically.

The next day a visitor asked Bhagavan, with reference to the words *dhimahi* in the *gayatri*, "What is the idea meant? I am not able rightly to grasp it."

B: The words only mean fixing the *aham* in the Self, though literally they mean, "We meditate".

Visitor: I am not able to form a conception of the '*Tat*' or the Self. Then, how am I to fix the *aham* in the *Tat*.

B: Why should you bother to conceive the *Tat* which you don't know? Try to find out the 'I' that you know, what it is and whence it arises. That is enough.

16-9-45 Afternoon

A visitor asked, "What should one, who is an absolute beginner, do in this (*i.e.*, spiritual) line?"

Bhagavan: The very fact that you put this question shows you know what to do. It is because you feel the want of peace, that you are anxious to take some steps to secure peace. Because I have a little pain in my foot, I am applying this ointment.

Visitor: What is the method to be adopted for securing peace?

B: The conception that there is a goal and a path to it, is wrong. We are the goal or peace always. To get rid of the notion that we are not peace is all that is required.

V: All books say that the guidance of a Guru is necessary.

B: The Guru will say only what I am saying now. He will not give you anything you have not already. It is impossible for anyone to get what he has not got already. Even if he gets any such thing, it will go as it came. What comes will also go. What always is will alone remain. The Guru cannot give you anything new, which you have not already. Removal of the notion that we have not realised the Self is all that is required. We are always the Self. Only, we don't realise it.

The Asramam compounder asked some questions about his experiences during meditation. Bhagavan explained that the Self is the one reality that always exists and it is by its light all other things are seen. We forget it and concentrate on the appearances. The light in the hall burns, both when persons are present there and when they are absent, both when persons are enacting something as in a theatre and when nothing is being enacted. It is the light which enabled us to see the hall, the persons and the acting. We are so engrossed with the objects or appearances revealed by the light that we pay no attention to the light. In the waking state or dream state, in which things appear, and in the sleep state, in which we see nothing, there is always the light of consciousness or Self, like the hall-lamp always burning. The thing to do is to concentrate on the seer and not on the seen, not on the objects, but on the Light which reveals them.

18-9-45 Afternoon

A group of Bengalis have come. One of them has recently lost a child. He put the question to Bhagavan, "Why did that child die so young? Is it his karma or our karma that we should have this grief?"

Bhagavan: The *prarabdha* which the child had to work out in this life was over and so it passed away. So we may call it the child's karma. So far as you are concerned, it is open to you not to grieve over it, but to remain calm and unaffected by it, being convinced that the child was not yours but always only God's, that God gave and God took away. And in this connection Bhagavan took out the *Yoga Vasishta* in English to refer to the story of Punya and Pavana. Strange to say, when he casually opened the book, it actually opened at the story he had in mind. And from the book he asked me to read out the portion where Punya advises his brother Pavana not to grieve foolishly over the death of their parents, pointing out that Pavana had had innumerable births in the past, in each one of which he had a number of relations and that exactly as he is not mourning for the death of all those relations now, he should not now mourn for the death of their father either.

The visitor asked, "When a person dies while yet a child and another lives long, which of them is the greater sinner?"

B: I cannot say.

I told the visitor that the data he had given could not by themselves enable anyone to judge which was the greater sinner.

Visitor: If a person lives long, he has greater chances of perfecting steps to reach realisation.

B: The person dying young may soon be reborn and have in that life better chances of striving towards realisation than the other person living long in this life.

A visitor asked, "When it is said that we must renounce all activities, is it meant that we should reduce our activities as much as possible?"

B: By giving up activities is meant giving up attachment to activities or the fruits thereof, giving up the notion 'I am the doer'. The activities for going through which this body has come, will have to be gone through. There is no question of giving up such activities, whatever one may or may not like.

27-9-45

Bhagavan suddenly seems to have felt like visiting Skandasramam, where for about a week now repairs are being done; and so without notice to anybody, after the midday meal, Bhagavan, on his usual after-lunch stroll, wended his way towards Skandasramam, followed by attendant Rangaswami. Few knew of this till about 3-30 p.m. But after 3-30 the news gradually spread and almost all the devotees went up to Skandasramam and found Bhagavan seated on the terraced platform in front, which overlooks the temple and town. We found Bhagavan in very good spirits and relating various events and incidents that happened during his stay there previous to his coming to Ramanasramam. Bhagavan had a mind even to continue stopping there and to spend the night there. But all the devotees had thronged there and none looked likely to move till Bhagavan moved. So at about 5-30 p.m. Bhagavan started, looked at the various parts of the Asramam, telling us where he used to sleep, where he used to sit, and where mother sat, where they cooked, where the old tap was, and so on, and then got down by the steps. On the way he visited Virupakshi Cave and explained about his life there also. Here he pointed out the மாடத்துப்

பிள்ளையார் மாடம் the niche, which is now a small window on the wall facing east in the verandah in front of the cave. மாடத்துப் பிள்ளையார் (*i.e.*, Ganesa in the niche) is an expression occurring in two stanzas, one composed by Iswara Swami and another composed by Bhagavan in praise of a Ganesa image placed in that niche at the time Bhagavan was staying in Virupakshi Cave. Some *sannyasi* who seems to have been living in that cave for some days now brought water from the well nearby and Bhagavan drank it with pleasure. Then Bhagavan left the cave for Ramanasramam, slowly wending his way down the steps. At the foot we all sat with him under a *pipal* tree around which there is a platform, close to Guha Namasivaya's Cave. Satakopa Naidu of Bangalore brought some பொரி (puffed rice) and groundnuts. All the crowd sat there with Bhagavan and enjoyed this picnic. By this time it was getting dark, and we all started along the hill track leading to the town through Guha Namasivaya's Cave and along the main road, and reached the Asramam about 8-30 p.m.

It was a marvel that Bhagavan did this trip all on foot in this way, the more so because his left big toe had become either dislocated or badly sprained on 26-8-45, and as a result thereof is still having some pain there.

Since Bhagavan left Skandasramam, he had gone there two or three times within about a year or two after his settling down here. But after that, *i.e.*, for nearly twenty-two years now, he has never gone there till today. Bhagavan was in great spirits and all the way down from Skandasramam to Ramanasramam he stopped once every few yards and related various incidents and made remarks about some trees having disappeared in the interval and about some cracks in the Virupakshi Cave, about the place where Jadaswami rolled stones down on Bhagavan (though Bhagavan would have it, it was all only in fun), and about the heavy rain and storm that came on one night and displaced huge boulders and created a spring for the convenience of Bhagavan and his followers.

6-10-45

It was reported to Bhagavan that somehow under cover of the leaves, two mangoes had escaped the notice of the monkeys and had grown to quite a big size and that they were discovered today, and that one was taken away by the monkeys and the other left behind. This made Bhagavan think of the expression 'இலை மறைவு' (under cover of leaves) and by association of ideas he thought of a stanza in 'பிரபுலிங்க லீலை' (*Prabhulinga Lila*), the 9th in 'மருள சங்கர தேவர் கதி' and read out to us a few stanzas, where it is related that once Marula Sankara was living like a madman near the place where leaf-plates, after eating, were thrown away in front of a mutt. Neither the head of the mutt nor the disciples knew anything about this man. But when Allama Prabhu went that way, Marula got up and prostrated himself at his feet and Allama Prabhu in turn took him up and embraced him. For, each knew the other's worth. Only a *jnani* can recognise a *jnani*. One who indulges in *kriya, charya*, or yoga can be recognised by these activities which he goes through. But in the case of a *jnani* there is no such external thing by which we can recognise him.

I note this incident, the more particularly because some who come here also sometimes have found it difficult to recognise Bhagavan's worth and have even asked me, "What is there about this Bhagavan of yours which makes you think he is a great man or a realised soul? He eats and sleeps and does everything else like us."

8-10-45 Afternoon

Janaki, daughter of Mr. A. Subbarayadu, the Deputy Superintendent of Police of this place, asked Bhagavan, "I want to do *nama smarana* always. But I am also keen on getting higher education. (She is in the first year College class). What should I do?".

Bhagavan: There is nothing contradictory between the two desires.

Janaki: If I am always doing *nama smarana*, how can I carry on studies for which the mind is required?

Bhagavan did not answer. But Frydman and I told the girl, "It was said both could be done at the same time." Frydman added, "Give the mind to studies and the heart to God."

9-10-45 Afternoon

Mr. K. Mahatani asked in continuation of the above, "If we want to succeed in any enterprise in the world, we must give our whole mind and heart to it. Otherwise we cannot succeed. So it is rather impracticable to devote one's mind both to God and worldly activity."

Bhagavan: If one keeps fixed in the Self, the activities will still go on and their success will not be affected. One should not have the idea that one is the doer. The activities will still go on. That force, by whatever name you may call it, which brought the body into existence will see to it that the activities which this body is meant to go through are brought about.

Mr. Mahatani was still not quite satisfied and thereupon Bhagavan referred him to read an article on renunciation which is found at the end of the Gita Press edition of *Bhagavad Gita*. This article mentions seven stages of renunciation and Bhagavan said, "Let Mr. Mahatani see if anything in this article appeals to him". I read out the whole article in the hall for the benefit of all, as Bhagavan desired. It is said there that one who has reached the seventh stage of renunciation will not feel even when his body is cut by a weapon or some other suffering is inflicted on him. When this portion was being read Bhagavan remembered the following poem.

வஞ்சகர் வேல்கொடு மார்பி னெறியினு
மெஞ்ச வேதழன் மூடி யெரியினு
நஞ்சி ஞுரழ ஞுகை நலியினு
மஞ்சி டாரது வானந்த மாவதே.

(*i.e.*, They won't be afraid even if guileful enemies stab their chest or they are surrounded by fire or bitten by a cobra, all will be bliss for them). This is found in Ponnambala Swami's commentary on *Bhagavad Gita* in Tamil stanzas, Chapter VI Verse 17 (Page 150 of the Asramam book). Continuing this topic, I said, "It is true such things are said in the books. But we see that the *jnani* feels pain. Even one like Sri Ramakrishna Paramahamsa felt pain when he had cancer of the throat and cried out, 'Why has mother sent this pain to me?' "

Bhagavan: It may be like that in the beginning, due to long association or habit. But afterwards it will pass off.

In this connection I must record that long ago, once when Bhagavan was suffering from some illness and I expressed concern, Bhagavan was pleased to explain to me that he felt the pain as in a dream and no more.

10-10-45 Morning

I came across the following on pages 110 and 111 in *Letters to my friends* by Gilbert Henry Gedge in the September 1945 issue of *Science of Thought Review*.

"Again, people sometimes say that when they are at work there is no time to be thinking about God; their mind has to be 'on the job'.

"Now, friend, I say to you once again that for all these different matters the remedy is the same. Seek first the kingdom of God. When that is done all things fall into their proper place and their proper perspective in our mind. God is in you and in all your circumstances now, and you and your own individual little world are in God now. Realisation of that fact involves also the realisation that all things in your life are in their right place and order, that the law of God rules your whole life and circumstances. Nothing whatever can be excluded from the rule of that law when we realise that our life is actually lived in God. Even when we are engaged in our daily work it helps to think of God, to recognise His presence with us, within and around us and in our job. It helps even more to see the job as God's work, for when we do so, we find new and better ways of doing it and are blessed in the doing."

I read this out to Bhagavan and he approved of it and even asked me to show it to Mr. Mahatani as bearing on last evening's discourse.

11-10-45 Morning

Mr. G.V. Subbaramayya arrived. Just then Bhagavan was reading a Telugu translation of his preface to *Dakshinamurti Stotra* in Tamil. A few days ago Mr. P.C. Desai brought to Bhagavan's notice a Gujarati book on *Dakshinamurti Stotra*, written by himself. And in connection with it Bhagavan asked me to make for Mr. P.C. Desai's benefit an English translation of Bhagavan's Tamil preface to the *Stotra*. This led Smt. Nagamma to make a Telugu translation. Reading and explaining the above Telugu translation, Bhagavan told Mr. G.V. Subbaramayya practically all that he had told Mr. P.C. Desai before. The gist of it is this: "Dakshinamurti, *i.e.*, the great Siva himself could not express the truth of the one Reality except by silence. But that silence could not be understood except by the very advanced. The others have to be told. And yet how is one to say in words that which God himself could not express? Sankara therefore advises the method of praising Dakshinamurti and with that as the ostensible object really seeks to explain that all is Brahman. In the first four stanzas he explains the nature of the world, since what prevents our knowing the reality is the world and if its (*i.e.*, world's) nature is understood, the obstacle in the way of realising truth will be removed. In the next four stanzas he explains the nature of the *jiva*. Then he explains the connection between the two and teaches that all is Self. Trying to explain the scheme and gist of Sankara's *Dakshinamurti Stotra*, I wrote the above brief preface."

18-10-45 Morning

A visitor from the Punjab asked Bhagavan, "When I meditate I feel a certain bliss at times. On such occasions, should I ask myself 'Who is it that experiences this bliss'?"

Bhagavan: If it is the real bliss of the Self that is experienced, *i.e.*, if the mind has merged really in the Self, such a doubt will not arise at all. The question itself shows real bliss was not reached.

All doubts will cease only when the doubter and his source have been found. There is no use removing doubts. If we clear one doubt, another doubt will arise and there will be no end of doubts. But if the doubter is found to be really non-existent, by seeking for the source of the doubter, then all doubts will cease.

Visitor: Sometimes I hear internal sounds. What should I do when such things happen?

Bhagavan: Whatever may happen, keep up the enquiry into the Self, asking 'Who hears these sounds?' till the reality is reached.

A second edition of *Sri Ramana, the Sage of Arunagiri* by Aksharajna has recently come out. Sampling it here and there, I came across the passage that Bhagavan blesses his disciples in various ways, the mild by sight, the middling by thought and the advanced by touch. Once when I was reading *Kaivalyam* in Tamil I asked Bhagavan, "Many books speak of Gurus blessing disciples or giving *diksha* by touching the head of the disciple with their hands or feet. How is it then Bhagavan never does any such thing?" Bhagavan then told me, "It is true the books mention the three ways of *diksha, viz.*, by sight, touch and thought. But *diksha* by thought is really the best." So I asked Bhagavan today about the above passage in Aksharajna's book, saying, "He also knew Bhagavan well. He must have had some reason for saying so." Bhagavan said, "I don't know," and added, "I might have touched some by accident or for other reasons, not with the intention of giving *diksha*." In this connection, I may record on the authority of Mr. G.V. Subbaramayya (who was present when the incident occurred) that some years ago, an old, venerable and distinguished-looking ascetic from North India was staying in the Asramam for about a month, that he used to repeat the entire *Bhagavad Gita* and that on the day of his departure Bhagavan touched him in the following circumstances:

Bhagavan returned to the hall after his morning stroll and sat on the couch. While his feet were still touching the ground, the above ascetic fell at Bhagavan's feet, his head almost touching Bhagavan's feet and prayed that Bhagavan should bless him with *diksha* by touch, adding he would not get up till Bhagavan did so. Bhagavan thereupon was pleased to put one of his hands on the old man's head and lifted him with the other hand.

While all this talk was going on, Dr. Srinivasa Rao was massaging Bhagavan's feet which had some rheumatic trouble. Bhagavan humorously remarked, "Doctor is now giving *diksha* to me by touch." About 15 days ago, when the Doctor was massaging Bhagavan's feet, Bhagavan asked him to stop, saying, "What you have done is enough. You may go and sit down. I shall do some massaging myself and get some *punya*. Why should you alone have all the *punya*?" and began massaging himself. (*punya* is spiritual merit earned, for example, by service to a Master).

19-10-45 Morning

A barrister from Bombay asked Bhagavan, "I have read the works of Bhagavan and others and, though I can understand them intellectually, I have not been able to realise anything in experience. I have tried Bhagavan's method for about six years and yet I have not made any progress. When I meditate, other thoughts come. For people like me, living in cities and doing our work and coming here only occasionally, what *sadhana* would Bhagavan advise so that we may succeed better than I have so far been able to do?"

Bhagavan: Your real nature is always there, your meditation, etc., come only temporarily. Reality being your Self, there is nothing for you to realise. All that is required is that you should give up regarding the unreal as real, which is what all are doing. The object of all meditation, *dhyana* or *japa* is only that, to give up all thoughts regarding the not-self, to give up many thoughts and to keep to the one thought.

As for *sadhana*, there are many methods. You may do *vichara*, asking yourself 'Who am I?' or, if that does not appeal to you, you may do *dhyana* 'I am Brahman' or otherwise, or you may concentrate on a *mantra* or name in *japa*. The object is to make the mind one-pointed, to concentrate it on one thought and thus exclude our many thoughts, and if we do this, eventually even the one thought will go and the mind will get extinguished in its source.

Visitor: In actual practice I find I am not able to succeed in my efforts. Unless Bhagavan's grace descends on me I cannot succeed.

Bhagavan: Guru's grace is always there. You imagine it is something, somewhere high up in the sky, far away, and has to descend. It is really inside you, in your heart, and the moment (by any of the methods) you effect subsidence or merger of the mind into its source, the grace rushes forth, spouting as from a spring, from within you.

Another visitor asked, "What is the reality of this world?"

Bhagavan: If you know your reality first, you will be able to know the reality of the world. It is a strange thing that most people do not care to know about their own reality, but are very anxious to know about the reality of the world. You realise your own Self first and then see if the world exists independently of you and is able to come and assert before you its reality or existence.

Another visitor asked, "Why is there so much pain even for the innocent, such as children for instance? How is it to be explained? With reference to previous births or otherwise?"

Bhagavan: As about the world, if you know your own reality, these questions won't arise. All these differences, the pains and miseries of the innocent, as you say, do they exist independently of you? It is you that see these things and ask about them. If by the enquiry 'Who am I'? you understand the seer, all problems about the seen will be completely solved.

Dr. Syed asked, "If a person prays for a spiritual good for say two years and yet is not answered, what should he do?"

Bhagavan: It may be it is for his good that the prayer is not granted.

Afternoon

Bhagavan related the following: "When my uncle Nelliappa Aiyar came to see me I was in the Mango *tope* (grove) near Gurumoortham. The direct and shortest route to that place from the Railway station lay through a place where a Swami (மாமரத்துச்சாமி) was living. My uncle, meeting that Swami, and in his anxiety (because I had come away directly from my schoolboy life and so could hardly know anything about religion or spiritual truths), enquired of the above Swami whether I really knew anything in the path on which I had entered. The Swami told my uncle that I knew nothing, but was sitting with eyes closed in a firm and obstinate manner, doing some sort of *hatha yoga*. So my uncle, who had a notion that none could know anything of value in spiritual life without reading Vedanta *sastras*, had a very poor opinion of me and felt only pity for me. Later, when I was in Virupakshi Cave, one day I was explaining the fourth stanza in *Dakshinamurti Stotra* to a young man who used to come to me frequently and who had requested me to explain the *Stotra*. In those days I was still generally silent and people thought I was observing *mauna*. My uncle suddenly appeared on the scene and I was caught in the act of explaining the *Stotra*. I was taken aback and for a moment hesitated whether I should continue the talk or observe *mauna*. But, seeing my uncle had already learnt that I did not mind talking, I continued the discourse. This convinced my uncle that I knew a great deal which he thought I could not have known." Bhagavan added, "The Swami who informed my uncle first that I knew nothing had also to change his opinion. This is how it happened. One day, returning from my *pradakshina* round the hill, I entered the Easanya Mutt and there I found this Swami. He showed the *Vivekachudamani* and asked me about some stanza there. When I explained it, quoting other portions from the same book and also other books, he completely changed his estimate of me."

I may also record here, since it does not seem to have been recorded so far, that Bhagavan told us that when his uncle came and had to send a written message to Bhagavan before he could get admittance, the poor gentleman had no ink or pen and wrote his message on a piece of paper with some twig for pen and the juice of prickly-pear fruit for ink.

26-10-45 Morning

Bhagavan told me that one morning, when he was sitting on the verandah in Virupakshi Cave, the words கருணையாலென்னை யாண்ட நீ came to him very insistently, but he took no special notice of them. It seems the same thing happened the following morning also. Then Bhagavan composed the first stanza of 'அருணாசல பதிகம்' (Eleven Verses on Arunachala). The next morning the words beginning the second stanza similarly came to him and he composed the second stanza; and so it went on every day, until the last two stanzas were composed on one day. On that day, after composing the two last stanzas Bhagavan, it seems, started for *giripradakshina* (going round the hill). One of his disciples, Aiyaswami, brought a piece of paper and pencil and told another disciple who was going with Bhagavan, "Bhagavan has been composing one stanza every morning for some days now, and today he has composed two stanzas. More may come to him today. In case they do, have this paper and pencil with you, so that the same may be recorded." And on the way round the hill Bhagavan actually composed the first six stanzas of the *Arunachala Ashtakam* (Eight Verses on Arunachala). It seems Echamma first got the 'அக்ஷர மணமாலை' (*The Marital Garland of Letters*) published and later Narayana Reddi. This Narayana Reddi came to know of the *Padhikam* and *Ashtakam* soon afterwards, and wanted to publish them. Then Bhagavan composed two more stanzas for completing the *Ashtakam*; and the *Padhikam* and *Ashtakam* were published by Narayana Reddi. This is how the *Padhikam* and *Ashtakam* in the *Five Hymns on Arunachala* came to be composed.

I asked Bhagavan: "I know that in the Madura house itself, Bhagavan had the dawn of *jnana* and that ever since then, Bhagavan had no 'தேகாத்ம புத்தி' (I-am-this-body consciousness). I know also that Bhagavan had a 'தாபம்' (a burning sensation) in the body which did not cease until he arrived at the temple here and reported His arrival to God Arunachala. But I don't believe this was the 'நின்னெறி' mentioned in *Marital Garland*; I also think that Bhagavan has gone through the severe pain or physical ordeal which I have read most Saints had to go through when the knot between body and spirit is sundered. I wish to know when this happened in Bhagavan's life. I know this information is not needed for my improvement. But for Bhagavan's history I think it is necessary."

Bhagavan kept quiet and only smiled. But after a time, he said the *Marital Garland* was written about 1914-1915. By that Bhagavan apparently meant to tell me that the knot was sundered long before that, about 1896 itself.

Afternoon

For some days now Bhagavan's rheumatic troubles have been pretty bad and so his legs are being occasionally massaged with some medicated oils. For about ten days now there has been in the town some Swami who professes to be able to cure with his *vibhuti* all kinds of diseases; and people from various villages have been flocking to see him and most of them also peep in at the Asramam to see Bhagavan. So Bhagavan said, "If all these people come and see I have all these physical ills myself and need to be massaged with medicated oils, they will know I am no good and won't come anymore. So this massaging is good in one way."

29-10-45 Afternoon

Dilip Kumar Roy, singer and author, who is on a visit here from Sri Aurobindo Ashram, asked Bhagavan, "According to the *Mahą Yoga* you say that the sages have not said anything to contradict each other. Yet, we find one advocating *bhakti*, another *jnana*, etc., leading thus to all sorts of quarrels."

Bhagavan: There is really nothing contradictory in such teachings. When for instance a follower of *bhakti marga* declares that *bhakti* is the best, he really means by the word *bhakti* what the *jnana marga* man calls *jnana*. There is no difference in the state or its description by attributes or transcendence of attributes. Only different thinkers have used different words. All these different *margas*, or paths or *sadhanas* lead to the same goal. What is once a means becomes itself the goal. When that happens *dhyana*, *bhakti* or *jnana*, which was at one time a conscious and painful effort, becomes the normal and natural state, spontaneously and without effort.

30-10-45 Afternoon

Dilip Kumar Roy read out a poem in English composed by him on Bhagavan and sang some songs before Bhagavan. Later he asked Bhagavan, "While all say Guru's direction is necessary it seems Bhagavan has said a Guru is not necessary."

Bhagavan: I have not said so. But a Guru need not always be in human form. First a person thinks he is an inferior and that there is a superior, all-knowing and all-powerful God who controls his own and the world's destiny, and worships him or does *bhakti*. When he reaches a certain stage and becomes fit for enlightenment, the same God whom he was worshipping comes as Guru and leads him on. That Guru comes only to tell him. 'The God is within yourself. Dive within and realise.' God, Guru and the Self are the same.

Roy: But in Bhagavan's case there was no Guru.

Bhagavan: The whole world was my Guru. It has been already said that Guru need not be in human form and that the Self within, God and Guru are the same.

Roy: I once asked my Gurudev (*i.e.*, Sri Aurobindo) about this and he said, 'A spiritual Hercules like Bhagavan needs no Guru'.

Bhagavan: Everything in the world was my Guru. Don't you know that Dattatreya, when he was asked by the king which Guru had taught him the secret of bliss, replied that the earth, water, fire, animals, men etc., all were his Gurus and went on explaining how some of these taught him to cling to what was good and others taught him what things he should avoid as bad.

31-10-45 Morning

Chella Battar (Daivasikamani Battar), temple priest of Tiruchuzhi, has come. Bhagavan pointed him out to me and said, "Whenever I see him I am reminded of the cut I received on my left finger and the scar it has left. I was about eight years old and he about three. His house was third from ours. Before his birth and when I was a child I used to be frequently taken to their house and petted as almost their child. It was Pongal time and this child came to our house with one hand holding a new 'அறிவாள் மணை' (blade fastened to a piece of wood for slicing vegetables), and the other hand dragging a long stout sugar cane. I hastened to cut the sugar cane for the child and accidentally got a cut between my thumb and left forefinger. I quietly asked the child to go back to his house and ran to the hospital and got my wound treated. It is this gentleman's son that was here sometime back, called Karpurasundaram, who is now doing puja in 'Sundara Mandiram' at Tiruchuzhi."

Afternoon

Ganapati Sastri brought a letter received by him from Grant Duff, who was here some years ago and is a great devotee of Bhagavan. In that letter Grant Duff says he is in California with the permission of the U.S.A. Government, that the country is pleasant, that he is nearing eighty, that he is anxious to make the best use of the very little time he may yet have in the world and that he hopes by Bhagavan's grace to visit the Asramam again, travelling by air.

Bhagavan drew my attention to Colombo Ramachandra's speech delivered at Colombo on the occasion of the Golden Jubilee of Vivekananda's speech at the Chicago Conference and printed in the *Ramakrishna Vijayam* of the Tamil month Aippasi. In it, Ramachandra says, "Vivekananda on his return from America said in his speeches that South India was going to take a leading part in the spiritual regeneration of the world, that in the 20th century there was going to rise in South India a flood of *atmic* power which would inundate not only the whole of India but the entire world. That force is what is now being generated and radiated by Aurobindo and Bhagavan in South India."

Bhagavan was reading an English translation of a French letter received from one Zikovsky and family, of Czechoslovakia, to this effect: "I and my family are grateful to Bhagavan for all his blessings so far. I hope to go and see Bhagavan, God willing. Meanwhile I pray Bhagavan may send such instructions or directions as he may deem fit." Bhagavan is not able to recognise the writer, but says he must be one of those who wrote from Europe (about the time Brunton first wrote about Bhagavan), that they knew long ago, *i.e.*, long before Brunton's writing about Bhagavan and his teaching and that they had been practising what Bhagavan taught. Bhagavan thinks the writer of the letter must be one of those who read about him and his teachings from what appeared from the pen of Humphreys (who became a devotee of Bhagavan about 1910-11) in some journals at that time.

2-11-45 Morning

Dilip Kumar Roy read out another poem composed by him on Bhagavan. Then he sang a few songs. Then he asked Bhagavan, "What is the best way of killing the ego?"

Bhagavan: To each person that way is the best which appears easiest or appeals most. All the ways are equally good, as they lead to the same goal, which is the merging of the ego in the Self. What the *bhakta* calls surrender, the man who does *vichara* calls *jnana*. Both are trying only to take the ego back to the source from which it sprang and make it merge there.

Roy: But which is the best way for me? Bhagavan must know.

Bhagavan did not reply. (This is only usual with Bhagavan. He leaves it to each devotee to find out what *sadhana* appears most easy to him).

Afternoon

Mr. Roy again sang a few songs. At the end he asked Bhagavan, "Music also helps one to develop *bhakti*, does it not?"

Bhagavan: Yes. Yes.

When Roy was taking leave, he asked Bhagavan whether *bhakti marga* could be followed with advantage and whether it would lead to *jnana.*

Bhagavan: Yes. Yes. *Bhakti* is *jnana mata i.e.*, the mother of *jnana.*

6-11-45 Evening

An elderly gentleman and a young man were sitting in front of Bhagavan. A little before Bhagavan was about to start for his evening stroll, the young man approached Bhagavan and said that his companion had lost his eyesight. Bhagavan nodded, as usual. Soon after, Bhagavan got up and told us, "He says he has lost his eyes. I have lost my legs. He comes and tells me. To whom am I to go and complain!" For nearly a month or more Bhagavan has been having more than usual trouble with his legs, either due to rheumatism or deficiency of B Vitamin. But how serious it is may be realised from his saying he has 'lost his legs'. This is not the first time he has said, "All of you come and complain to me. To whom am I to go and complain?" This is quite consistent with his teaching, that there is nothing but the Self and that he is That!

8-11-45 Morning

When (on 2-11-45) Mr. Roy asked Bhagavan the best way of killing the ego, Bhagavan said, "To ask the mind to kill the mind is like making the thief the policeman. He will go with you and pretend to catch the thief, but nothing will be gained. So you must turn inward and see where the mind rises from and then it will cease to exist." In reference to this answer, Mr. Thambi Thorai of Jaffna (who has been living in Palakothu for over a year) asked me, whether asking the mind to turn inward and seek its source is not also employing the mind. So, I put this doubt before Bhagavan and Bhagavan said, "Of course we are employing the mind. It is well known and admitted that only with the help of the mind the mind has to be killed. But instead of setting about saying there is a mind, and I want to kill it, you begin to seek the source of the mind, and you find the mind does not exist at all. The mind, turned outwards, results in thoughts and objects. Turned inwards, it becomes itself the Self. Such a mind is sometimes called *arupa manas* or *suddha manas*."

Today, the doorway on the south facing Bhagavan's seat has been closed and a window constructed in its place; and the middle window on the northern wall has been replaced by the doorway removed from the southern wall. Going through this doorway, Bhagavan need not climb any steps.

11-11-45 Morning

Maha Vir Prasad, Chief Engineer, U.P., who has been staying here for about twenty days, asked Bhagavan, "I find it said in *Maha Yoga* that in the beginning of meditation one may attend to the breath, *i.e.*. its inspiration and expiration, and that after a certain amount of stillness of the mind is thereby attained, one can dive into the heart seeking the source of the mind. I have been badly in want of some such practical hint. Can I follow this method? Is it correct?"

Bhagavan: The thing is to kill the mind somehow. Those who have not the strength to follow the enquiry method are advised *pranayama* as a help to control the mind. And *pranayama* is of two kinds, one of controlling and regulating the breath and the other of simply watching the breath.

Prasad: During meditation I sometimes attain a state lasting for about fifteen minutes, during which I am not aware of anything and am free from all thoughts. Some have told me that such a state is what may be called *yoga nidra* and that one should guard against such a state as bad.

Bhagavan: One should endeavour to get beyond sleep. (For some reason Bhagavan did not answer further the query put by Prasad). I thereupon advised Prasad to read *Crumbs from the Table*, where this particular matter is dealt with. Bhagavan also asked us to take a copy of the book and give it to Prasad. We did so.

Evening

A visitor: I don't know what *kundalini* is.

Bhagavan: Kundalini is one name given by the *yogic* people for what may be called the *atma sakti* inside the body. The *vichara* school calls the same power *jnana*. The *bhakta* calls it love or *bhakti*. The yogic school says that this power is dormant in *muladhara* at the base of the spinal cord and that it must be roused and taken through the various *chakras* on to *sahasrara* at the top, in the brain, to attain *moksha*. The *jnanis* think this power is centred in the heart, and so on.

12-11-45 Morning

A visitor from the Punjab asked Bhagavan, "When the mind or *ahankar* is killed, is that stage an inert stage?"

Bhagavan: Why do you bother about the *jnani's* state? You understand your present state.

Visitor: The *mumukshu* naturally wants to know about the *mukti* state which is his goal.

Bhagavan kept quiet for a little while and then said, "You admit mind has to be killed. Why don't you do it first and see for yourself then whether that stage is inert or without consciousness?"

Visitor: When *ahankar* goes, will *aham vritti* exist?

Bhagavan: That which is, always is. If the *ahankar* dies, It, the Reality, exists as It has always existed. You may speak of It as having *aham vritti* or simply *aham*. It is all the same. That which exists is 'I am' or '*aham*'.

18.11.45

This morning about 6 a.m. Vaikunta Vasar, an attendant, was massaging Bhagavan's legs. After he had been massaging for about half an hour, Bhagavan expressed 'என்னத்தையோ பிடிக்கிருப் போலிருக்கிறது' (I vaguely feel that something is being massaged). This is perhaps a glimpse into the inner life of Bhagavan. He was not in any trance or special *samadhi* then, but in his usual state.

20-11-45 Afternoon

One Rishikesananda Swami of the Ramakrishna Mission is here. It seems he has been advised by Swami Siddheswarananda to visit Bhagavan. Bhagavan spoke about Siddheswarananda and showed two books, one containing his lectures (causeries) and another which was received only three weeks back though despatched from France in 1941. Rishikesananda said that Siddheswarananda had learnt French very well and spoke fluently in that language. He also said that one Vijayananda Swami was working in South America and was very popular there in spite of hostile propaganda by Christian missionaries. Two ladies of affluence supported the Swami and asked him to remain there. One of the ladies was Mrs. Guirellis, (known to the Asramam as Mamita, who had adopted the Canarese boy Raman and who is staying at Bangalore now near the Ramakrishna Mission). Siddheswarananda intends to come to India for a few months and hopes to visit Ramanasramam also then. The talk drifted to the clothes these Swamis wear in foreign countries. Rishikesananda told Bhagavan that generally they wear European clothes and that, while delivering lectures, they wear long and flowing ochre-coloured robes and a turban such as Vivekananda is seen wearing in some pictures.

21-11-45 Morning

The Swami was asking Bhagavan about the characteristics of a *jnani*. Bhagavan said they are all described in books, such as the *Bhagavad Gita*, but that we must bear in mind that the *jnani's* state being one which transcends the mind cannot be described with the help merely of the mind and that all description therefore must be defective. Only silence can correctly describe their state or characteristics. But silence is more effective than speech. From silence came thought, from thought the ego and from the ego speech. So if speech is effective, how much more effective must its original source be? In this connection Bhagavan related the following story: "Tattvaraya composed a *bharani* (a kind of poetic composition in Tamil) in honour of his Guru Swarupananda and convened an assembly of learned pandits to hear the work and assess its value. The pandits raised the objection that a *bharani* was only composed in honour of great heroes capable of killing a thousand elephants, and that it was not in order to compose such a work in honour of an ascetic. Thereupon the author said, 'Let us all go to my Guru and we shall have this matter settled there'. They went to the Guru and, after all had taken their seats, the author told his Guru the purpose of their coming there. The Guru sat silent and all the others also remained in *mauna*. The whole day passed, night came, and some more days and nights, and yet all sat there silently, no thought at all occurring to any of them and nobody thinking or asking why they had come there. After three or four days like this, the Guru moved his mind a bit, and thereupon the assembly regained their thought activity. They then declared, "Conquering a thousand elephants is nothing beside this Guru's power to conquer the rutting elephants of all our egos put together. So certainly he deserves the *bharani* in his honour!"

Afternoon

A lady visitor from Sri Aurobindo's Ashram asked Bhagavan, "When I concentrate, all sorts of thoughts rise and disturb me. The more I try, the more thoughts rise up. What should I do?"

Bhagavan: Yes. It will be so. All that is inside will try to come out. There is no other way except to pull up the mind each time it wants to go astray and to fix it on the Self. Bhagavan quoted the verse in the *Bhagavad Gita* which says that as often as the wavering mind goes after anything, it should be drawn away and fixed in the Self.

Siva Mohan Lal asked Bhagavan, "When I concentrate here in Bhagavan's presence, I am able to fix my thought on the Self easily. But in my place it takes a long time and much trouble to do so. Now why should it be so, especially as I feel convinced that Bhagavan is everywhere and is my *antaryami*?" I said, "It must of course be so. Though we are told that God is immanent everywhere, are we not also told that he is more manifest in some objects or places than in others, *e.g.*, in temples, and images or *avatars*?" Bhagavan said, "Ask Muruganar, who is here. He has sung a song where he says Ramanasramam is not simply here for him, but everywhere." Thereupon Muruganar read out the following stanza from 'ரமண தேவமாலை' (*Ramana Devamalai*):

ஆண்டெனவே யாண்டு மடங்கிமன நிற்றலால்
ஈண்டுபுனல் சூழுலக மெங்கணுமே-வேண்டி
அமரர் பலரு மடையும் பெரிய
ரமணதே வாச்சி ரமம்.

Which means, 'Because (by His grace) the mind has attained quiescence and remains calm everywhere as it used to remain at Ramanasramam, wherever I may go in this world it is to me Ramanasramam, to which even *devas* go with keen desire.' In other words, Ramanasramam is *chid akasa* which is everywhere and to which we gain access by killing the mind. Bhagavan added, "Time and place really do not exist. Even in the radio we have a hint of this truth. We have Hyderabad here. What is sung there, we hear here at the same time as it is sung there. Where is time and place?"

Dr. Srinivasa Rao asked Bhagavan, "What is the meaning of 'தூங்காமல் தூங்குவது', *i.e.*, being in sleepless sleep?"

Bhagavan: It is the *jnani's* state. In sleep our ego is submerged and the sense organs are not active. The *jnani's* ego has been killed and he does not indulge in any sense activities of his own accord or with the notion that he is the doer. So he is in sleep. At the same time he is not unconscious as in sleep, but fully awake in the Self; so his state is sleepless. This sleepless sleep, wakeful sleep, or whatever it may be called, is the *turiya* state of the Self, on which as the screen, all the three *avasthas*, the waking, dream and sleep, pass, leaving the screen unaffected." Bhagavan said that instead of holding on to that which exists, we are looking for that which does not. We bother about the past and the future, not realising the truth of the present. We do not know the 'ஆதி' (beginning) or the 'அந்தம்' (end). But we know the middle. If we find out the truth of this, we shall know the beginning and the end. Bhagavan quoted from *Bhagavad Gita*: "I am in the heart of all beings and am their beginning, middle and end." Bhagavan also said the reality is only *mauna* and quoted Thayumanavar:

வேறுபடுங் சமயமெல்லாம் புகுந்து பார்க்கின்
விளங்குமரம் பொருளேநின் விளையாட் டல்லால்
மாறுபடுங் கருத்தில்லை முடிவில் மோன
வாரிதியில் நதித்திரள்போல் வயங்கிற் றம்மா

(கல்லாலின்-25)

(*i.e.*, If we scrutinise all the religions which look so different, we find nothing discrepant at all in them, but they are only your (Lord's) sport. They all end in quiescence or *mauna*, as rivers merge in the sea).

In this connection Bhagavan also said, when one talks of *brahmakara vritti* for the mind, it is something like saying *samudrakara nadi*, about the river which has merged in the ocean.

Night

Following Bhagavan's quotation from the *Gita*, Rishikesananda referred to a verse from *Mandukya Upanishad* in which the words *adi* and *anta* occur. Bhagavan took it out and explained the text, which says: "That which was not in the beginning and which won't be at the end, but which is only in the middle, can't be real. Only that can be real which is not only in the middle, but also at the beginning and the end".

Dr. Srinivasa Rao asked Bhagavan, "When we enquire within 'who am I?' what is that?"

Bhagavan: It is the ego. It is only that which makes the *vichara* also. The Self has no *vichara*. That which makes the enquiry is the ego. The 'I' about which the enquiry is made is also the ego. As the result of the enquiry the ego ceases to exist and only the Self is found to exist.

I asked Bhagavan, "It seems this morning Rishikesananda quoted some text which says wherever the mind goes, that is *samadhi*. How can that be? Our mind goes after whatever it likes. Can that be *samadhi*?"

Bhagavan: That passage refers to *jnanis*. Whatever they may be doing, there is no break in their *samadhi* state. Their bodies may be engaged in whatever activities they were intended by *prarabdha* to go through. But they are always in the Self. We associate or identify ourselves with the body; whatever it does, we say we do. The *Bhagavad Gita* says, 'The wise man will think the senses move among the sense objects and be unattached to the activities of the sense organs.' I would go farther and say that the *jnani* does not think even that. He is the Self and sees nothing apart from himself. What the *Bhagavad Gita* says in the above passage is for the *abhyasi* or the practiser. There is no harm in engaging in whatever activities naturally come to one. The hindrance or bondage is in imagining that we are the doers and attaching ourselves to the fruits of such activities.

In this connection Bhagavan also said, "A man says 'I came from Madras'. But in reality 'he' did not come. The *jutka* or some other vehicle brought him from his house to the railway station, the train brought him to Tiruvannamalai railway station, and from there some other cart brought him here. But he says 'I came'. This is how we identify ourselves with the acts of the body and the senses." Bhagavan also quoted from the *Vedanta Chudamani* to the effect that the activities of the *jnani* are all *samadhi*, *i.e.* he is always in his real state, whatever his body may happen to be doing. Bhagavan also referred to Rajeswarananda and said that once he planned to take a big party of pilgrims with Bhagavan in their midst. Bhagavan said, "I did not consent to go and the thing had to be dropped. What is there I could go and see? I see nothing. What is the use of my going anywhere?" ("பார்த்தால் ஒன்றும் தெரிகிறதில்லை") This is one of those self-revealing statements, which sometimes escape Bhagavan's lips.

The following remarks were also made by Bhagavan this night:

"The *jnani* sees he is the Self and it is on that Self as the screen that the various cinema-pictures of what is called the world pass. He remains unaffected by the shadows which play on the surface of that screen.

"See with the 'ஊனக்கண்' (the physical eye), and you see the world. See with the 'ஞானக்கண்' (the eye of realisation), everything appears 'பிரம்மமயம்' (as the Self).

"To see an object that is in the dark, both the eye and the light of a lamp are required. To see the light only, the eye is enough. But to see the sun, there is no need of any other light. Even if you take the lamp with you, its light will be drowned in the light of the sun. Our intellect or *buddhi* is of no use to realise the Self. To see the world or external objects, the mind and the reflected light (or *chidabhasa*) which always arises with it are necessary. To see the Self, the mind has simply to be turned inside and there is no need of the reflected light.

"If we concentrate on any thought and go to sleep in that state, immediately on waking the same thought will continue in our mind. People who are given chloroform are asked to count one, two, etc. A man who goes under after saying six for instance will, when he again comes to, start saying seven, eight, etc.

"In some books, the ego is compared to a leech; before leaving one body it takes hold of another."

22-11-45 Morning

Bhagavan explained how it is said in books that the highest possible happiness, which a human being can attain or which the ten grades of beings higher than man, ending with gods like Brahma can attain, is like foam in the deluging flood of the bliss of the Self.

Imagine a man in robust health; of vigorous adult age, endowed with unsurpassed wealth and power, with intellect and all other resources, and married to a fair and faithful wife, and conceive of his happiness.

Each higher grade of being above man is capable of a hundred-fold greater happiness than that of the grade below. But the highest happiness of all the eleven grades of being is only the foam in the flooding ocean of divine bliss.

In this connection Bhagavan narrated the following story:

"A king was passing through a forest in all his pomp and pageantry, with his army and retinue behind him. He came across a man with not even a cod-piece on him, lying on the ground, with one leg cocked over the other and laughing away, apparently supremely happy and contented with himself and all the world. The king was struck with the man's happy state and sent for him. But when the king's men approached the nude ascetic and delivered the king's message, he took absolutely no notice and continued in his ascetic bliss. On being told of this, the king himself went to the man and even then the man took no notice. Thereupon it struck the king that this must be no common man, and said: 'Swami, you are evidently supremely happy. May we know what is the secret of such happiness and from which Guru you learnt it?' Thereupon the ascetic told the king: 'I have had twenty-four Gurus. Everything, this body, the earth, the birds, some instruments, some persons all have taught me.' All the things in the world may be classed as either good or bad. The good taught him what he must seek. Similarly, the bad taught him what he must avoid. The ascetic was Dattatreya, the *avadhuta*."

After Bhagavan returned from his morning stroll about 8 a.m., some visitor prostrating himself seems to have spilled out his entire stock — a good quantity — of snuff. Attendant Krishnaswami noticed it and collected the snuff and threw it out. This reminded Bhagavan of some incidents in his life. He said, "Tobacco is a germicide. When I was in Virupakshi Cave, one day I suddenly found one tooth gave sharp pain when the cold rice came in contact with it and I could eat no more. I stopped eating and thought I would have to die of starvation. Vasudeva Sastri was then living with me. He had gone out at the time. When he returned to the cave I told him of my toothache. He said it was nothing and that a little tobacco would cure it, killing the germs. As we had no tobacco with us, somebody who had snuff with him gave me a little snuff and advised me to press it against the tooth and it gave immediate relief, so much so that I was able to eat my next meal. When I examined the tooth there appeared to be something like a dot on it. Gradually it became a hole. Later on a gentleman who was a District Munsiff at Tirukoilur and visiting me came to know of it, and sent a dentist from Madras. The dentist came, stayed here three days, charging Rs.300-0-0 for his stay and did nothing substantial, except cleaning my teeth, pulling out one tooth and a part of another.

"Even before I came here I knew of the power of tobacco. When the Periyar dam was constructed and the water first allowed to pass in the canals, the water came on in a flood and there was plenty of fish in the water. The fishermen used to divert the water by means of a side channel and let it into a pond into which they had thrown a number of bundles of tobacco stems, *i.e.*, the stumps after the leaves had been utilised for making cigars. The moment the fish got into the pond they became unconscious or dead on account of the poison of the tobacco and began to float. And the fishermen got heaps of fish in this way. Afterwards I came across the following stanza in தாயுமானவர் (Thayumanavar) which alludes to the above practice of fishermen (in திடமுறவே 4).

உள்ளத்தி னுள்ளே யொளித்தென்னை யாட்டுகின்ற
கள்ளக் கருணையையான் காணுந் தரமாமோ
வெள்ளத்தை மாற்றி விடக்குண்பார் நஞ்சூட்டும்
பள்ளத்தின் மீன்போற் பதைத்தேன் பராபரமே.

Translation: I am struggling like the fish caught in the pond whose waters diverted from the flood had been poisoned by flesh-eaters. Is it possible for me to understand your hidden kindness. Oh Almighty, who lying concealed in my heart is moving me about like a puppet?"

After this, at Dr. Srinivasa Rao's request, Bhagavan explained the stanza occurring at the end of 'சுகவாரி' commencing 'எந்நாளும் உடலிலே' and the last four stanzas in 'மண்டலத்தின்' of தாயுமானவர் (Thayumanavar).

Later in the morning, at Rishikesananda's request Bhagavan recounted his first experience of the Self in his upstairs room at

Madura. "When I lay down with limbs outstretched and mentally enacted the death scene and realised that the body would be taken and cremated and yet I would live, some force, call it *atmic* power or anything else, rose within me and took possession of me. With that, I was reborn and I became a new man. I became indifferent to everything afterwards, having neither likes nor dislikes." Dr. Srinivasa Rao asked Bhagavan how he first came to have *bhakti*. Bhagavan replied, "The first thing that evoked *bhakti* in me was the book '*Periya Puranam*', which I came across in my house, which belonged to a neighbour and which I read through. It was however only after the experience described above that I used to go daily to the temple and pray that I should become devoted like one of the sixty-three saints (Nayanmar) of '*Periya Puranam*'."

Afternoon

Dr. Srinivasa Rao told the Swami, "I have heard from one, who said he saw it, that when Bhagavan was in Skandasramam, a snake once crept over his body." Bhagavan said, "Snakes raise their hoods and look into our eyes and they seem to know when they need not be afraid, and then they pass over us. It did not strike me either that I should do anything to it."

Later Bhagavan said, "Even though we usually describe the reality as *Sat, Chit, Ananda*, even that is not quite a correct description. It cannot really be described. By this description all that we endeavour to make plain is that it is not *asat*, that it is not *jada* and that it is free from all pain."

Again Bhagavan said, "We are all in reality *Sat-Chit-Ananda*. But we imagine we are bound and are having all these pains."

I asked, "Why do we imagine so? Why does this ignorance or *ajnana* come to us?"

Bhagavan said, "Enquire to whom has this ignorance come and you will find it never came to you and that you have always been that *Sat-Chit-Ananda*. One performs all sorts of penances to become what one already is. All effort is simply to get rid of this *viparita buddhi* or mistaken impression that one is limited and bound by the woes of *samsara*."

Later Bhagavan said, "The spark of *jnana* will easily consume all creation as if it were a mountain-heap of cotton. All the crores of worlds being built upon the weak (or no) foundation of the ego, they all topple down when the atomic bomb of *jnana* comes down upon them." Bhagavan said, "All talk of surrender is like pinching jaggery from the jaggery image of Lord Ganesa and offering it as *naivedya* to the same Lord Ganesa. You say you offer your body, soul and all possessions to God. Were they yours that you could offer them? At best, you can only say, 'I falsely imagined till now that all these which are yours (God's) were mine. Now I realise they are yours. I shall no more act as if they are mine.' And this knowledge that there is nothing but God or Self, that I and mine don't exist and that only the Self exists, is *jnana*." He added, "Thus there is no difference between *bhakti* and *jnana*. *Bhakti* is *jnana mata* or mother of *jnana*."

Talking of the innumerable ways of different seekers after God, Bhagavan said, "Each should be allowed to go his own way, the way for which alone he may be built. It will not do to convert him to another path by violence. The Guru will go with the disciple in his own path and then gradually turn him into the supreme path at the ripe moment. Suppose a car is going at top speed. To stop it at once or to turn it at once would be attended by disastrous consequences."

The talk then turned to the names of God and Bhagavan said, "Talking of all *mantras*, the *Brihadaranyaka Upanishad* says 'AHAM' is the first name of God. The first letter in Sanskrit is A 'अ' and the last letter Ha 'ह' and 'Aha' thus includes everything from beginning to end. The word 'Ayam' means that which exists, Self-shining and Self-evident. 'Ayam', 'Atma', 'Aham', all refer to the same thing. In the Bible also, 'I AM' is given as the name of God."

24-11-45 Morning

Bhagavan spoke about the way in which in the old days he used to climb to the peak at any time he felt like it, and that by any route or even no route. He said only the grass-cutters knew some of the routes he used. "Sometimes people would come from Madras and other parts and, setting out to reach the top of the hill, would stray near Skandasramam. Finding me seated there, they would ask me for the route to the hill top. When I told them the route was to their right and turned northward, some would say. 'Do you know who we are and wherefrom we come? We are from Madras. None of your tricks with us. The top is here straight above us and you want to lead us astray.' I used to keep quiet. They would try to climb in a straight line, and after a long time, they would return tired out, finding that all their efforts to reach the peak were in vain. Nearing me, they would bow their heads in shame and go away, avoiding me."

25-11-45

Bhagavan related how, while he was living in Skandasramam, cheetahs used to visit him. He mentioned two such instances. "In one, the cheetah made a terrific roar which clearly appeared aggressive, but it did nothing to us and went chasing monkeys. On the other occasion, the cheetah walked up slowly and majestically and on nearing the Asramam gave a loud roar, but one in which only peace and no aggression could be detected, just as if it wanted to announce its arrival and no more. It came very near, where the hill stream is now flowing in Skandasramam, and after a time, slowly walked away, giving another roar, as it were to announce its leave-taking."

After breakfast Bhagavan went to Skandasramam attended by only one attendant as usual. Skandasramam has been completely repaired and put into perfect condition recently and the path to it on the hill behind Ramanasramam has also been improved. To celebrate the occasion and to give Bhagavan a chance of spending some time in his old Asramam, which we knew he thoroughly enjoys, it had been arranged that Bhagavan and all his devotees should spend the day there and return here only in the evening. There were some two hundred people crowded into Skandasramam by about 9-30 a.m., and we all returned only in the afternoon. Bhagavan left at about 4-15 and reached Ramanasramam about 5-30 p.m. At Skandasramam Bhagavan was in a happy and cheerful mood. The weather however was a bit too cloudy and chill, with biting cold winds blowing most of the time. Bhagavan related at great length and in minute detail various incidents that occurred during his life at Skandasramam and Virupakshi Cave. He explained that the name Skandasramam was given because the Asramam was originally planned and built by one Kandaswami, an old disciple, at great self-sacrifice and by his unaided physical efforts. He remarked, "It is a miracle how, on this hill, when need arises water springs up where there was none before and where none could have been suspected. After the need passes, the water also disappears." He traced the history of the hill stream now flowing in Skandasramam, how he first discovered its source further up and worked with his then disciples to lead it down. There was a terrific storm and rain one night and it appeared to the townsmen in the morning, from that distance, as if a big road had been made overnight. It seems during this occurrence a tank called Pada Thirtham (பாத தீர்த்தம்) was completely filled up and there was mud and rock heaped up to a height of about fifteen feet where the tank originally stood. (I learnt later, on 12-12-45, from Bhagavan that half or three-quarters of this tank was again restored by a devotee).

Bhagavan also narrated at length the history of the monkeys associated with his stay in Virupakshi Cave and Skandasramam, explaining in particular how நொண்டிப் பையன் ('The lame boy,' Bhagavan's pet name for him) came under Bhagavan's influence. It seems, while Bhagavan was in Virupakshi Cave, a monkey had been bitten and mauled badly by the then king monkey and left for dead near the cave. Bhagavan took pity on him and tended him and he recovered. Afterwards, he was attached to Bhagavan and was always with him, getting his daily feed at Bhagavan's Asramam. When the other monkeys came there, the lame one would not allow them to approach Bhagavan and he pointed out to Bhagavan the king who had made him lame. But later on, all the monkeys used to come there and used to show regard and love to their erstwhile enemy, the lame-monkey. In course of time the lame one became the monkey-king. One day Bhagavan and his party had left Skandasramam for *giripradakshina*, leaving the Asramam in charge of one or two who stayed behind. During Bhagavan's absence the lame one and a host of other monkeys came and broke the twigs and small branches of all the trees at Skandasramam and played havoc with all they found there. Bhagavan was wondering why they did so. The next day the monkeys again came and the lame one got up the highest tree, reached its highest point and shook it and then got down. This it seems is a sign of royal precedence among the monkeys. When Bhagavan offered food as usual to the lame one, he would not take it, but led the man offering it to where three other monkeys were sitting, and there he shared his food with them. The three monkeys were the queens of the deposed king, who were now the lame one's queens according to their custom and usage. Then Bhagavan knew that the lame one had become king, that the previous day they all came to have his coronation in Bhagavan's presence and finding Bhagavan absent expressed their disappointment and chagrin by breaking branches, etc. The lame one had afterwards six children by the three queens and all the six would get a morsel each from Bhagavan when he took his meal every day. It seems the lame one misbehaved on two occasions and hurt Bhagavan by hitting him. Each time Bhagavan thought of punishing him by denying him admission to his presence. But finding his pet repentant, and seeing that it was only his monkeyish nature that was responsible, Bhagavan excused him. One of the occasions was when Bhagavan took up a plate of milk intended for the monkey and was about to blow into it to make it cool, as it was too hot for the monkey. The monkey thought that Bhagavan was taking the milk near his mouth to drink it himself. Bhagavan said that, at Skandasramam, sometimes a peacock and serpent used to play side by side before him, the one with its tail spread out and the other with its hood raised. Those who played host to all the numerous devotees on this day were Prof. T.K. Doraiswami Aiyar and Mr. Satakopa Naidu of Bangalore, both great devotees of Bhagavan. Of Mr. Naidu, the following is worth narrating as an interesting study in psychology.

Mr. Naidu has known Bhagavan for about thirty-five years now. After he had known Bhagavan for some years, it seems he once came to Virupakshi Cave and, finding Bhagavan had gone out, sat down at a certain place. After a little time Bhagavan returned and Mr. Naidu discovered that the place he had been seated, was the very place that Bhagavan generally used for his seat. This, it is said, gave Mr. Naidu such a shock that, though he has become an almost permanent resident of the Asramam, and has a permanent room of his own inside the Asramam, he would not come before Bhagavan at all, much less sit in the hall or dine with Bhagavan. Even earlier, when Mr. Naidu used to visit the Asramam once or twice a year, he felt too shy to appear before Bhagavan. He never speaks about the original incident. I have therefore to be content with narrating what I have heard from others.

27-11-45 Morning

Miss Sarojini Hathee Singh (sister of Mr. Hathee Singh, brother-in-law of Jawaharlal Nehru), who is here now on her second visit to this place, expressed a desire to have the daily life of Bhagavan filmed and shown to the world. I told her Mr. K.K. Nambiar had a similar idea and even took a few shots with a cine camera a few months back, but either because there was something wrong with the film or with the operator, nothing came of it. Miss Hathee Singh said she would arrange for this after returning from here this time. At meal time Miss Indumati (a relation of Ambalal Sarabhai), who with her mother and others had come here from Aurobindo's *darshan* on the 24th instant, asked me if there was any book dealing with the ordinary life of Bhagavan, including any light or humorous incidents or remarks. I replied in the negative and she said there ought to be one. She said, "Before we came here we did not know Bhagavan was so human and that he moved so freely, talked and even made humorous remarks. We knew only of his spiritual eminence. There ought to be a book which reveals all these aspects which bring him closer to us as a man."

29-11-45

I went to Vellore on the 27th evening and met Mr. A.Lobo, District Judge, and his wife at their place this morning. Both made enquiries about Bhagavan and Mr. Lobo suggested that there should be some record of Bhagavan's life and doings at the Asramam.

From Mr. Lobo's house I went to Sir Norman Strathie, Adviser, who was then camping at Vellore. There again naturally we were talking of the Asramam. He said he had heard of Bhagavan's teaching through silence, and added, "we can understand that."

1-12-45

I returned here last night. Maha Vir Prasad, Chief Engineer to the U. P. Government who had been staying here for about twenty days in October and November and who went on a pilgrimage to Rameswaram and other places, is back here. In continuation of an old question of his with reference to a certain passage in *Maha Yoga*, he asked Bhagavan whether it was necessary and a condition precedent for a man to watch his breathing before beginning the mental quest 'Who am I?'

Bhagavan: All depends on a man's *pakva*, *i.e.*, his aptitude and fitness. Those who have not the mental strength to concentrate or control their mind and direct it on the quest are advised to watch their breathing, since such watching will naturally and as a matter of course lead to cessation of thought and bring the mind under control.

Breath and mind arise from the same place and when one of them is controlled, the other is also controlled. As a matter of fact, in the quest method — which is more correctly 'Whence am I?' and not merely 'Who am I?' — we are not simply trying to eliminate saying 'we are not the body, not the senses and so on,' to reach what remains as the ultimate reality, but we are trying to find whence the 'I' thought for the ego arises within us. The method contains within it, though implicitly and not expressly, the watching of the breath. When we watch wherefrom the 'I'-thought, the root of all thoughts, springs, we are necessarily watching the source of breath also, as the 'I'-thought and the breath arise from the same source.

Mr. Prasad again asked whether, for controlling breath, the regular *pranayama* is not better in which 1:4:2 proportion for breathing in, retaining, and breathing out is prescribed. Bhagavan replied, "All those proportions, sometimes regulated not by counting but by uttering *mantras*, etc., are aids for controlling the mind. That is all. Watching the breath is also one form of *pranayama*. Retaining breath, etc., is more violent and may be harmful in some cases, *e.g.*, when there is no proper Guru to guide the *sadhak* at every step and stage. But merely watching the breath is easy and involves no risk."

An old gentleman, Mr. Swaminatha Aiyar, a vakil from Dindigul, had come. With him was a male child about three years old, called Ramana. Apparently the child had not until then seen Bhagavan, though he had heard a good deal about Bhagavan. So the boy said in the hall ரமணனைக் கண்டு பிடிச்சுவிட்டேன் (*i.e.*, I have now discovered Ramana). This naturally caused laughter amongst us all and Bhagavan joined in the laugh.

The old gentleman asked Bhagavan whether one should not first go through *nirvikalpa samadhi* before attaining *sahaja samadhi*. Bhagavan replied, "When we have *vikalpas* and are trying to give them up, *i.e.*, when we are still not perfected, but have to make conscious effort to keep the mind one-pointed or free from thought it is *nirvikalpa samadhi*. When through practice we are always in that state, not going into *samadhi* and coming out again, that is the *sahaja* state. In *sahaja* one sees always oneself. He sees the *jagat* as *swarupa* or *brahmakara*. What is once the means becomes itself the goal, eventually, whatever method one follows, *dhyana, jnana* or *bhakti*. *Samadhi* is another name for ourselves, for our real state."

In the evening, after *parayana*, Bhagavan was looking into a book. Bhagavan turned to me and said it was *Glimpses of Sai Baba* by Mr. B.V. Narasimha Aiyar and that Mr. Shroff had bought it for Bhagavan's perusal. I said, "Yes, I saw it in Shroff's house this morning. I wonder if it contains anything new, not contained in his previous works on Sai Baba." Bhagavan read out the introduction to the book by Justice Kuppuswami Aiyar. Dr. Syed, who was in the hall, said he had read the book and that it contained nothing new. He also said that

Mr. Narasimha Aiyar, when questioned on the subject, could not say whether Sai Baba taught Self-realisation to anybody. Almost immediately as if to contradict Dr. Syed, Bhagavan read out from the introduction to the book a sentence which says that Sai Baba not only granted boons for material relief to his devotees, but also gave them a push towards their ultimate goal of Self-realisation.

2-12-45

This morning the Dowager Rani of Vizianagaram with two or three others came to the hall, having arrived at the Asramam last night. Dr. Srinivasa Rao was massaging Bhagavan's feet. Bhagavan told Dr. Srinivasa Rao, "You go and sit; otherwise they would come and ask what is the matter with Bhagavan's health." Doctor accordingly stopped massaging. Bhagavan does not like any fuss to be made about him on any account.

In the afternoon I showed a book called *Wonderful India* to Bhagavan. It contained many pictures and Bhagavan went through the book for more than an hour, looking at the pictures.

4-12-45

About the middle of last month certain rearrangements were made in the hall, a railing put round Bhagavan's couch on the western and southern sides, all the shelves removed to the eastern half of the hall, etc. When all this was done I remarked such crowding of furniture near Bhagavan's couch might increase the bug-pest. Then we spoke of insecticides and about DDT, the most effective insecticide discovered during the war. This morning Lt. Shroff brought some DDT and sprayed it in the hall and on the furniture, including Bhagavan's sofa. Bhagavan advised it should be tried on the cow-shed and he was very solicitous that if possible the cows should be rid of all flies now troubling them. Lt. Shroff left some

DDT in the Asramam with instructions as to how it should be used. We found the *Mauni* had already with him a cutting from some paper in which full instructions about the use of DDT were given.

6-12-45 Afternoon

Mr. G. Subba Rao spoke to Bhagavan about the late Mauna Swami of Courtallam. He was with Bhagavan originally in 1906. He was called Sivayya then. Today Bhagavan recalled that it was Sivayya who first gave him a *kamandalam*. It seems Sivayya stayed with Bhagavan for about a year or so, then went to Courtallam, and when he again came to Bhagavan about 1909 or 1910, he brought a coconut *kamandalam*, the first Bhagavan ever used. Bhagavan took out the picture in the book 'ரமண விஜயம்' (*Ramana Vijayam*) in which there is a picture of Bhagavan sitting on a rock, holding this particular *kamandalam* in his right hand and resting his left hand on his left thigh. Bhagavan is at the peak of health and strength in this picture.

Night

Referring to the stanza 'அங்கியுரு வாயுமொளி' (3rd stanza of *Sri Arunachala Mahatmya* in *Collected Works of Ramana Maharshi*) I asked Bhagavan, whether the cave mentioned in it is inside God or inside the mountain (which of course is also said to be God). Bhagavan replied, "Of course, in the context, it means the cave is inside the hill and that there, in the cave, are all enjoyments." Bhagavan added, "The stanza says you are to believe that inside this hill there is a cave, which is brilliance itself or which is glorious with light, and that all enjoyments are to be found there." I also asked Bhagavan, "I have read somewhere that this place is called *bhoga kshetra*. I wonder what is meant thereby." Bhagavan replied, "Yes, it is said so. But what does it mean? If thinking of this *kshetra* can itself give *mukti*, what wonder if this place can give all other enjoyments one may desire?" Dr. Srinivasa Rao asked whether after putting oneself the question "Who am I?" one should remain quiet or whether one should go on to give the answer, such as "I am not this body, senses, etc." or whether one should go on repeating the question "Who am I?"

Bhagavan: "Why should you go on repeating 'Who am I?' as if it is a *mantra*. If other thoughts arise, then the questions, 'To whom do these thoughts arise?', 'Whence does the 'I' to which these thoughts come arise?' have to be asked, *i.e.*, to keep away other thoughts. Even in *mantra japam*, when the man fails to repeat the *mantra*, *i.e.*, when other thoughts begin to occupy his mind, he reminds himself 'I have left off the *mantra*' and begins repeating it. The object in all paths is to keep off all other thoughts except the thought of God or Self."

In this connection Bhagavan again said "The Name is God," and quoted the Bible, 'In the beginning was the word, and the word was with God, and *the word was God*'." Swami Ramdas often preaches the importance of *Nama smarana*, the Name he uses being Sri Ram Jai Ram Jai Jai Ram. In the latest issue of *Vision* Swami Ramdas has written about 'That thou art', and Bhagavan referred me to it.

7-12-45

The September 1937 number of *Vision* contains an article on the Philosophy of the Divine Name according to Nam Dev. Bhagavan frequently refers to it with approval. Today also Dr. Srinivasa Rao brought it and Bhagavan explained it to him. Bhagavan remarked, "All this must have been uttered by Nam Dev after he attained complete realisation, after touching the feet of Vishopakesar to whom Vithoba sent him for enlightenment." Bhagavan then related the following story:

"Vithoba found Nam Dev had not yet realised the Supreme Truth and wanted to teach him. When Jnaneswar and Nam Dev returned from their pilgrimage, Gora Kumbhar gave a feast to all the saints in his place and among them were Jnaneswar and Nam Dev. At the feast, Jnaneswar in collusion with Gora, told Gora publicly, 'You are a potter, daily engaged in making pots and testing them to see which are properly baked and which are not. These pots before you (*i.e.*, the saints) are the pots of Brahma. See which of these are sound and which not.' Thereupon Gora said, 'Yes Swami, I shall do so', and took up the stick with which he used to tap his pots to test their soundness; and holding it aloft in his hand he went to each of his guests and tapped each on the head as he usually did to his pots. Each guest humbly submitted to such tapping. But when Gora approached Nam Dev, the latter indignantly called out: 'You potter, what do you mean by coming to tap me with that stick?' Gora thereupon told Jnaneswar, 'Swami, all the other pots have been properly baked. This one, (*i.e.*, Nam Dev) alone is not yet properly baked.' All the assembled guests burst into laughter. Nam Dev felt greatly humiliated and ran up to Vitthal with whom he was on the most intimate terms, playing with him, eating with him, sleeping with him, and so on. Nam Dev complained of this humiliation which had happened to him, the closest friend and companion of Vitthal. Vitthal (who of course knew all this) pretended to sympathise with him, asked for all the details of the happenings at Gora's house and after hearing everything said, 'Why should you not have kept quiet and submitted to the tapping, as all the others did? That is why all this trouble has come.' Thereupon Nam Dev cried all the more and said, 'You also want to join the others and humiliate me. Why should I have submitted like the others? Am I not your closest friend, your child?' Vitthal said, 'You have not yet properly understood the truth. And you won't understand if I tell you. But go to the saint who is in a ruined temple in such and such a forest. He will be able to give you enlightenment.' Nam Dev accordingly went there and found an old, unassuming man sleeping in a corner of the temple with his feet on a Siva *lingam*.

Nam Dev could hardly believe this was the man from whom he — the companion of Vitthal — was to gain enlightenment. However, as there was none else there, Nam Dev went near the man and clapped his hands. The old man woke up with a start and, seeing Nam Dev, said, 'Oh, you are Nam Dev whom Vitthal has sent here. Come!' Nam Dev was dumb-founded and began to think, 'This must be a great man.' Still he thought it was revolting that any man, however great, should be resting his feet on a *lingam*. He asked the old man, 'You seem to be a great personage. But is it proper for you to have your feet on a *lingam*?' The old man replied, 'Oh, are my feet on a *lingam*? Where is it? Please remove my feet elsewhere.' Nam Dev removed the feet and put them in various places. Wherever they were put, there was a Siva *lingam*. Finally, he took them on his lap and he himself became a Siva *lingam*. Then he realised the truth and the old gentleman said, 'Now you can go back'." Bhagavan added, "It is to be noted that only when he surrendered himself, and touched the feet of his guru, enlightenment came. After this final enlightenment Nam Dev returned to his house and for some days did not go to Vitthal at the temple, though it had been his habit not only to visit Vitthal every day, but to spend most of his time with Vitthal at the temple. So after a few days, Vitthal went to Nam Dev's house and like a guileless soul enquired how it was that Nam Dev has forgotten him and never visited him. Nam Dev replied, 'No more of your fooling me. I know now. Where is the place where you are not! To be with you, should I go to the temple? Do I exist apart from you?' Then Vitthal said, 'So you now understand the truth. That is why you had to be sent for this final lesson'."

Bhagavan referred to the article in the *Vision* of December, 1945 on *Sthita Prajna* and to the lines from *Sat Darshana* quoted in that article. Dr. Syed thereupon asked Bhagavan when *Reality in Forty Verses* was made by Bhagavan. Bhagavan said, "It was recently something like 1928. Muruganar has noted down somewhere the different dates. One day Muruganar said that some stray verses composed by me now and then on various occasions should not be allowed to die, but should be collected together and some more added to them to bring the whole number to forty, and that the entire forty should be made into a book with a proper title. He accordingly gathered about thirty or less stanzas and requested me to make the rest to bring the total to forty. I did so, composing a few stanzas on different occasions as the mood came upon me. When the number came up to forty, Muruganar went about deleting one after another of the old collection of thirty or less on the pretext they were not quite germane to the subject on hand or otherwise not quite suitable, and requesting me to make fresh ones in place of the deleted ones. When this process was over, and there were forty stanzas as required by Muruganar, I found that in the forty there were but two stanzas out of the old ones and all the rest had been newly composed. It was not made according to any set scheme, nor at a stretch, nor systematically. I composed different stanzas on different occasions and Muruganar and others afterwards arranged them in some order according to the thoughts expressed in them to give some appearance of connected and regular treatment of the subject, *viz.*, Reality." (The stanzas contained in the old collection and deleted by Muruganar were about twenty. These were afterwards added as supplement to the above work and the Supplement too now contains 40 verses).

Bhagavan also said, "*Marital Garland of Letters* was composed partly at the Virupakshi Cave and partly on my walks round the hill. *Upadesa Saram* alone was written with a scheme and a set purpose and at a stretch at one sitting. That was because Muruganar had set a limit of one hundred stanzas for the entire theme of the poem and in it had planned that the particular subject of *Upadesa* should be confined to thirty stanzas, of which again he had already composed three stanzas, leaving thus only twenty-seven stanzas within the brief compass of which I was required to deal with the whole subject."

In the afternoon Bhagavan explained to Dr. Srinivasa Rao the significance of the name Rama. "The 'Ra' stands for the Self and 'ma' for the ego. As one goes on repeating 'Rama', 'Rama', the 'ma' disappears, getting merged in the 'Ra' and then 'Ra' alone remains. In that state there is no conscious effort at *dhyana*, but it is there, for *dhyana* is our real nature."

8-12-45 Morning

Dr. Srinivasa Rao took this notebook and read out yesterday's entry. Thereupon Bhagavan asked Krishnaswami to take out the notebook in which Muruganar and others had noted down the dates on which various stanzas were composed. We found it was only in 1928 that the *Reality in Forty Verses* was composed.

Bhagavan showed me the Tamil paper *Hindustan* which contained an article by Tilak Sastri on Bhagavan's visit to Skandasramam on 25-11-45, explaining the origin of the name, among other things.

Afternoon

When I went to the *Pathasala* to bring some Sanskrit books at Bhagavan's instance, an incident occurred in the hall which is recorded below. Miss Kamdin (now Mrs. McIver) was sitting next to a lady who went into a trance and purported to have received sugar candy from Narayana *i.e.*, God. She thinks that there was no trickery at all in it and that the candy came mysteriously into the lady's hands. I also was given a bit of the candy.

The incident is thus recorded by Mr. K.A. Mahatani:

On 8th December 1945 at about 3-45 p.m., I saw a Gujarati widow aged about 50 years sitting in the hall with two girls of about eight and ten years in the front row on the side reserved for ladies. I could see that she was in *samadhi*.

After a few minutes she fell on her back quietly in *samadhi* posture without stretching her legs. People in the hall thought that she was in a hysterical fit, but those two girls said that she was in *samadhi* and that it often happened to her. Then those two girls started singing a Gujarati *bhajan* song in a nice tune. (The song begins 'Haji mare gher thaya lila ler').

Bhagavan was all the time attentively looking at the lady and enjoying the tune, keeping time by beating his knee with his hand. I had never before noticed Bhagavan so interested in any song.

After a few minutes the lady got up without anybody's help and sat in *samadhi* in the same posture, and began to mutter something in Gujarati. I asked her whether she saw any vision. She said in Hindustani "Yes," and added that Sri Narayan gave a message for all in the hall. "Let them close their eyes, be still, without any *pravritti* (*i.e.*, without any thought or action) and I will give *darshan* to one and all."

I translated to Bhagavan what she said. For two or three minutes she was bowing her head with hands clasped towards Bhagavan. Then we noticed that she handed over a piece of sugar candy to one of the two girls sitting near her.

Before that we had seen her open hands quite empty. I asked the girl what was that sugar candy and how it came into her hands.

The girl replied, "This is *prasad* given to the lady by Bhagavan Narayan; and whenever she goes into *samadhi* she gets different things (such as fruit, flowers, garlands, *sandal, kumkum* and sweets) on different occasions."

Then the lady said that she used to get such moods since she was six years old. The girl presented the piece of sugar candy to Bhagavan. He partook a little of it and the rest was distributed among the others who were present in the hall.

I remarked that this was very miraculous. Bhagavan indicated, 'Yes', with only a gesture of his hand, but said nothing. After a few minutes, the lady left the hall with the two girls. Before leaving she bowed low to Bhagavan and asked for his blessings and his permission to go back to Bombay.

I learnt that she had come that morning and left the same evening. She gave her name in the office as Mataji Maniben Samadhiwallah, C/o. R.G. Raval, Purshottam Building, opposite Opera House, Bombay.

9-12-45 Morning

When yesterday Bhagavan referred to Tilak's article in *Hindustan*, I said, "Our Nagamma has also written an account in Telugu of the visit of Bhagavan to Skandasramam on 25-11-45 and the happenings there." Nagamma had told me previously about this. This morning, Nagamma brought the writing and showed it to Bhagavan. He read a little and then said, "Let her read it. We shall all listen," and returned the paper to her. Before she could read it out, Bhagavan began talking to us about other matters. Bhagavan said that the old disciple Kandaswami was anxious to build a separate Asramam for Bhagavan. He inspected various places on the hill and in the forests to select a site, and finally suggested the present Skandasramam site and then Bhagavan also approved of it. Thereupon Kandaswami began converting what was a thick forest of prickly pear on the mountain slope. The result of his labours, unaided by any at the time, is the Asramam we see now. He added, "You cannot imagine the state the site was in originally. Kandaswami worked with almost superhuman effort, achieved by his own hands what even four people together could not have done. He removed all the prickly pear, reduced stone and boulder to level ground, created a garden and raised the Asramam. We got four coconut trees for planting. To plant them properly Kandaswami dug huge square pits about ten feet deep. That would give you an idea of the amount of labour he put into the work he took on hand. He was a strong, well-built man." Then Bhagavan showed us a group photo in *Self-Realisation* in which the above Kandaswami, Perumalswami, Palaniswami, Sivaprakasam Pillai, Narayana Reddi, Iswara Swami, etc., are sitting with Bhagavan. The photo was taken on a rock behind Virupakshi Cave. He then added, "Kandaswami looks like a weak and lean man in this photo. That is because he went away from us for more than a month and was doing *tapas* at 'ஏழு சுனை' (Seven Springs) and was purposely underfeeding himself. Before that, he was a muscular, well-built man. He went away with only some flour and a little jaggery to Seven Springs and lived there for about one and a half months, living only on these scanty provisions. One night at about 7 p.m. myself, Perumalswami, Nagappa Chetti and possibly one or two others went in search of Kandaswami and found him sleeping inside the rocks at Seven Springs. Perumalswami went inside and brought out Kandaswami's conch. Kandaswami and Perumalswami were adepts at blowing long, continuous blasts on the conch. Perumalswami blew a loud, long blast outside the cave. Kandaswami woke up and, recognising that it was Perumalswami that was blowing the conch, came out. Seeing me, he prostrated himself. We all spent the night there. We finished what was left of the flour and jaggery which he had, and burnt away the firewood he had gathered, made it impossible for him to continue there and persuaded him to come away with us. It was because of his fasting and *tapas* that you find him lean in this photo."

Bhagavan proceeded to describe how Perumalswami and Kandaswami used to blow in concert on the conch and how when Bhagavan was in Virupakshi Cave, Perumalswami, Kandaswami and Palaniswami used to go about begging in the streets for food and bring it up the hill and all there used to share it. Before Perumalswami joined them, Palaniswami and Ayyaswami and Kandaswami would go to a *chattram* and the *manigar* would give food for all. But when Perumalswami also joined, the *manigar* began questioning why an addition was necessary. Thereupon Perumalswami laid down that they should no longer go to the *chattram* or be at the mercy of the *manigar*, but would go and beg in the town. Accordingly, a party of four or more would leave the cave on this errand. When leaving the cave, they would blow a long blast on their conches. This was an announcement to the town's people that Bhagavan's party had left the cave on their begging mission. The party would give another blast when they reached the foot of the hill. A third call would be sounded at the entrance to the street. All the residents of the street would be ready with their offerings and the party would march along the street singing some *Sivanamavali* and collecting the offerings. The food collected was ample, it seems, for all who gathered near Bhagavan and all the monkeys, etc. *Marital Garland of Letters* was specially composed for use by the begging party. Bhagavan humorously added, "*Marital Garland of Letters* fed us for many years."

10-12-45

Yesterday or the day before, in the morning, a snake was seen by Chinnaswami and others in the Asramam premises somewhere near Bhagavan's hall. We heard the cries, "What kind of snake is it?" "Beat it! Beat it!" When we heard the noise of actual beating, Bhagavan cried out 'யார் அடிக்கிறது?' 'யார் அடிக்கிறது?' ("Who is beating it?") Apparently this remonstrance of Bhagavan was not heard by the party, and the snake was killed. Bhagavan, added, 'இவங்களை அப்படி ரெண்டு கொடுத்தால் அப்போ தெரியும்' ("If these persons are beaten like that, then they will know what it means.")

Night

Mr. P. C. Desai read out in the hall the manuscript prepared by Mr. M. Venkatarama Ayyar on *Arunachala Mahatmyam.*

11-12-45

About 6-30 p.m. a young man, Mr. Ramachandra Reddi of Begampet, Hyderabad (Deccan), who came here a few months back and stayed a day or two and took some pictures of Bhagavan with his cine camera, told Bhagavan that he had a film of about 100 feet ready and, if permitted, he would project it before Bhagavan. Bhagavan had no objection and so he made two persons hold a white sheet at the western end of the hall and on that screen projected the pictures he had taken — Bhagavan coming from the hall, meeting Narayana Iyer's son Ramanathan, holding their youngest child, touching with his stick and speaking to him, etc., Bhagavan coming from the cow-shed, climbing the hill and then returning from there, being followed by Mrs. Taleyarkhan and Miss Soona Dorabji and some other scenes. We all appreciated the pictures. But Bhagavan could not see them clearly. It was a revelation to us how poor his sight was. Then for his benefit the screen was held near the southern window opposite Bhagavan's sofa and the pictures were projected again, but he could not see them clearly even then.

Bhagavan said in this connection that once Mr. Grant Duff or someone else wrote to the Asramam that they saw some film of Bhagavan in Hollywood. Bhagavan said, "We knew nothing about it. But apparently someone had come and snapped me when I was moving on the hill."

Mr. K. K. Nambiar also took about 100 feet of film some 6 months back. But it seems to have been a failure. Our Venkatoo said in the hall that some years ago Jayadevlal's friend took some pictures with a cine camera, but as they had heard nothing more of them, they too must have been a failure.

12-12-45 Morning

Mr. Desai continued his reading about 10 a.m. When he read about one Kuppaiyar who was lame and afterwards got the use of his legs, about 40 years ago, and Bhagavan said he knew of the incident and that he had seen Kuppaiyar after he got better, I said "அது பகவான் செய்ததுதானும். நமக்கு சொல்றதில்லை. அதனுடைய திருட்டுத்தனம் தான் அது" (*i.e.*, it would appear that it was really done by Bhagavan, though he does not speak to us about it. It is his stealthy way). I said so because Bhagavan's old classmate Ranga Aiyar and one other at least who could be trusted to know about it had assured me that, from what Bhagavan had told them of this incident, they were convinced that it was only Bhagavan who had worked the miracle. When I made the above remark in the hall to those near me in Bhagavan's presence and hearing, he did not deny my assumption. Bhagavan related to me once the following incident that happened when he was living on the hill: "A cartman was engaged one night by a lady new to this town to take her to some street. The cartman purposely took her to some out-of-the-way place near the hill and was about to attack her for her jewels or molest her. Then two constables appeared on the scene and threatened the cartman and escorted the lady to her proper destination. The lady noted the numbers of the constables and made enquiries afterwards about them and it was ascertained that no human police constable had ever done such a service on that night." Ranga Aiyar believes that this was also really Bhagavan's work. I concur with him now. For from the way Bhagavan narrated the incident, even at the time I first heard it from his lips, I had the same suspicion, though Bhagavan ascribed the incident to Arunachala. We cannot tax Bhagavan with falsehood. He describes what he did as having been done by Arunachala, because he and Arunachala are one.

Afternoon

As I was entering the hall about 2-50 p.m., Bhagavan was reading out from the Tamil *Arunachala Puranam* the verses in which it is said that Gauri, after crossing the several streets of Arunachalam, reached Gautama's Asramam. When Bhagavan came to the verses dealing with Gautama's joy at Gauri's coming to his Asramam, Bhagavan could not go on, for tears filled his eyes and emotion choked his voice. So he laid aside the book and Desai continued his reading of the manuscript. I may here record that I have noticed on more than one occasion in the past how Bhagavan could not proceed with the reading of any deeply devotional portions of Tamil works such as *Thevaram* and devotional hymns of Thayumanavar. This afternoon when I took from Bhagavan the above *Arunachala Puranam* and referred to the portion which moved him so deeply and told him, in effect, that I had discovered his plight which he tried to hide from us all, he remarked, "I don't know how those people who perform *kalakshepam* and explain such passages to audiences manage to do it without breaking down. I suppose they must first make their hearts hard like stone before starting their work."

In the course of Mr. Desai's reading of the manuscripts, he read about the holy hill having eight faces. To a question of mine whether as a matter of fact this hill has eight faces, Bhagavan replied, "The *purana* says that the *Ashta Vasus* having flattered themselves in Brahma's presence lost all their merit, and to regain it they came and did penance here all round Arunachala. They were given *darshan* by Siva at one and the same time by Siva assuming eight faces in this hill. All those eight *Vasus* are still in the shape of eight spurs round this hill. What is meant by saying all those *Vasus* are still here as hills and doing penance round this holy hill, it is difficult to understand. Does it only mean they are living on these hills and doing penance, or are they themselves these hills?" He added, "It is difficult now for us to locate where the *Ashta Dikpalakas* actually stood sentry, whether at the spots where the *Ashta Dik Lingams* are now found or whether the *lingams* are those which were installed and worshipped by them. We cannot be sure where exactly Gauri did penance and where Gautama had his Asramam. But it would be safe to assume that Gauri did her penance in the region covered by Pavalakunru, Durga temple and Pachaiamman Koil and that Gautama's Asramam must have also been near this region."

Bhagavan also said that whatever temple might have originally existed on or about Pavalakunru would seem to have disappeared probably on account of Tippu's invasion, that the present temple there was built only about fifty years ago and that he once discovered the remains of an old cannon between Pavalakunru and the northern wall of the Big Temple. It would appear that Tippu Sultan placed cannon near Pavalakunru and attacked the northern wall of the temple which was then used as a fort. The northern wall still bears traces of cannon shots. It seems the information given by Bhagavan was conveyed to the Government and the cannon was carried away and kept as a relic.

Night

For the benefit of those who could not see Bhagavan's film on the 11th night, it was again shown today at about 6-30 p.m. in the dining hall. Before we went there Bhagavan said that Yogananda and also one Shukla who was a Guru of the American lady (Mrs. Noye) had taken cine pictures of Bhagavan and that the latter's pictures might have eventually reached Hollywood and come to the notice of Grant Duff or others who wrote to the Asramam.

16-12-45

In the *Sunday Times* of 16-12-45 an article entitled "In silent adoration of Sri Maharshi", by V.F. Gunaratna, of Ceylon had appeared. I perused it in the hall. Bhagavan remarked, "Dr. Syed has read it and thinks it insipid." Thereupon I said,

"There is nothing to complain of in it. In fact, I read it long ago, probably about last *Jayanti* time, when Mr. Ramachandra of Colombo showed me the manuscript." The article states Bhagavan's teaching, correctly if briefly, though it has nothing new to tell us who are already well acquainted with him and his teaching.

17-12-45 Morning

An article in the *Sunday Herald* of 16-12-45 entitled 'The Maharshi who transforms man's life' by Dr. Syed was read out in the hall. Dr. Syed said the title he gave was different but the editor had changed it. Bhagavan also perused another article by Dr. Syed on the significance of Mohurrum which appeared in *Free India* of 16-12-45.

Evening

Dr. Syed said that the title he gave was 'Ramana Maharshi's invisible work'.

19-12-45 Afternoon

Some lady introduced another lady to Bhagavan, saying "Subbu has come". Bhagavan could not make out who this Subbu was. But, when it was explained to him who the lady was, he said, "சுப்புகுட்டியா" (Is it Subbukutti?) and recognised her as the younger sister of Chellam Bhattar of Thiruchuzhi who had visited him recently. This lady seems to have been a small girl with whom Bhagavan had played in his boyhood. He told us, "This lady had an aunt who used to take me to her house and pet me when I was a child." I asked, "Where is that lady now?" Bhagavan said, "She died long ago and her husband married again and had several children."

Dr. Syed is old and has various ailments which render it very difficult for him to go round the Hill. However, as he found that

Bhagavan sets great store by his disciples going round the Hill he and his wife decided to try it about a month back. They took Bhagavan's permission and went round and came back without any difficulty or untoward incident. Today again they both came to Bhagavan and took permission to go round the Hill. Bhagavan used to say that if one went round the Hill once or twice, the Hill itself would draw one to go round it again. I have found it true. Now this is happening to Dr. Syed.

My two sons and their wives and children and about ten more relations of mine arrived this night and when I introduced them, Bhagavan made kind inquiries whether I had been able to get suitable accommodation, etc., for them. Bhagavan is equally solicitous about the comfort of everybody who comes here. How can one help loving him and becoming bound to his feet?

21-12-45

This is Bhagavan's *Jayanti* (65th birthday). The crowd of devotees is greater than usual, many of them having come from distant parts. There were the usual decorations, music, feast and feeding of the poor. In the afternoon a number of prayers and verses in honour of Bhagavan specially composed for the occasion were read out. A message sent by Swami Sivananda (of Rishikesh) was also read out.

23-12-45 Afternoon

Mons. Georges Le Bot, Private Secretary to the Governor of Pondicherry, and Chief of Cabinet of the French Government there, came to Bhagavan. He could not easily squat down on the floor and so Bhagavan asked us to give him a seat. We placed for him a chair opposite to Bhagavan. He had brought with him his request written in French. After expressing his greetings to Bhagavan through some interpreters who came with him and who spoke Tamil, he produced his French writing. Our Balaram Reddi tried to interpret the same to Bhagavan. But he found it rather difficult, as the French was rather high-flown. So we sent for Mr. Osborne (whose wife and three children have been living for nearly five years here and who himself returned from Siam about a month back) and he came and explained the gist as follows: "I know little. I am even less. But I know what I am speaking about. I am not asking for words, explanations or arguments, but for active help by Maharshi's spiritual influence. I did some *sadhana* and attained to a stage where the ego was near being annihilated. I wanted the ego to be annihilated. But at the same time I wanted to be there to see it being killed. This looked like having contradictory desires. I pray Maharshi may do something by his influence, in which I fully believe, to enable me to reach the final stage and kill the ego. I do not want mere arguments or explanations addressed to the mind, but real help. Will Maharshi please do this for me?"

He had also written out another question: "I have been having for my motto 'Liberate yourself'. Is that all right or would Maharshi suggest any other motto or ideal for me?"

Bhagavan kept silent for a few minutes, all the while however steadily looking at the visitor. After a few minutes the visitor said, "I feel that I am not now in a state in which I can readily receive any influence which Maharshi may be pleased to send. After some time, I shall come again when I am in that state of exaltation in which I may be able to assimilate his influence or spiritual help." He added, "May I have a little conversation with this interpreter (Mr. Osborne) and come here some other time?" Bhagavan said, "Yes, you can certainly go and have some talk." They both went out. The *Sarvadhikari* gave the visitor some fruits and coffee and he took leave expressing his desire to come here some other time. After the visitor left the hall, Bhagavan said, "He seems to have read about all this and to have done some *sadhana*. He is certainly no novice." Someone suggested that the books in French, in our library, on Bhagavan's teachings might be shown to the visitor.

They were accordingly taken out and shown to him while he was still with the *Sarvadhikari*, having coffee. He looked at them and said he had read them all.

Mr. Subramania Iyer (Assistant Director of Public Health Madras, who has been coming to Bhagavan for some years now) brought an album, containing 41 photos (taken by Dr. T.N. Krishnaswami on 25-11-45) of Bhagavan at Skandasramam and presented it to the Asramam. Bhagavan looked at the pictures, which were all good, except one or two spoiled slightly by the sunlight.

24-12-45 Morning

Bhagavan asked Mr. T.P. Ramachandra Aiyar to read out a letter written by Mr. Subramania Iyer (Dindigul), a brother of our Viswanatha Brahmachari. It gave an account of the grand way in which Bhagavan's *Jayanti* was celebrated at Tiruchuzhi on the 21st instant. Mr. Subramania Iyer was writing a letter to Mr. S. Doraiswamy Iyer, giving an account of the conversation between Georges Le Bot and Bhagavan. It was read out in the hall for the benefit of all assembled. I also read out the account of the same happening recorded in this diary.

A visitor asked if he could do both *pranayama* and *dhyana*. Bhagavan said, "One is a help to the other. Whether one need do *pranayama* depends on one's *pakva* or fitness."

Evening

After *parayana*, Mr. Osborne said that before Mons. Georges Le Bot left, he said the following: "I had the experience described by me, twice, first by my own efforts, and the second time under the silent influence of a French philosopher now dead, who held my wrist and brought me to the same stage without any effort on my part. Both times I kept approaching the breaking point in waves but shrank back. It was because of the second experience that I decided that Maharshi could again bring me to that point."

To the visitor who pursued the question about *pranayama*, Bhagavan said, "The aim is to make the mind one-pointed. For that *pranayama* is a help, a means. Not only for *dhyana* but in every case where we have to make the mind one-pointed, it may be even for a purely secular or material purpose, it is good to make *pranayama* and then start the other work. The mind and *prana* are the same, having the same source. If one is controlled, the other is also controlled at the same time. If one is able to make the mind one-pointed without the help of *pranayama*, he need not bother about *pranayama*. But one who cannot at once control the mind, may control the breath and that will lead to control of the mind. It is something like pulling a horse by the reins and making it go in one direction."

Bhagavan asked Mr. Osborne if Mons. Le Bot had mentioned the name of the French philosopher who had helped him to attain the experience referred to by him. Mr. Osborne could not give the name, but said the philosopher, now dead, seems to have been one trained in and following the ancient Greek philosophy. Bhagavan remarked, "It could not be Guenon, as that philosopher is said to be dead."

Bhagavan continued, "He says he has 'Liberate Yourself' for his motto. But why should there be any motto? Liberation is our very nature. We are that. The very fact that we wish for liberation shows that freedom from all bondage is our real nature. That has not got to be freshly acquired. All that is necessary is to get rid of the false notion that we are bound. When we achieve that, there will be no desire or thought of any sort. So long as one desires liberation, so long, you may take it, one is in bondage." He also said, "People are afraid that when ego or mind is killed, the result may be a mere blank and not happiness. What really happens is that the thinker, the object of thought and thinking, all merge in the one Source, which is Consciousness and Bliss itself, and thus that state is neither inert nor blank. I don't understand why people should be afraid of that state in which all thoughts cease to exist and the mind is killed. They are every day experiencing that state in sleep. There is no mind or thought in sleep. Yet when one rises from sleep one says, 'I slept happily'. Sleep is so dear to everyone that no one, prince or beggar, can do without it. And when one wants to sleep, nothing however high in the range of all the worldly enjoyments can tempt him from much desired sleep. A king wants to go to sleep, let us say. His queen, dear to him above all other things, comes then and disturbs him. But even her, he then brushes aside and prefers to go to sleep. That is an indication of the supreme happiness that is to be had in that state where all thoughts cease. If one is not afraid of going to sleep, I don't see why one should be afraid of killing the mind or ego by *sadhana*." Bhagavan also quoted during the above discourse the Tamil stanza (quoted already in this diary) which ends by saying that so long as the cloud of ego hides the moon of *jnana*, the lily of the Self will not bloom.

25-12-45 Afternoon

When I went into the hall to take permission from Bhagavan to go round the hill. Mr.N. Pisharoti, our compounder, was reading out some verses recently composed by him in Malayalam.

Mr. Chinta Dikshitulu's Telugu composition *Ramana Gopala* was read out in the hall. It was greatly enjoyed by all. Bhagavan also appreciated it and thought it worthwhile being read out to all. It was done accordingly.

26-12-45 Afternoon

Pointing to Mr. Venkatachalam, (father of the girl Souris who visited Bhagavan a few years ago for the first time and wrote an account of her experiences in the form of a letter to a friend in the Telugu journal *Bharati*) Bhagavan said, "He came this morning. I at once asked Dr. Srinivasa Rao also to come and stand by Mr.Venkatachalam and showed them both to all so that none should afterwards mistake the one for the other. They are so much alike. The resemblance was even greater two or three years ago." A book has recently been received by Bhagavan in which Mr.Venkatachalam's letters to Mr.C. Dikshitulu during one year (1938 or 1939?) are published. The portions relating to Bhagavan in those letters were read out by Mr. Venkatachalam in the hall.

27-12-45 Morning

Bhagavan was reading an account written by Nagamma to her brother on Bhagavan's visit to Skandasramam on 25-11-45. Bhagavan had read only a little when I suggested it might be read out, so that all might hear it. Accordingly it was read by Nagamma and translated by Mr. Venkatachalam. We all appreciated it.

Night

It was reported to Bhagavan that Echamma was seriously ill for three days and unconscious for two days. Bhagavan said, 'அப்பப்போ அப்படி யிருக்கிறதுண்டு, அப்படியே கண்ணை மூடிண்டு இருந்திடுவா' ('She used to be like that now and then. She would remain like that, closing eyes'). From these words I imagined that Bhagavan meant she would recover.

28-12-45 Morning

It seems Echammal passed away at about 2-30 a.m. and the matter was reported to Bhagavan only about 8 a.m. in the hall. The talk naturally was about Echammal and how from 1907 she persevered in offering food to Bhagavan without any break. Bhagavan also remembered three other persons who fed him when he was under the *iluppai* tree in the Big Temple. One was Dasi Rajambal who, it seems, took a vow that she would not eat before feeding Bhagavan and was feeding him for about two months until he moved away to Gurumoortham. It seems she continued to send food even to Gurumoortham for a day or two. But Bhagavan asked her to discontinue it. It seems this lady died only recently. Bhagavan mentioned also Meenakshi Ammal, a Kammala woman, and said, "She was like a *rakshasi*. She would daily go round the hill and then come and cook and bring food to me. After some time she began assuming control over everybody including Palaniswami. If others brought food, etc., she would give some to me and whatever remained she used to take away with her." (Bhagavan said, in the afternoon, "Our Nagappa's mother Ratnamma also used to bring food in those days"). Of food supplied regularly, கட்டளை (*Kattalai*) as Bhagavan put it, he said, "You don't know what trouble all such regular supply involves. Those who make it expect some control over you. It also creates some *aham* in them. Everyone of them expects you to take something. One would say 'அடியே, உன் கையாலே கொஞ்சம் வையடி' ('I say, serve something with your own hand'), and then each would serve something. The quantity would become too great. Any number of people bring any number of things, and at all times, and you must take them. Sometimes we used to mix up all things received, milk, food, porridge, etc., and drink it if the resulting mixture was a liquid. 'Swami-hood' is very difficult. You cannot realise it. I am speaking from fifty years' experience. After such experience in Gurumoortham I wanted to avoid it by not remaining in any one place."

Afternoon

Santhamma came and reported to Bhagavan that Echamma passed away peacefully and people did not even know when exactly life departed and that though she was unconscious for nearly two days, when she had a little consciousness at one time during these two days, the one question she asked was, "Has food been sent to Bhagavan?" (Later I learnt from Nagamma that this was not quite correct. It seems that somebody, to test whether Echamma's mind was clear and not wandering, asked the question "Has food been sent to Bhagavan today?" and Echammal at once showed recognition). Her body was cremated. I thereupon asked Bhagavan, "It is said in the case of such people they should not be cremated, but buried". Bhagavan replied, "It seems she herself had mentioned that her body should be cremated and that her bones alone should be taken and buried in her village." I also asked Bhagavan what he meant by his statement last night that "she would often remain with closed eyes". He explained, "She practised concentrating on the head centre and would be in a trance-like state for even two or three days with breath fully controlled. I told her it was only *laya* and one should not be satisfied with it, but must get out of it and beyond it."

One Mr. Joshi, introduced by our Chaganlal Yogi, put the following questions and Bhagavan gave the following answers:

Question 1: When I think 'Who am I?', the answer comes 'I am not this mortal body but I am *chaitanya, atma,* or *paramatma.*' And suddenly another question arises — 'Why has *atma* come into *maya*?' or in other words 'Why has God created this world?'

Answer: To enquire 'Who am I?' really means trying to find out the source of the ego or the 'I' thought. You are not to think of other thoughts, such as 'I am not this body, etc.' Seeking the source of 'I' serves as a means of getting rid of all other thoughts. We should not give scope to other thoughts, such as you mention, but must keep the attention fixed on finding out the source of the 'I' thought, by asking (as each thought arises) to whom the thought arises and if the answer is 'I get the thought' by asking further who is this 'I' and whence its source?

Question 2: Is *atma* a subject of *sakshatkara*?

Answer: The *atma* is as it is. It is *sakshat* always. There are not two *atmas*, one to know and one to be known. To know it is to be it. It is not a state where one is conscious of anything else. It is consciousness itself.

Question 3: I do not understand the meaning of "*brahma satyam jagat mithya* (Brahman is real, the world is unreal)". Does this world have real existence or not? Does the *jnani* not see the world or does he see it in a different form?

Answer: Let the world bother about its reality or falsehood. Find out first about your own reality. Then all things will become clear. What do you care how the *jnani* sees the world? You realise yourself and then you will understand. The *jnani* sees that the world of names and forms does not limit the Self, and that the Self is beyond them.

Question 4: "I do not know how to worship. So kindly show me the way to worship."

Answer: Is there a 'worshipper' and a 'worshipped'? Find out the 'I', the worshipper; that is the best way. Always the seer must be traced.

29-12-45 Morning

Mr. Viswanatha Brahmachari brought a Tamil translation of Mr. C. Dikshitulu's *Ramana Gopala* and Bhagavan perused it.

Night

Mr. P.C. Desai introduced Mr. P.C. Dewanji (Retd. Sub-Judge) who was returning from Trivandrum, where he had presided over a section of the Philosophical Conference. Mr. Dewanji asked Bhagavan, "What is the easiest way to attain one-pointedness of mind?" Bhagavan said, "The best way is to see the source of the mind. See if there is such a thing as the mind.

It is only if there is a mind that the question of making it one-pointed will arise. When you investigate by turning inwards, you find there is no such thing as the mind."

Then Mr. P.C. Desai quoted Bhagavan's *Upadesa Sara* in Sanskrit to the effect, "When you investigate the nature of mind continuously or without break, you find there is no such thing as the mind. This is the straight path for all." The visitor again asked, "It is said in our scriptures that God it is that creates, sustains and destroys all and that He is immanent in all. If so and if God does everything and if all that we do is according to God's *niyati* (law), and had already been planned in the Cosmic Consciousness. is there individual personality and any responsibility for it?"

Bhagavan: Of course, there is. The same scriptures have laid down rules as to what men should or should not do. If man is not responsible, then why should those rules have been laid down? You talk of God's *niyati* and things happening according to it. If you ask God why this creation and all, He would tell you it is according to your karma again. If you believe in God and His *niyati* working out everything, completely surrender yourself to Him and there will be no responsibility for you. Otherwise find out your real nature and thus attain freedom.

Mr. Sundaresa Iyer brought two copies of 'கந்தர் அனுபூதி' (*Kandar Anubhuti*) to Bhagavan and said they were sent by Dasi Rajambal's son (Shanmuga Sundaram, teacher in a school here) who had published for free distribution 500 copies of the book in honour of his mother's memory. Bhagavan again said in this connection, "Though she was a young woman and born in that caste, she took a vow that she would not take her meal before giving me food."

30-12-45

Ramana Gopala has been translated into Tamil and the final copy was read out in the hall this morning.

Afternoon

A devotee brought and gave to Bhagavan a cutting from *The Bombay Chronicle* in which an account was given of how Ramana *Jayanti* was celebrated this year at Matunga, Bombay, by the Ramana Satchidananda Sangh and how one Vijayaraghava Bhagavatar of Mannargudi and his party performed an excellent *kalakshepam* on Bhagavan and his life and teachings. The cutting was read out in the hall for the benefit of all. It said that a *harikatha* was held on Ramana. Bhagavan said, "*Harikatha* on Ramana is a misnomer. *Kalakshepam* would have been more appropriate."

Tilak Sastri wanted to know from Bhagavan about Echammal, so that he could send an article to the press about her. Bhagavan said, "You may write what you like. *Vijayam* and other books contain a reference to her." Bhagavan said, "Our Venkatakrishniah's mother also seems to have passed away the same night. I find it in today's Telugu paper *Zamin Ryot*."

R.Narayana Iyer asked Bhagavan if Echammal was conscious to the last. Though people (including myself) had told Bhagavan that Echammal was unconscious for the last two days of her existence, not having been able to recognise those around her, Bhagavan said in reply, "Yes, She was. She remained as in *samadhi* and passed away. It is even said they did not know when exactly life expired." Mysore Ramachandra Rao added, "The corpse did not look like a corpse at all. It looked very much as she used to look here."

31-12-45 Morning

Mr. Chinta Dikshitulu is here. Bhagavan said, "We were talking of Chinta Dikshitulu yesterday. He is here now." Later another gentleman arrived. A Muslim from the Punjab, he was born blind, but has learnt Arabic, Persian, Urdu and English and knows by heart the whole of the *Quran*. It seems he heard of

Bhagavan from some friend, who also translated to him in Urdu the English book *Who am I?* and thereupon he decided he should go and visit Bhagavan. Accordingly he has come all the way from the Punjab, all alone. Somebody suggested to him here that he should hear some other works of Bhagavan. He replied, "No. It is not necessary. That one book is enough."

1946

2-1-46 Afternoon

Mr. Joshi has submitted what Bhagavan calls a question paper, and Bhagavan answers the same.

First about the *jnani's* doing work, without the mind: "You imagine one cannot do work if the mind is killed. Why do you suppose that it is the mind alone that can make one do work. There may be other causes which can also produce activity. Look at this clock, for instance. It is working without a mind. Again suppose we say the *jnani* has a mind. His mind is very different from the ordinary man's mind. He is like the man who is hearing a story told with his mind all on some distant object. The mind rid of *vasanas*, though doing work, is not doing work. On the other hand, if the mind is full of *vasanas*, it is doing work even if the body is not active or moving."

Question 2: Is *soham* the same as 'Who am I?'

Answer: Aham alone is common to them. One is *soham*. The other is *koham*. They are different. Why should we go on saying *soham*? One must find out the real 'I'. In the question 'Who am I?', by 'I' is meant the ego. Trying to trace it and find its source, we see it has no separate existence but merges in the real 'I'.

Question 3: I find surrender is easier. I want to adopt that path.

Answer: By whatever path you go, you will have to lose yourself in the One. Surrender is complete only when you reach the stage 'Thou art all' and 'Thy will be done'.

The state is not different from *jnana*. In *soham* there is *dvaita*. In surrender there is *advaita*. In the Reality there is neither *dvaita* nor *advaita*, but That which is, is. Surrender appears easy because people imagine that, once they say with their lips 'I surrender' and put their burdens on their Lord, they can be free and do what they like. But the fact is that you can have no likes or dislikes after your surrender and that your will should become completely non-existent, the Lord's Will taking its place. Such death of the ego is nothing different from *jnana*. So by whatever path you may go, you must come to *jnana* or oneness.

Question 4: How am I to deal with my passions? Am I to check them or satisfy them? If I follow Bhagavan's method and ask, 'To whom are these passions?' they do not seem to die but grow stronger.

Answer: That only shows you are not going about my method properly. The right way is to find out the root of all passions, the source whence they proceed, and get rid of that. If you check the passions, they may get suppressed for the moment, but will appear again. If you satisfy them, they will be satisfied only for the moment and will again crave satisfaction. Satisfying desires and thereby trying to root them out is like trying to quench fire by pouring kerosene oil over it. The only way is to find the root of desire and thus remove it.

Another visitor asked Bhagavan, "If I try to make the 'Who am I?' enquiry, I fall into sleep. What should I do?"

Bhagavan: Persist in the enquiry throughout your waking hours. That would be quite enough. If you keep on making the enquiry till you fall asleep, the enquiry will go on during sleep also. Take up the enquiry again as soon as you wake up.

Another visitor asked Bhagavan if it was not necessary that the *varnasrama* differences should go if the nation was to progress.

Bhagavan: How can one say whether it is necessary or not necessary? I never say anything on such subjects. People often come and ask me for my opinion on *varnasrama*. If I say anything they will at once go and publish in the papers, 'So and so also is of such and such an opinion.' The same scriptures which have laid down *varnasrama dharma* have also proclaimed the oneness of all life and *abheda buddhi* as the only reality. Is it possible for anyone to teach a higher truth than the Unity or Oneness of all life? There is no need for anyone to start reforming the country or the nation before reforming himself. Each man's first duty is to realise his true nature. If after doing it, he feels like reforming the country or nation, by all means let him take up such reform. Ram Tirtha advertised, 'Wanted reformers — but reformers who will reform themselves first.' No two persons in the world can be alike or can act alike. External differences are bound to persist, however hard we may try to obliterate them. The attempts of so-called social reformers, to do away with such classes or divisions as *varnasrama* has created, have not succeeded, but have only created new divisions and added a few more castes or classes to the already existing ones, such as the Brahmo-Samajists and the Arya-Samajists. The only solution is for each man to realise his true nature.

Another visitor said, "*Jnanis* generally retire from active life and do not engage in any worldly activity."

Bhagavan: They may or may not. Some, even after realising, carry on trade or business or rule over a kingdom. Some retire into forests and abstain from all acts except those absolutely necessary to keep life in the body. So, we cannot say all *jnanis* give up activity and retire from life.

Visitor: I want to know if Bhagavan can give concrete examples, like the butcher *Dharmavyadha* mentioned in our books, of *jnanis* now living and doing their ordinary daily work in life.

Bhagavan did not answer.

Visitor: Is renunciation necessary for Self-realisation?

Bhagavan: Renunciation and realisation are the same. They are different aspects of the same state. Giving up the non-self is renunciation. Inhering in the Self is *jnana* or Self-realisation. One is the negative and the other the positive aspect of the same, single truth. *Bhakti, jnana, yoga* — are different names for Self-realisation or *mukti* which is our real nature. These appear as the means first. They eventually are the goal. So long as there is conscious effort required on our part to keep up *bhakti, yoga, dhyana*, etc., they are the means. When they go on without any effort on our part, we have attained the goal. There is no realisation to be achieved. The real is ever as it is. What we have done is, we have realised the unreal, *i.e.*, taken for real the unreal. We have to give up that. That is all that is wanted.

Visitor: How has the unreal come? Can the unreal spring from the real?

Bhagavan: See if it has sprung. There is no such thing as the unreal, from another standpoint. The Self alone exists. When you try to trace the ego, based on which alone the world and all exist, you find the ego does not exist at all and so also all this creation.

3-1-46 Afternoon

When I entered the hall Bhagavan was already answering a question which, I gathered, was to the effect "Is the theory of evolution true?" and Bhagavan said, "The trouble with all of us is that we want to know the past, what we were, and also what we will be in the future. We know nothing about the past or the future. We do know the present and that we exist now. Both yesterday and tomorrow are only with reference to today. Yesterday was called 'today' in its time, and tomorrow will be called 'today' by us tomorrow. Today is ever present. What is ever present is pure existence. It has no past or future. Why not try and find out the real nature of the present and ever-present existence?"

Another visitor asked, "The present is said to be due to past karma. Can we transcend the past karma by our free will now?"

Bhagavan: See what the present is, as I told you. Then you will understand what is affected by or has a past or a future and also what is ever-present and always free, unaffected by the past or future or by any past karma.

Another visitor asked, "Can one person create an urge for anything in another. Can a Guru transform a disciple as if by magic?"

Bhagavan: What is your idea of a Guru? You think of him in human shape as a body of certain dimensions, colours, etc. A disciple after enlightenment told his Guru, "I now realise you lived in my innermost heart as the one reality in all my countless births and have now come before me in human shape and lifted this veil of ignorance. What can I do for you in return for such great kindness?" And the Guru said, "You need not do anything. It is enough if you remain as you are in your real state" This is the truth about the Guru.

Mr. Joshi put five questions. I give below the questions and Bhagavan's answers.

Question 1: Should I go on asking 'Who am I?' without answering? Who asks whom? Which *bhavana* (attitude) should be in the mind at the time of enquiry? What is 'I' the Self or the ego?

Answer: In the enquiry 'Who am I?', 'I' is the ego. The question really means, what is the source or origin of this ego? You need not have any *bhavana* in the mind. All that is required is, you must give up the *bhavana* that you are the body, of such and such a description, with such and such a name, etc. There is no need to have a *bhavana* about your real nature. It exists as it always does; it is real and no *bhavana*.

Question 2: I cannot be always engaged in this enquiry, for I have got other work to do, and when I do such work I forget this quest.

Answer: When you do other work, do you cease to exist? You always exist, do you not?

Question 3: Without the sense of doership — the sense 'I am doing' — work cannot be done.

Answer: It can be done. Work without attachment. Work will go on even better than when you worked with the sense that you were the doer.

Question 4: I don't understand what work I should do and what not.

Answer: Don't bother. What is destined as work to be done by you in this life will be done by you, whether you like it or not.

Question 5: Why should I try to realise? I will emerge from this state, as I wake up from a dream. We do not make an attempt to get out of a dream during sleep.

Answer: In a dream, you have no inkling that it is a dream and so you don't have the duty of trying to get out of it by your effort. But in this life you have some intuition, by your sleep experience, by reading and hearing, that this life is something like a dream, and hence the duty is cast on you to make an effort and get out of it. However, who wants you to realise the Self, if you don't want it? If you prefer to be in the dream, stay as you are.

With reference to question 4, Mrs. P. C. Desai quoting the *Bhagavad Gita* asked Bhagavan, "If (as Arjuna was told) there is a certain work destined to be done by each and we shall eventually do it however much we do not wish to do it or refuse to do it, is there any free will?"

Bhagavan said, "It is true that the work meant to be done by us will be done by us. But it is open to us to be free from the joys or pains, pleasant or unpleasant consequences of the work, by not identifying ourselves with the body or that which does the work. If you realise your true nature and know that it is not you that does any work, you will be unaffected by the consequences of whatever work the body may be engaged in according to destiny or past karma or divine plan, however you may call it. You are always free and there is no limitation of that freedom."

4-1-46 Morning

Among the letters etc., received was a small pamphlet called *Divine Grace Through Total Self-Surrender* by Mr. D.C. Desai. Bhagavan read out to us a few extracts from it, *viz.*, the following quotation from Paul Brunton: "I remain perfectly calm and fully aware of who I am and what is occurring. Self still exists, but it is a changed, radiant Self. Something that is far superior to my unimportant personality rises into consciousness and becomes me. I am in the midst of an ocean of blazing light. I sit in the lap of holy bliss"; and also the following: "Divine grace is a manifestation of the cosmic free-will in operation. It can alter the course of events in a mysterious manner through its own unknown laws, which are superior to all natural laws, and can modify the latter by interaction. It is the most powerful force in the universe."

"It descends and acts, only when it is invoked by total self-surrender. It acts from within, because God resides in the heart of all beings. Its whisper can be heard only in a mind purified by self-surrender and prayer."

Paul Brunton describes its nature as follows: "Rationalists laugh at it and atheists scorn it, but it exists. It is a descent of God into the soul's zone of awareness. It is a visitation of force unexpected and unpredictable. It is a voice spoken out of cosmic silence . . . . It is cosmic will which can perform authentic miracles under its own laws."

Afternoon

Dr. Syed read out to Bhagavan a Sufi story from this month's *Vision* whose moral is that there must be implicit, unquestioning faith in and obedience to the Master's direction.

When all others would not obey Muhammad Ghazni's command to destroy a precious gem of his, one servant unhesitatingly destroyed it and, when taken to task for it by the others, said, "Nothing is more precious to me than my master's command." I was reminded by this of the following incident in Ramanuja's life and so related it to Dr. Syed and others. It seems God Ranganatha was being taken out in procession in Srirangam and Ramanuja called out to a disciple to come out and see the procession. The disciple was boiling Ramanuja's milk and would not come out however often he was called, and later explained to his Master, "Ranganatha is your Master and he is important to you. You alone are important to me and I couldn't leave off your service, *i.e.*, boiling milk for you, to go and see Ranganatha."

With reference to Bhagavan's answer to Mrs. Desai's question on the evening of 3-1-46, I asked him, "Are only important events in a man's life, such as his main occupation or profession, predetermined, or are trifling acts in his life, such as taking a cup of water or moving from one place in the room to another, also predetermined?"

Bhagavan: Yes, everything is predetermined.

I: Then what responsibility, what free will has man?

Bhagavan: What for then does the body come into existence?

It is designed for doing the various things marked out for execution in this life. The whole programme is chalked out. 'அவனன்றி ஓரணுவும் அசையாது' (Not an atom moves except by His Will) expresses the same truth, whether you say அவனன்றி அசையாது (Does not move except by His Will) or கர்மமின்றி அசையாது (Does not move except by karma). As for freedom for man, he is always free not to identify himself with the body and not to be affected by the pleasures or pains consequent on the body's activities.

5-1-46 Afternoon

When I entered the hall Bhagavan was answering some question saying, "There is no difference between dream and the waking state except that the dream is short and the waking long. Both are the result of the mind. Because the waking state is long, we imagine that it is our real state. But, as a matter of fact, our real state is what is sometimes called *turiya* or the fourth state which is always as it is and knows nothing of the three *avasthas, viz.*, waking, dream or sleep. Because we call these three *avasthas* we call the fourth state also *turiya avastha*. But it is not an *avastha*, but the real and natural state of the Self. When this is realised, we know it is not a *turiya* or fourth state, for a fourth state is only relative, but *turiyatita*, the transcendent state called the fourth state."

A visitor asked Bhagavan, "Priests prescribe various rituals and pujas and people are told that unless they properly observe these with fasts, feasts, etc., sin will accrue, and so on. Is there any necessity to observe such rituals and ceremonial worship?"

Bhagavan: Yes. All such worship is also necessary. It may not be necessary for you. But that does not mean it is necessary for nobody and is no good at all. What is necessary for the infant class pupil is not necessary for the graduate. But even the graduate has to make use of the very alphabet he learnt in the infant class. He knows the full use and significance of the alphabet now.

The same visitor asked, "I do *Omkara* puja. I say 'Om Ram'. Is that good?"

Bhagavan: Yes. Any puja is good. 'Om Ram' or any other name will do. The point is to keep away all other thoughts except the one thought of Om or Ram or God. All *mantra* or *japa* helps that. He who does the *japa* of Ram, for example, becomes *Rama-maya*. The worshipper becomes in course of time the worshipped. It is only then that he will know the full meaning of the *Omkar* which he was repeating.

Our real nature is *mukti*. But we are imagining we are bound and are making various strenuous attempts to become free, while we are all the while free. This will be understood only when we reach that stage. We will be surprised that we were frantically trying to attain something which we have always been and are. An illustration will make this clear. A man goes to sleep in this hall. He dreams he has gone on a world tour, is roaming over hill and dale, forest and country, desert and sea, across various continents and after many years of weary and strenuous travel, returns to this country, reaches Tiruvannamalai, enters the Asramam and walks into the hall. Just at that moment he wakes up and finds he has not moved an inch but was sleeping where he lay down. He has not returned after great effort to this hall, but is and always has been in the hall. It is exactly like that. If it is asked, why being free we imagine we are bound, I answer, "Why being in the hall did you imagine you were on a world adventure, crossing hill and dale, desert and sea? It is all mind or *maya*."

Another visitor, who said that he was from Sri Aurobindo's Ashram, asked Bhagavan: "But we see pain in the world. A man is hungry. It is a physical reality. It is very real to him. Are we to call it a dream and remain unmoved by his pain?"

Bhagavan: From the point of view of *jnana* or the reality, the pain you speak of is certainly a dream, as is the world of which the pain is an infinitesimal part. In the dream also you yourself feel hunger. You see others suffering hunger. You feed yourself and, moved by pity, feed the others that you find suffering from hunger. So long as the dream lasted, all those pains were quite as real as you now think the pain you see in the world to be. It was only when you woke up that you discovered that the pain in the dream was unreal. You might have eaten to the full and gone to sleep. You dream that you work hard and long in the hot sun all day, are tired and hungry and want to eat a lot. Then you get up and find your stomach is full and you have not stirred out of your bed. But all this is not to say that while you are in the dream you can act as if the pain you feel there is not real. The hunger in the dream has to be assuaged by the food in the dream. The fellow beings you found in the dream so hungry had to be provided with food in that dream. You can never mix up the two states, the dream and the waking state. Till you reach the state of *jnana* and thus wake out of this *maya*, you must do social service by relieving suffering whenever you see it. But even then you must do it, as we are told, without *ahamkara, i.e.*, without the sense "I am the doer," but feeling, "I am the Lord's tool." Similarly one must not be conceited, "I am helping a man below me. He needs help. I am in a position to help. I am superior and he inferior." But you must help the man as a means of worshipping God in that man. All such service too is for the Self, not for anybody else. You are not helping anybody else, but only yourself.

Mr. T.P. Ramachandra Aiyar said in this connection, "There is the classic example of Abraham Lincoln, who helped a pig to get out of a ditch and in the process had himself and his clothes dirtied. When questioned why he took so much trouble, he replied, 'I did it to put an end not so much to the pig's trouble, as to my own pain in seeing the poor thing struggle to get out of the ditch'."

Mr. Joshi asked: I am a householder. I have dependants and obstacles in the way of my spiritual progress. What should I do?

Bhagavan: See whether those dependants and obstacles are outside you, whether they exist without you.

Joshi: I am a beginner. How should I start?

Bhagavan: Where are you now? Where is the goal? What is the distance to be covered? The Self is not somewhere far away to be reached. You are always that. You have only to give up your habit, a long-standing one, of identifying yourself with the non-self. All effort is only for that. By turning the mind outwards, you have been seeing the world, the non-Self. If you turn it inwards you will see the Self.

After this discourse, Lokamma began singing a Tamil song. Bhagavan at once said: "Mother used to sing this song very often. This repeats the very same thing we have been talking about now." Thereupon I asked Bhagavan who the author of the song was.

He said, "Avudai Ammal. She has composed a great many songs. They are very popular in those parts (Madura and other nearby districts). Some of them have been published. Still so many remain unpublished. They have been handed down orally from generation to generation, mostly through women, who learn them by heart, hearing them from others and singing them along with those who already know them." I learnt now that Bhagavan's mother was illiterate. Bhagavan told me that, in spite of it, she had learnt by heart a great many songs. The song and its meaning are given below:

பல்லவி

சச்சிதா னந்தமாய் தானிருந்தும் மறந்தவர்போல்
எப்படிமுன் னிருந்த தன்னமே — ஆ ஆ — (சச்சி)

அனுபல்லவி

அற்புதமீ தற்புதபீ தற்புதபீ தென்னிடத்தில்
அச்சமுற இடமில்லையே — ஆ ஆ — (சச்சி)

சரணம்

1. மனசுண்டோ மறந்தறிய வபுசுண்டோ பிறந்திறக்க
மலமுண்டோ நிர்மலத்திலே
சரிபெரிசு சிறுசுண்டோ ஜாதிவர்ண மதிலுண்டோ
சாக்ஷியென்ன சாக்ஷிய முண்டோ
நிறைந்தசுக சாகரத்தில் நிஷ்களம் சகளமென்ன
அற்புதமீ தற்புத மிதுவே — ஆ ஆ — (சச்சி)

2. வாய்திறக்க இடுமில்லை மௌனசங் கல்பமில்லை
வந்ததில்லை போனது மில்லை
ஆதியந்தம் நடுவுமில்லை ஜோதியென்று பேருமில்லை
உபாதியில்லை என்னிடத்திலே
பாதியென்றும் பீதியென்றும் உபாதிவந்த சொப்பனமி(து)
அற்புதமீ தற்புத மிதுவே — ஆ ஆ — (சச்சி)

3. உட்புறம்பு உயரம்கீழ் தசதிக்கும் பூரணமாய்
ஒளியாகி வெளியாகியே
நிற்குண நிராதரமாய் நிறைவாய் உபசாந்தமுமாய்
பிரஞ்ஞான கனமாகியே
அக்ஷயா னந்தமாய் அகம்பதலக்ஷி யார்த்தமுமாய்
அபரோக்ஷ சுகமாகியே — ஆ ஆ — (சச்சி)

How did the Self that ever is
Awareness — bliss,
How did It till now behave
As if It had forgotten this?

Wonder of wonders, beyond understanding
Is your strange fear,
My Swan, my dear,
Your fear of me!

Mind learning, knowing and forgetting,
Body begotten, begetting and then dying,
Whence these impurities in Purity?
Bigness, smallness, class, rank, sight and seer —
Why these darkling waves in the full deep sea of bliss?

No need for speech or vow of silence;
No coming or going; no beginning, end or middle.
Nor light nor sound; no quality.
No separateness and hence no fear.
Oh wonder of wonders, the things that seem
In a dream!

In and out, high and low, and all the ten directions
Lost in light illimitably vast,
Unbroken, unsupported, full and calm,
Pure Awareness, Bliss immutable,
The once-remote, long — longed — for goal
Now here, joy, joy!

6-1-46 Morning

Mr. Lakshmana Sarma (known as 'Who') has come. Bhagavan was looking into a note-book in which Mr. Sarma had written out an English translation of his *Vedanta Saram* (Sanskrit). I was curious to know what this *Vedanta Saram* deals with and so was asking Mr. Sarma's son Kameswaran about it. Bhagavan heard this and turning to me said, "This is the same as *Maha Yoga*."

There was some talk about Sarma's birthday and Bhagavan said, "He says he is born always or daily" and referred to the eleventh stanza in the supplement to *Ulladu Narpadu* in Tamil which has been translated into English under the title *Reality in Forty Verses*. For looking up this song he picked up 'நூற்றிரட்டு' (*Collected Works* in Tamil) from the revolving shelf by his side and before putting it back, detected that moths had been at work on the cover. He remarked, "We have not been studying these books. So these insects have been digesting them."

Afternoon

Mr. L. Sarma came and sat next to me. This morning he could not recognise me, though I was only about three feet from him. So I was advising him to undergo an operation for his cataract. He said that he had been able to retard the development of this disease and that, if he could do so in the future also, he would rather manage for the rest of his life with partial eyesight than risk an operation. Then I told him it all depended on what further lease of life he had and in this connection I asked what the reading of his horoscope in this matter was. Thus we talked about astrology and I asked Bhagavan for his view on astrology. He said, "It is all right (அது சரிதான்). Why not? If one accepts the theory of karma, one will have to accept the theory of astrology and horoscope also." After this, Sarma, Dr. Syed, G. Subba Rao and myself talked about the science of astrology and whether there was any use or sense in knowing our future and so on; and then Mr. Subba Rao told us that in the books on astrology it is clearly laid down that what is destined to happen according to the horoscope may be modified to some extent by propitiatory *pujas* etc. Mr. S. Rao went on to say how the mere dust of the feet of men like Bhagavan, how a look from them, can burn away all our sins etc. At this I asked, "I have also come across some of these writings which extol the virtues of *sat sang*. I should like to know whether these writings are to be understood as literally true and whether there is not some exaggeration in them." Mr. S. Rao said they were literally true, but that one must have faith. And I asked him why, if that were so, those who were responsible for those texts about *sat sang* did not add the proviso themselves but left it to commentators like Mr. S. Rao to add it. Thus a number of us wrangled for a few minutes; but Bhagavan kept silent studiously, as usual on such occasions. Then we too became silent. Once before I had put the question to Bhagavan himself, with reference to the five stanzas on *sat sang* in the Supplement to the *Reality in Forty Verses* and Bhagavan only said then, "அதென்னமோ, நான் இருந்ததை அப்படியே தான் எழுதினேன்;" meaning, "I have translated the verses as I found them (in Sanskrit). Don't ask me!"

7-1-46 Morning

Mr. Mahatani asked Bhagavan, "It is said in *Advaita Bodha Deepika*, that the Supreme Self identifying itself with the mind appears changeful. How can the mind coming from *maya* which itself comes from the Self be able to alter or change the changeless Self?" Bhagavan answered, "There is in reality no change, no creation. But for those who ask, 'How has this creation come about?' the above explanation is given."

Afternoon

Mr. Ramachandra Rao of Bangalore read before Bhagavan his Canarese work just being prepared called *The Ramana I have known*. After he had finished reading, I asked him when he first came to Bhagavan and he said, '1918'. I then asked him if he was narrating all his experiences since then and if he was doing so with the help of any notes or memoranda. He replied he was writing of all that had happened since 1918, and that only from memory. I was wondering at such memory. Bhagavan said, "Nayana (Kavyakantha Ganapathi Muni) would remember and give you the hour and date for every incident at which he was present."

Night

Mr. G.L. Sarma seems to have prepared a manuscript on *Gita Saram*. Bhagavan asked Mr. Balaram Reddi to read it out.

As it was said in that, "Only when there is complete devotion, the Lord will respond and take complete charge of the devotee," Mr. P. Bannerji (who has recently come after a stay at Aurobindo's) asked Bhagavan, "Is it a condition precedent for the Lord showing grace that one must be completely devoted? Would not the Lord naturally in his grace be kind towards all his children whether they are devoted or not?"

Bhagavan: How can one help being devoted? Everyone loves himself. That is experience. If the Self were not his dearest object, would one love it? The Self or Lord is not somewhere else but is inside each of us and in loving oneself, one loves only the Self.

The visitor could not understand how this was an answer to his question. I explained, "Bhagavan has told us more than once, 'The Lord's grace is always flowing. There is no time at which it is not flowing, and no person towards whom it is not flowing. But only those can receive it who have developed the capacity. Devotion is a condition precedent, not for the flowing of grace from the Lord, but for your being able to receive and assimilate the grace which is there always flowing'."

In this connection Dr. Syed quoted the verse in *Bhagavad Gita* which says that the Lord is the friend of all, the sinner and the saint alike, but that he is specially in the heart of those who cherish him and that such people are dear to Him.

8-1-46 Afternoon

Mr. Mahtani again asked Bhagavan about his question (found recorded under 7-1-46). Bhagavan replied, "The very sentence you quote says that mind is a superimposition, that it has no reality but is like the appearance of the snake in the rope. The text also says the Supreme Self, when identified with the mind, appears changeful. To the seer, the ego, the Self seems changeful. But the Self is the same ever, unchanging and unchangeable. It is like this: There is a screen. On that screen first appears the figure of a king. He sits on a throne. Then before him in that same screen a play begins with various figures and objects and the king on the screen watches the play on the same screen. The seer and the seen are mere shadows on the screen, which is the only reality supporting these pictures. In the world also, the seer and the seen together constitute the mind and the mind is supported by, or based on, the Self."

9-1-46 Afternoon

Mr. P. Bannerji asked Bhagavan, 'What is the difference between *jivanmukti* and *videhamukti*?

Bhagavan: There is no difference. For those who ask, it is said, 'A *jnani* with body is a *jivanmukta* and he attains *videhamukti* when he drops off this body.' But this difference is only for the onlooker, not for the *jnani*. His state is the same before and after the body is dropped. We think of the *jnani* as a human form or as being in that form. But the *jnani* knows he is the Self, the one reality which is both inside and outside, and which is not bound by any form or shape. There is a verse in the *Bhagavata* (and here Bhagavan quoted the Tamil verse) which says, "Just as a man who is drunk is not conscious whether his upper cloth is on his body or has slipped away from it, the *jnani* is hardly conscious of his body, and it makes no difference to him whether the body remains or has dropped off."

Mr. P.B. asked, "What is the difference between a devotee and a disciple? A friend here told me I should not call myself a disciple of Bhagavan and that I can only be a devotee."

Bhagavan: If we worship an object or person then we are devotees. If we have a Guru then we are disciples.

I added that his friend must have told him so, for the reason that Bhagavan takes no disciples, *i.e.*, formally initiates none, and so it may be misleading if any one says, 'I am Bhagavan's disciple.'

P.B.: But what if I accept his teaching and regard myself as his disciple because I try to follow his teaching?

I replied, "Of course you may do that, as Ekalavya learnt archery from an image of Drona."

Bhagavan then added, "After all, as in the above case everything comes from within. First the man feels that he is bound, in the bondage of *samsara*, that he is weak and miserable and that unless he leans upon and gets help from God who is all-powerful and can save him, he cannot get out of bondage and misery. Thus he makes *bhakti* to *Ishwara*. When this *bhakti* develops and the intensity of his devotion is so great that he forgets his entire self and becomes *Iswaramaya* and complete surrender has been achieved, God takes human shape and comes as Guru and teaches the devotee that there is but one Self and that That is within him. Then the devotee attains *jnana* by realizing the Self within him and then he understands that the *Ishwara* or Lord whom he worshipped and had *bhakti* for, the Guru who came in human shape, and the Self are all the same."

Mr. P.B.'s first question led Bhagavan to speak further about realisation and he said, "There are no stages in realisation or *mukti*. There are no degrees of *jnana*. So that there cannot be one stage of *jnana* with the body and another stage when the body is dropped. The *jnani* knows he is the Self and that nothing, neither his body nor anything else exists, but the Self. To such one what difference could the presence or absence of body make?

"It is false to speak of Realisation. What is there to realise? The real is as it is, ever. How to real-ise it? All that is required is this. We have real-ised the unreal, *i.e.*, regarded as real what is unreal. We have to give up this attitude. That is all that is required for us to attain *jnana*. We are not creating anything new or achieving something which we did not have before. The illustration given in books is this. We dig a well and create a huge pit. The *akasa* in the pit or well has not been created by us. We have just removed the earth which was filling the *akasa* there. The *akasa* was there then and is also there now. Similarly we have simply to throw out all the age-long *samskaras* which are inside us, and when all of them have been given up, the Self will shine, alone." He also said, "*Mukti, jnana, dhyana* is our real nature. They are other names for the Self".

10-1-46 Afternoon

Bhagavan was perusing some verses in Tamil (கண்ணிகள்) composed by Mr. Venkatesa Sastrigal. He and his wife (Salammal) had been staying in the Asramam. But about a fortnight back they moved to Adiyannamalai and settled down there. When I and T. P. Ramachandra Aiyar and some others went round the hill on the 1st January, Mr. Sastriar and his wife met us on the road and took us to their house and there we had these verses read out to us. I mentioned, therefore, that the verses were not new to us. Thereupon Mr. Sastriar said the verses stood at 27 then and were now 108. A few days back Mr. Venkatrama Aiyar brought news to Bhagavan that Sastriar and his wife intended coming here on Thursday. After Bhagavan heard it, he said in connection with some letter which had arrived here for Sastriar, "It seems they are coming here on Thursday. Whether they will stay here or whether intend to go back we don't know." When Sastriar came to the hall, I told him about Bhagavan's remarks and added, "I mention this to you as I too don't like your having shifted there." Bhagavan said, "They came and said they were going to Adi Annamalai and live there. I did not say anything. Why should we interfere? They want to live free, without being under any restraint or regulations as in the Asramam. They must have peace of mind, wherever they may be."

Speaking of Adiyannamalai, where Mr. Venkatesa Sastrigal was staying, Bhagavan said, "It is a good place. I used to stay there occasionally. Once on a *giri-pradakshina* we were caught in the rain and we stayed the whole night in the temple there. It was then I heard the Sama Veda chant."

11-1-46 Afternoon

A young man from Colombo asked Bhagavan, "J. Krishnamurti teaches the method of effortless and choiceless awareness as distinct from that of deliberate concentration. Would Sri Bhagavan be pleased to explain how best to practise meditation and what form the object of meditation should take?"

Bhagavan: Effortless and choiceless awareness is our real nature. If we can attain it or be in that state, it is all right. But one cannot reach it without effort, the effort of deliberate meditation. All the age-long *vasanas* carry the mind outward and turn it to external objects. All such thoughts have to be given up and the mind turned inward. For that, effort is necessary for most people. Of course everybody, every book says, "சும்மா இரு" *i.e.*, "Be quiet or still". But it is not easy. That is why all this effort is necessary. Even if we find one who has at once achieved the *mauna* or Supreme state indicated by "சும்மா இரு", you may take it that the effort necessary has already been finished in a previous life. So that, effortless and choiceless awareness is reached only after deliberate meditation. That meditation can take any form which appeals to you best. See what helps you to keep away all other thoughts and adopt that method for your meditation.

In this connection Bhagavan quoted verses 5 and 52 from "உடல் பொய்யுறவு" and 36 from "பாயப் புலி" of Saint Thayumanavar. Their gist is as follows. "Bliss will follow if you are still. But however much you may tell your mind about this truth, the mind will not keep quiet. It is the mind that won't keep quiet. It is the mind which tells the mind, 'Be quiet and you will attain bliss'. Though all the scriptures have said it, though we hear about it every day from the great ones, and though even our Guru says it, we never are quiet, but stray into the world of *maya* and sense objects. That is why conscious, deliberate effort or meditation is required to attain that *mauna* state or the state of being quiet."

Another young man from Colombo asked Bhagavan, "How are the three states of consciousness inferior in degree of reality to the fourth? What is the actual relation between these three states and the fourth?"

Bhagavan: There is only one state, that of consciousness or awareness or existence. The three states of waking, dream and sleep cannot be real. They simply come and go. The real will always exist. The 'I' or existence that alone persists in all the three states is real. The other three are not real and so it is not possible to say they have such and such a degree of reality. We may roughly put it like this. Existence or consciousness is the only reality. Consciousness plus waking, we call waking. Consciousness plus sleep, we call sleep. Consciousness plus dream, we call dream. Consciousness is the screen on which all the pictures come and go. The screen is real, the pictures are mere shadows on it. Because by long habit we have been regarding these three states as real, we call the state of mere awareness or consciousness as the fourth. There is however no fourth state, but only one state. In this connection Bhagavan quoted verse 386 from 'பராபரக் கண்ணி' of Thayumanavar and said this so-called fourth state is described as waking sleep or sleep in waking — meaning asleep to the world and awake in the Self.

Mr. O. P. Ramaswami Reddiar (the Congress leader) asked Bhagavan, "But why should these three states come and go on the real state or the screen of the Self?"

Bhagavan: Who puts this question? Does the Self say these states come and go? It is the seer who says these states come and go. The seer and the seen together constitute the mind. See if there is such a thing as the mind. Then, the mind merges in the Self, and there is neither the seer nor the seen. So the real answer to your question is, "Do they come and go? They neither come nor go." The Self alone remains as it ever is. The three states owe their existence to 'அவிசார' (non-enquiry) and enquiry puts an end to them. However much one may explain, the fact will not become clear until one attains Self-realisation and wonders how he was blind to the self-evident and only existence so long.

Another visitor asked Bhagavan, "What is the difference between the mind and the Self?"

Bhagavan: There is no difference. The mind turned inwards is the Self; turned outwards, it becomes the ego and all the world. The cotton made into various clothes, we call by various names. The gold made into various ornaments, we call by various names. But all the clothes are cotton and all the ornaments gold. The one is real, the many are mere names and forms.

But the mind does not exist apart from the Self, *i.e.*, it has no independent existence. The Self exists without the mind, never the mind without the Self.

18-1-46 Morning

This is தை பூசம் (Thai Poosam) day. That led me to ask why Ramalinga Swami's memory was celebrated on that day, whether he shook off his mortal coil on Thai Poosam. Bhagavan could not say. I also wanted to know if Bhagavan knew anything authentic as to how exactly Ramalinga Swami ended his life on earth. Bhagavan said nothing about this either.

Afternoon

In the English abridgement of *Srimad Bhagavatam* I found it said that Prithu let his body be dissolved into the several elements of which it was composed. As this sounds very much like what is generally reported of Ramalinga Swami, (*viz.*, that he got into a room and locked himself up and that, when after some days the room was broken open, it was found empty), I asked Bhagavan whether 'realised' men could make their bodies disappear thus. He said, "The books tell us that some saints went away with their bodies to heaven, riding on elephants, etc., sent specially to take them. They also speak of saints disappearing as light or flame, as *akasa* or ether, and as stone lingam. But it must be remembered that all this is only in the view of the onlooker. The *jnani* does not think he is the body. He does not even see the body. He sees only the Self in the body. If the body is not there, but only the Self, the question of its disappearing in any form does not arise." In this connection Bhagavan again quoted the Tamil verse from *Bhagavatam* already referred to in the entry under 9-1-46; and at this time he made us take out both the Sanskrit verse and the Tamil verse from the books, I give below the two verses:

சாற்றிய குணமு மாக்கையு மனமுந்
தானல வென்பதை யுணர்ந்தாற்
போற்றிய வாக்கை யுடனிருப் பதுவும்
போவது மறந்திடா ராகி
யேற்றதம் புயமேற் றுகில்கழி வதுவு
மிருப்பதும் வெண்ணறை பருகி
மாற்றரு மதத்தி னறிந்திடா தொழுகு
மக்களைப் போலுவர் மாதோ.

deham cha nasvaram avasthitam utthitam va
siddho no pasyati yatodhyagamat svarupam
daivadapetam uta daiva vasad upetam
vaso yatha parikrtam madira madandhah.

(22, *Hamsa Gita: The Bhagavata*, Ch. XI)

(The meaning of this stanza is given on page 113).

Bhagavan added, "There is a certain school of thinkers who would not call anyone a *jnani* whose body is left behind at death. It is impossible to conceive of a *jnani* attaching such importance to the body. But there is such a school — the Siddha School. In Pondicherry they have a Society." Soon after this a boy of about seventeen years from Pondicherry came and asked Bhagavan, "After hearing the *pranava* sound, what is the stage beyond it that one should reach?" Bhagavan said, "Who is it that hears the *pranava* or talks of the stage beyond? See and find out, and then all will be clear. What is *pranava*, and what is that stage beyond hearing *pranava* of which you speak? Where is it? About all those things we don't know. But you are. So find out first about your self, the seer, and then all will be known."

The boy again asked, "I wish to know what is the way to *mukti*."

Bhagavan: That is all right. But what is *mukti*? Where is that and where are you? What is the distance between the two, so that we can speak of a path? First find out about yourself and where you are and then see if these questions arise.

Night

The talk turned to various recipes suggested by various people about *kaya kalpa*. Bhagavan mentioned a few *kalpas* based on camphor, a hundred year old neem tree, etc., and said, "Who would care to take such trouble over this body? As explained in books, the greatest malady we have is the body, the பவ நோய் (the disease of birth), and if one takes medicines to strengthen it and prolong its life, it is like a man taking medicine to strengthen and perpetuate his disease. As the body is a burden we bear, we should on the other hand feel like the coolie engaged to carry a load, anxiously looking forward to arrival at the destination when he can throw off his burden."

19-1-46 Morning

Bhagavan told me that my question about Thai Poosam and Ramalinga Swami was answered in today's *Bharata Devi*, which says that the Swami entered into the room for his end on Thai Poosam day. Mr. Viswanatha Aiyar read out the long article which compared the Swami to Mahatma Gandhi and quoted largely from his *Arutpa*.

Afternoon

Yesterday I suggested to Bhagavan that he might make a Tamil translation of the Sanskrit verse from Chap. XI of the *Bhagavata*, as he felt that the Tamil verse did not closely follow the Sanskrit original. So, today seeing Muruganar in the hall and talking to him about it, he casually composed the following stanza without paper or pencil in his hand.

தனுநிலை யிலதே சரிக்கினு மிருக்கினும்
வினையினாற் கூடி விலகிடு மாயினும்
தனையறி சித்தன் றானுணர் கின்றிலன்
புனைதுகி லினைக்கள் வெறியினன் போலவே.

(An English translation of this stanza is given on page 113).

Night

Bhagavan wants to improve the Tamil rendering and bring it nearer the original Sanskrit. He discussed some alterations with Muruganar, and told me that I was not to regard the above stanza as final.

20-1-46 Morning

Mr. Balaram Reddi asked Bhagavan about the Sanskrit verse whose translation is found in the supplement to *Reality in Forty Verses* beginning 'தேகங்கட நிகர்சடம்' and Bhagavan explained how he used the word *Abhavam* and Kavyakantha preferred *Abhedam*. Bhagavan further told us that this verse seeks to establish in two ways the proposition that the body is not 'I'. First, by saying that the body is *jada* (inert) and never is able to feel or say 'I', and secondly by saying that when we have no body, *i.e.*, even when we have no consciousness of body, 'I' exists. The talk about this verse began under the following circumstances. It seems one Bernard Duval of Morocco was here for about fifteen days some eight years ago. He recently wrote to Major A.W. Chadwick (who has been living in the Asramam for ten years now) that when he was a prisoner during this war, he learnt Sanskrit and even translated Bhagavan's *Upadesa Saram* into English, that later he had lost all those papers, and that he would like all Sanskrit works of Bhagavan to be sent to him. In connection with this request of Mr. Duval, Balaram was finding out what were all the works composed by Bhagavan in Sanskrit, and Bhagavan seems to have told Balaram that the above verse was also composed by him.

Mr. Viswanatha Aiyar's mother came and told Bhagavan, "Nagamma has written an account in Telugu of what took place in our Asramam at the *goshala* on *Mattu Pongal* day. It is very good." Bhagavan said, "Is it so? Her brother has asked her to write accounts of what takes place here. Is she here?" Thereupon we asked Nagamma to read it out and she did so. Bhagavan asked V's mother if she had read *Ramana Gopala*. She said, "I have read only the Tamil rendering made by my son and want to hear the Telugu original." Thereupon we asked Nagamma to read out the Telugu and it was done.

One Mr. Gokul Bhai D. Bhatt, a Public Accountant of Bombay, composed a few verses on Bhagavan and read them out in the hall. At my request he also translated them for the benefit of all assembled in the hall. One Mr. Govindaramaiya, P. W. Inspector from Chittoor, took Bhagavan's permission and read out Sage Angirasa's *Gurupadaka*. It seems he was advised to do so by one Subramania Sastri, a very aged *jnani*, past eighty years, belonging to Conjeevaram originally, whom he met recently at Ambattur.

This morning, before returning to the hall at about 10 a.m., Bhagavan gave *darshan*, near the cowshed, to one Mr. Ramaswami Iyengar who, it seems, has been having a Ramanasramam at Kumbakonam for several years, who is now aged and infirm, and who has come with great trouble to see Bhagavan after many years, during which the *Sarvadhikari* had denied him access to Bhagavan for various alleged misdeeds on his part. The poor man had to remain in his car which was brought to the cowshed and Bhagavan, on his way to the hall, stood a few minutes near the car and gave *darshan* to his old disciple. The disciple just wept and said nothing. Bhagavan gave him one of his well-known gracious looks.

Afternoon

I was very late in going to the hall. But before going for his evening stroll Bhagavan himself was pleased to ask me, "You have not seen the final form into which we have cast that stanza?" and showed me the following.

தனுநிலை யிலதால் தங்கினு மெழினும்
வினையினு லடுத்து விடுத்திடு மேனும்
புனைதுகி லினுக்கள் வெறிக்குரு டனைப்போற்
றனையுணர் சித்தன் றனுவுணர் கிலனே.

(An English translation of this stanza is given on page 113.)

Night

I understood எழினும் in the first line as rising into the air or sky and so asked Bhagavan how it was appropriate; but he explained that it only meant 'moving'. He also told me, "We have it concisely in the Sanskrit. But in the *Sita Rama Anjaneya Samvadam* it is given in great detail and elaborately." This remark was due to the fact that yesterday, when Bhagavan could not find in the Tamil *Bhagavatam* anything corresponding to the Sanskrit verse, G. Subba Rao said that he remembered the same thing occurring in the Telugu *Sita Rama Anjaneya Samvadam*. Today the book was produced and the relevant portion was shown to Bhagavan. Balaram Reddi told me that *Sita Rama Anjaneya Samvadam* is to the Telugus what *Kaivalyam* is to the Tamilians.

When Kunjuswami arrived in the hall, Bhagavan asked him whether Ramaswami Iyengar of Kumbakonam had left and what he intended to do. K. said that R. intended to stay for a month or two at Palakottu till he recovered his health and that the others alone would go back the following day.

21-1-46

Gokul Bhai read out the Gujarati *Ramana Gita* Chapter XI and then the Gujarati *Upadesa Saram*. Mr. P.C. Desai asked Bhagavan, "In verse 14, they have translated the second line of the Sanskrit verse as 'If the mind is continuously fixed on meditation of the Self, etc.' Is that all right, seeing that neither 'continuously' nor 'Self' is found in the original?"

Bhagavan: Eka chintana involves continuous thought. If no other thought is to come, the one thought has to be continuous. What is meant by the verse is as follows. The previous verses have said that for controlling the mind breath-control or *pranayama* may be helpful. This verse says that the mind so brought under control or to the state of *laya* should not be allowed to be in mere *laya* or a state like sleep, but that it should be directed towards *eka chintana* or one thought, whether that one thought is of the Self, the *ishta devata* or a *mantram*. What the one thought may be will depend on each man's *pakva* or fitness. The verse leaves it as one thought.

Mr. Desai wanted to know if in the next edition verse 14 in the Gujarati should be corrected or if it might stand as now. Bhagavan said nothing. He had said enough on the subject. (I concluded that there could be no harm in introducing 'continuous' in the second line, but there was no justification for bringing in 'thought or Self' as all that Bhagavan said in the original was that the mind brought to *laya* should be made to occupy itself with *eka chintana*, one thought).

Night

When Bhagavan was still engaged in making the Tamil Stanza recorded under 20-1-46, Mr. Balaram Reddi requested him to compose one in Telugu as well. So Bhagavan made one and discussed some alternatives with Balaram. I again asked Bhagavan about the meaning of the first line in the Tamil stanza, "There seems to be no point in saying 'whether the body remains in a place or moves about, it is impermanent.'" Thereupon, he told me that the first line is not to be read as though the whole of it was one sentence and that the first sentence stops with half the line. I give below a literal translation for the correct understanding of the stanza:

"The body is impermanent (not real). Whether it is at rest or moves about and whether by reason of *prarabdha* it clings to him or falls off from him, the Self-realised *siddha* is not aware of it, even as the drunken man blinded by intoxication is unaware whether his cloth is on his body or not."

22-1-46

Early in the morning, immediately after *parayana*, Bhagavan gave Balaram the Telugu stanza and asked for his suggestions for improving it. Balaram replied, "What suggestions are there for me to make?" Bhagavan said, "I don't know. I must ask people like you," and put the verse in the revolving shelf.

23-1-46 Night

Dr. Srinivasa Rao asked whether in Stanza 10 of the Supplement to *Reality in Forty Verses* Bhagavan does not teach us to affirm *soham.* Bhagavan explained it as follows:

It is said the whole Vedanta can be compressed into the four words, *deham, naham, koham, soham*. This stanza says the same. In the first two lines, it is explained why *deham* is *naham, i.e.*, why the body is not 'I' or *na aham*. The next two lines say, 'If one enquires *ko aham, i.e.*, Who am I, *i.e.*, if one enquires whence this 'I' springs and realises it, then in the heart of such a one the omnipresent God Arunachala will shine as 'I', as *sa aham* or *soham*: *i.e.*, he will know 'That I am,' *i.e.*, 'That is "I".'

In this connection Bhagavan also quoted two stanzas, one from Thayumanavar and the other from Nammalvar, the gist of both of which is: "Though I have been thinking I was a separate entity and talking of 'I' and 'mine', when I began to enquire about this 'I', I found *you* alone exist." The two stanzas and their meaning are given below:

1. நானான தன்மையென்று நாடாமல் நாடவின்ப
   வானாகி நின்றனை நீ வாழி பராபரமே—(தாயுமானவர்)

2. யானே யென்னை யறிய கிலாதே
   யானே யென்றன தேயென் றிருந்தேன்
   யானே நீஎன் னுடைமையு நீயே
   வானே யேத்துமெம் வானவ ரேறே.—(நம்மாழ்வார்)

(1) Searching who this 'I' was,
Soon I found
You only standing as the heaven of bliss,
You only, blessed Lord! — (*Thayumanavar*)

(2) Not knowing who I was,
I used to speak of 'I' and 'mine'
But I am You and mine is You,
Lord whom all the gods adore. — (*Nammalvar*)

24-1-46 Morning

Bhagavan picked out the above two verses for me and also quoted the following two lines from the 7th stanza of 'ஆனந்த மானபரம்' in Thayumanavar:

* நானாகி நின்றவனா நீயாகி நின்றிடவு
நானென்ப தற்றி டாதே
நான்நான் எனக்குளறி நானா விகாரியாய்
நானறிந் தறியா மையாய்

Though I have become You and You alone exist
Undestroyed the 'I' persists
As I within that knows

And I that turns to what is known,
The many things knowing and unknowing —

Bhagavan added that many similar quotations could be found elsewhere among Alwar's songs. Dr. S. Rao took the book 'திருவாய்மொழி' (*Tiruvoimozhi*) from Bhagavan's hand and said, "I see there is a commentary also." On this stanza which says, "I discover that I am You, and all that I called mine is You," the *Visishtadvaita* commentator said, "I reached so near God as to regard I and mine as God himself."

Dr. S. Rao said, "The Self-realised ones could not possibly differ among themselves and the leaders of the various schools, if they were Self-realised men, could not have said anything contradictory to each other's teachings. But their followers must have misunderstood or misinterpreted their teachings in such a way as to lead to all these schisms and latter day quarrels." Dr. S. Rao said that, while he was at Salem, a gentleman often quoted to him a verse from Saint Nammalvar in which the Alwar describes the deity at Tirupati as both Vishnu and Siva.

The post brought an English translation from Mr. D.S. Sastri of his sister's Telugu letters regarding Bhagavan's trip to Skandasramam on 25-11-45, and the same was read out in the hall by Mr. Viswanatha Aiyar. The *pathasala* boys had shown Bhagavan a printed picture, "Four rabbits make a great leader." When I came to the hall about 10-15, Bhagavan asked if I had seen it. I said 'No', and thereupon he sent for it and showed it to me. Bhagavan said, "You must first see the four rabbits and then see how they make up Gandhi."

Afternoon

When I entered the hall about 3 p.m., Bhagavan was already searching for the stanza that Dr. S. mentioned. In a little time we got at the stanza. It begins 'தாழ்சடையும்' and is said to have been composed by Peyazhvar when he saw the deity at Tirupati.

Night

Attendant Krishnaswami told Bhagavan that he wanted to go to Madras to see Mahatma Gandhi and that he would return on Sunday. Bhagavan said, "Ask *Sarvadhikari*. Don't say afterwards I gave you permission to go." He added, "If he goes away now, the *Sarvadhikari* may not admit him when he comes back. If he objects to taking him back on his return from Madras, what can I do? What authority have I here?" In spite of all this K. went away, informing Bhagavan he would go and return.

25-1-46 Afternoon

Lokammal sang *Tirukkazhukkunra Pathigam* from *Tiruvachakam*. Muruganar thereupon asked what the meaning of 'நாணொணாததோர் நாணமெய்தி' (became ashamed without becoming ashamed) was. Bhagavan said it might be one of those expressions like நாடாமல் நாடி நினையாமல் நினைந்து (searched without searching; thought without thinking) and நினையாமல் எப்படி நினைக்கிறது. இதெல்லாம் என்னமோ சொல்றது. வேறே சொல்ல வழியில்லை. (How is one to think without thinking? These are all ways of saying. There is no other way of saying.) Similarly Muruganar asked what the allusion was in 'இயக்கி மாற ருபத்து நால்வரை எண் குணம் கொண்ட ஈசனே' (O Lord, who bestowed the eight spiritual attainments on the sixty-four Yakshas). Bhagavan was not sure, but thought it was one of the stories in *Tiruvilaiyadal Puranam*. I went and brought my copy of *Tiruvachakam* with commentary by Subramaniam Pillai. On 'நாணொணாத' etc., the book threw no light at all. As for the latter line, the book said the allusion was to the story of Uttrakosamangai. Bhagavan got the *Tiruvilaiyadal Puranam* but could not find the story there. The story found there was another, though also about six 'இயக்கர்' (*Yakshas*). Muruganar remarked, "This story of Uttarakosamangai does not seem to have been published. It appears that many things in saint Manikkavachagar's life and many sayings or songs of his would be better elucidated if we could get at the above book. We must enquire to see if that book can be had."

Night

After *parayana*, Bhagavan asked Viswanatha Iyer, "What places did you visit?" V. replied, "We went to Guha Namasivayar's Cave, the Mango Tree Cave, Virupakshi Cave and Skandasramam. We returned by the new path which is so well made that we could return without effort. It is such a slope." Bhagavan asked whether they went by a cross cut from Mulaipal Thirtham and V. said 'Yes'. Bhagavan said, "When I now see those places, I wonder how we lived in those places which were then all rocks, stones and thorns. But then, we were quite comfortable and at home. We never felt any inconvenience. There would be no light. We would walk even in the dark among all those rocks and shrubs. As one remarked, we had both lights and eyes in our feet". When I stepped out of the hall Miss Soona Dorabji (she and her father are frequent visitors to the Asramam and ardent devotees of Bhagavan) told me it was she who was escorted by Mr. V. to all the above caves.

26-1-46 Morning

Bhagavan mentioned a book about the Madhva school. Dr. S. Rao took out from the shelf and gave me two pamphlets by one B. N. Krishnamurti Sarma, formerly of Annamalai University, on "Certain philosophical bases of Madhva's theistic realism". Bhagavan said that the gentleman came the day before yesterday and gave these pamphlets in person. "He came and spoke in Sanskrit. He is the Principal of the Sanskrit College at Tiruvaiyar. He says everyone must speak in Sanskrit. He says he has read a lot and is not able to realise the truth. We advised him to read our books and see if they help. He has taken some books from here."

Bhagavan looked into these pamphlets for a few minutes here and there. But he was not interested and said, "This is all for scholars." Dr. S. pointed out a certain passage dealing with *mukti* and saying that, even after *mukti*, each *jiva* retains its individuality, that among those who have attained *mukti* there are several grades, with a hierarchy of *jivas*, and so on. Dr. S. said, "So long as there are others, one will have fear. So long as there are higher stages, one will have a desire to reach them. So this can't be that stage without fear or desire which alone can yield perfect peace." Bhagavan approved of this and quoted a Sanskrit text about that Supreme State without fear or desire.

The blind Muslim from the Punjab (already referred to) again came to the hall today. Bhagavan read an account only a few minutes ago in the *Swadesamitran* of a blind man of Nellore, aged 41, who had *darshan* of Mahatma Gandhi at Madras and who could repeat the entire *Gita* with Sankara's commentary. This led us to talk about the similarity in the two cases, as this Muslim can repeat the whole *Quran*. Bhagavan was reading the Telugu paper *Zamin Ryot* and came across some verses in Telugu by Kanakamma and Lakshmi Bai of Nellore (devotees of Bhagavan and frequent visitors here). He asked Balaram to cut the verses and paste them in the file book. "These verses were composed and read out here last *Jayanti* but are published now in the paper," Bhagavan told us. The verses were read out in the hall by Nagamma today, at Mrs. Taleyarkhan's request. When the bell rang for lunch, Bhagavan said about the blind Muslim, "See if he will stay for lunch; and if so, somebody who knows Hindi must take charge of him and be with him", and he was satisfied only after we said that he would be looked after carefully by us.

Afternoon

At Mrs. Taleyarkhan's request, Nagamma read out, and Balaram translated into English, her account of what took place here on *Mattu Pongal* day. She also read out another account of what took place one day in September when some Bangalore devotees brought two pigeons and requested Bhagavan to keep them in the Asramam. How the pigeons had the great good fortune to be caressed by Bhagavan and to be seated on his lap, and how for nearly one hour they remained quiet as if in *samadhi*, was all beautifully recorded by Nagamma and Mr. Balaram translated this also.

I had the pamphlet on Madhva's Philosophy in my hand and Bhagavan asked me, "Have you read it?" I said, "This does not interest me. As Bhagavan remarked, it might interest only great scholars. But I find this author also asks, as I sometimes used to feel, 'Why should we refuse to treat anything as real unless it exists always'?" Bhagavan said, "How can anything be said to be real which is only a passing show?" Somebody in the hall said, "All this difficulty arises because of translation into English. The Sanskrit word is *satyam* which means, not reality, but that which exists always." Balaram also quoted *Bhagavad Gita* which says, "That which exists never ceases to exist. That which does not exist (at any time) has no existence (இல்லாததனுக்கிருப்பில்லை, உள்ளதனுக் கில்லாமை யென்பதில்லை)". Sometime later, Subbu Lakshmi Ammal (a Brahmin widow who has long been doing service in the kitchen here) told Bhagavan, "I had not so far seen the cave where the Keerai Patti lived. So I went and saw the place yesterday." Bhagavan asked, "Which is the cave you saw?" S. said, "It is called Alamarathu Guhai. I saw it. Bhagavan said on the day we all returned from Skandasramam, 'It is here Keerai Patti lived.' So I thought it was that cave." Bhagavan said, "No. That is not the cave where she lived. She lived only in the *mantapam* in the Guhai Namasivayar Temple nearby. I lived in the cave now called Alamarathu Guhai for some time. There was no *banyan* tree then. That tree as well as all the trees on both sides up to Virupakshi Cave were all planted and watered by Kandaswami who planned and created Skandasramam later." Then Bhagavan, in a reminiscent mood, added, "This Keerai Patti was at the Big Temple even when I first came and was sitting at the Subrahmanyar Temple there. She used to provide food to Sadhus in the Temple. Later, she began bringing food to me from one Kammala (blacksmith) lady who used to send it. After some time that Kammala lady herself began bringing the food to me, instead of sending it through Keerai Patti. Then Keerai Patti used to have a big *jata* (matted locks). When I afterwards came to live in Virupakshi Cave, she was living in the Guhai Namasivayar Temple and she had then removed all her hair. She lived in the *mantapam* there and used to worship the images of Namasivayar, etc., carved on the walls and pillars of the *mantapam*. The priest would come and worship the image inside. But she worshipped and offered food to the images on the wall in the *mantapam* where she lived. She would get up in the morning, go out for a stroll on the small hill, proceed towards the place where our Asramam is now and go round to where Skandasramam is and come down to her place. By that time she would have collected fuel, cow-dung, etc., and bundle them up behind her back; and in her lap she would have gathered a lot of green leaves of all sorts for cooking. She had only one pot. She would first boil water in that pot and bathe. In the same pot she would cook her rice, make her sauce, prepare any side dish such as the leaves she had brought, each by turns, offer the food to the images on the wall or pillar, bring them to me and then go and have her own meal. In the evening she would go into the town. There was not a house in the town which she did not know. She would go and ask for various things and get them. Coming to me, she would say, 'A good soul gave me a handful of broken rice. I have made porridge out of it.'

"But if one went and looked, there would be in her place various provisions and a big pot full of broken rice. That was the sort of woman she was. She was very fond of me. I also used to go to her now and then. I would help her sometimes to gather green leaves, *e.g.*, from a drumstick tree. I would also help her sometimes in cleaning and plucking the leaves preparatory to their being cooked. Sometimes I used to stay there and eat with her." I asked Bhagavan when she died. He said, "She died before we came here. She was buried only here, opposite the Dakshinamurti Temple under a tamarind tree."

Soon after *parayana* was over, about 6-15 p.m., the monkeys (seeing that the window near Bhagavan at which they used to come and beg for fruits and nuts was closed) came near the doorway on the same side, and the ladies and children who wanted to go out of the hall by that doorway were frightened. In connection with this, Mr. Viswanatha Aiyar used the word *manthi* and said it denoted a male monkey. I said, "I believe it means the very reverse. See this from Pillai Perumal Aiyangar, 'மண்மூலந் தாவென்று மந்தி கடுவற்குரைப்ப' (the *manthi* asked her mate to give her roots from the earth)." Thereupon Muruganar said, *manthi* is used generally to denote both sexes and especially to denote the female sex. Bhagavan quoted மந்திகுறளை யொத்தேனில்லை (I am not like the little one of a monkey) of Saint Pattinathar and said, "There evidently it must refer to the mother monkey" and went on to recollect one song from *Thiruppugazh* and another from Pattinathar's உடற்கூற்று வண்ணம் (*Udarkkotruvannam*) in which the word *manthi* occurs. These two songs were picked out at once. The first one is *Palani Vaguppu*. The portion referred to in it was read out by Bhagavan and explained to us. It is in praise of the fertility of Palani and says, "The *manthi* sitting on the areca-nut tree sees the flowers on the sandalwood trees nearby and, thinking they are hoods of snakes, jumps in fear on to another tree, and the branches so vacated, first bending down and then rising up strike against the fully ripe plantain fruits hanging in bunches in the plantain trees nearby and scatter the plantains, which in their turn fall on the jack fruits lying underneath and set flowing the honey forming in them, so that the same honey released in huge quantities flows in streams and waters the adjoining forest of *shambaga* trees." All this was explained by Bhagavan. On previous occasions too I have heard Bhagavan give this as an example of our poets exaggerating the fertility of a country. The other lines in Pattinathar were also picked out. They are: வருவது போவ தொருமுது கூனு மந்தி யெனும்படி குந்தி நடந்து, மதியு மிழந்து செவி திமிர் வந்து. Bhagavan read this song right up to the end, reading the same according to the metre.

27-1-46 Morning

Krishnaswami returned this morning, as he had promised to do. Bhagavan was making kind enquiries about his trip to see Gandhiji at Madras. K. said there were huge crowds in the train and that he had to stand all the way from here to Madras, that there again there was a crowd of more than a lakh, that there was an ocean of cars parked at one corner, that anyhow through the kind offices of some of our friends he sat quite near Mahatma Gandhi with a 6-rupee ticket, that later all the crowd rushed in breaking the gates, that Gandhi refused to speak in any language except Hindi, and so on. Bhagavan said, "You have seen Gandhi. Now you know and have enjoyed the pleasure to be got out of such trips," and so saying he gave back the ticket with the remark, "Keep it safe. It is worth six rupees". K. also brought a number of photographs, big and small, presented to him by Dr. T.N.K., in many of which he and Bhagavan are found together. In this connection, Nagamma told Bhagavan that Viswanatha Iyer's mother wanted to see Bhagavan's pictures taken recently at Skandasramam. He ordered the album to be brought and shown to the lady and it was done.

K. told Bhagavan, "Dr. T.N.K. said he would send some medicines through me to Bhagavan, but I had no time even to meet him again and take them. T.P.R. will bring them." Bhagavan said, "Why medicines? What is wrong with me now? I am all right. All this is unnecessary fuss. Why did you go and ask him to send me medicines?" K. said, "I did not ask. He himself said he would send them; and he is also planning to come and see Bhagavan." Bhagavan remarked, "He would have asked you, 'How is Bhagavan?' and you would have said something. Otherwise why should he send medicine?" K. said, "When one is asked like that, how can one keep quiet? We have to speak." K. also told Bhagavan, "Some of our friends wished to suggest to Mahatma Gandhi that he should visit our Asramam. But when they consulted Mr. O. P. Ramaswami Reddi, he said: 'Here none of us has any access to Mahatma Gandhi. Rajaji alone has influence'." Bhagavan thereupon said, "He won't be allowed to come to such places" (அவாயெல்லாம் இங்கேயெல்லாம் வரவிடமாட்டா). About a week ago, Bhagavan was mentioning that once the Mahatma came to this place, was near the cattle fair site (a furlong or less from our Asramam), finished his business there in less time than the time fixed for it, collected a purse and left the place. K. also brought news that the Mahatma told people that he was frequently thinking of Bhagavan and had great reverence for him. Bhagavan said, "Yes. Yes. That may be so. Whenever anybody tells him he has no peace of mind, he packs them off here, telling them, 'Go and stay at Ramanasramam for a time.' They come and tell us."

Later, after 10 a.m. Bhagavan was reading *Dinamani* and, coming across an article there on the temple at Perur (near Coimbatore), read it out to us and said, "It is news to me. We do not hear of this in the life of Sundaramurti or in the *Periyapuranam*. But it may be in the *Sthalapuranam*." This is the story: On a particular day in the year, the God and the Goddess are taken out to an adjoining field and the festival of the God and Goddess transplanting seedlings on behalf of a devotee is celebrated, in memory of the fact, that one day Sundaramurti Swami entered the temple and found to his dismay that neither God nor Goddess was there and that on searching for them he found them in a field working at transplanting for this devotee, a Harijan.

28-1-46 Morning

Mr. P. B. Ray, who has been staying here for about a month now, has finished his Bengali life of Bhagavan. He read his dedication, translated into English, before Bhagavan, and said he had first heard of Bhagavan from somebody in Madras some years ago, and soon after, he began writing this life and it has taken him four years to complete this. Bhagavan said that long ago some Bengali had written a small life of his in a Bengali journal and that some more articles had also appeared in some Bengali papers or journals about him. Mr. Ray said he had written the two articles now mentioned by Bhagavan. Thereupon Bhagavan searched for the other Bengali article and traced it and gave it to Mr. Ray for perusal. It was in a journal called *Amrut* and published in 1934. The author of the article was Jagadishananda Swami of the Ramakrishna Mission. Mr. Ray perused it and told me in the evening that the article touched on all points, but somehow omitted to make any mention of the experience of Bhagavan arising from the idea of death and resulting in his Self-realisation, which happened at Madura before his coming here.

One Gokul Bhai, who was here recently, has written that he tried to bring Gandhiji here, but he found that Gandhiji peremptorily ordered that nothing at all should be added to his programme which was already too crowded. Bhagavan added, "They can't find time for all this."

29-1-46 Afternoon

Bhagavan took up the new edition of *Ramana Lila* (Telugu life of Bhagavan) and, casually opening it, came across odd stanzas composed by him, (like those about drinking water before, during and after meals, and about those who run after *siddhis* being even worse than the magicians) and expressed surprise, "He has added all these in this edition. I have not seen it so far. When did he take all this and add it in this edition?"

While Bhagavan was still looking into this new edition, a visitor asked, "I came here about a year ago and ever since I have been trying to follow Bhagavan's instructions. I am not however succeeding very well. I try to look at all women as mothers. But I don't succeed." Bhagavan did not reply and the visitor continued, "While I am at home, it is all right. But when I go out and see women, I am not able to control my mind and am swept off my feet. What should I do?" He also added, "I want *atma sakshatkaram*; what should I do? I pray for Bhagavan's blessings." After a pause, Bhagavan replied, "You say you are all right when at home. Be at home, at home in the mind. Don't allow it to go outwards, but turn it inwards and keep it at home there. Then all will be well and you will have *atma sakshatkaram*. The trouble is we think we are the mind. See if we are the mind."

The visitor said, "I am a *grahasta*. Still I want to practise *brahmacharya* even with my wife. But I am not able to succeed. What should I do?" Bhagavan replied, "That is because of age-long *vasanas*. The *sankalpas* are so powerful because they have existed so long. But they will go."

30-1-46 Afternoon

Bhagavan was reading a letter from Mr. Appu Sastri, who had visited one Haridyal Maharaj living in a boat on the Ganges at Benares. The Maharaj (Swami) is reputed to be two hundred years old. In this connection, Bhagavan said, "When I was at Gurumurtham my nails had grown about an inch long and I had a long flowing *jata* (matted hair) and people used to talk I was very old in years, though so young in appearance, and that I had existed like that for centuries!"

The visitor (referred to in the last entry) told Bhagavan, "I am going back to my place this night. I have mentioned my difficulties."

Bhagavan: Yes. They will go gradually.

Visitor: I pray for Bhagavan's *kripa drishti.*

Bhagavan did not reply. Only a few minutes before this Colombo Ramachandra's two small girls had finished singing and almost the last song (composed by their father, an ardent and long-standing devotee) contained the lines — கண்ணாலே பார்த்தவர்கள் கவலகற்றிக் கதிகாட்டும், அண்ணா மலைரமண அருட் குருவா யிருப்பவற்கு, மங்களம் மங்களமே (He who remains at Annamalai as the gracious Guru who casts his glance on them, dissipates their sorrows and directs them to salvation).

Night

A visitor, Ananda Swami, brought a reprint from *The Hindu* of some date in 1940, in which Maurice Frydman (a devotee of Bhagavan for the last ten years) gives an account of how, under circumstances beyond suspicion of fraud, two women prayed, went into a sort of trance, and then got into their hands mysteriously and from nowhere some sugar candy and almonds. The Swami also mentioned that he had seen other instances himself like this where people received fruits, etc., and asked Bhagavan what could be the explanation of such occurrences. Bhagavan replied: "We hear of so many things. There are certain sects which work for such things. They may see or get such things. But who sees or gets them? You must see that. In the *Periyapuranam* also is mentioned a similar occurrence. A merchant sent his wife two mangoes saying he would eat them later with his meal. Before he returned from his business, a *sadhu* came saying he was very hungry and the wife, pitying him, gave him some rice, and, as she had nothing else ready to give with the rice, one of the mangoes. She hoped the husband would be satisfied with only one mango. The husband returned later and during the meal asked for the mangoes, finished one and finding it very sweet asked for the other one also. The wife was in a fix, dreaded her husband's fury and went into the room where she had kept the two fruits before and prayed to God for help in this situation. And lo! One more fruit lay where she had kept the two fruits, and so she brought it and gave it to her husband. He ate it and found it much more delicious and giving him an ecstasy and *shanti* which he had never before known. So he pressed the wife to tell the truth about this fruit and got it out of her. In wonder and still a little incredulous, he asked his wife to pray for and get another fruit. The wife said she would try, and by God's grace got another fruit also. Then it dawned on him she was a saint and he prostrated himself before her and thinking it was sacrilege for him to treat her further as his wife, left the village, and went and lived in some other village. The wife after some time traced him out and thinking that, as he was her Lord, it was her duty to go to him, and it was for him to do what he liked with her, she went towards that village. The husband, getting scent of it, told the villagers there, 'A great saint is coming. We must receive her with due respect, ceremony and pomp, taking out a palanquin and music with drums, etc.' Thus he organised a big welcome and marching at the head of the reception party prostrated himself first before his wife.

"The wife did not know what to do. She shed the mortal body and lived in the astral body and eventually reached heaven taking her husband also there. The woman saint is Karaikkal Ammaiyar, whose story is found in *Periyapuranam*."

We also recalled an incident similar to that narrated by Frydman and this Ananda Swami, which occurred in Bhagavan's hall only a few months back, and which has been recorded in this diary. Then a Gujarati lady got sugar-candy in her palm after praying. At Mr. Balaram's request, the earlier volume of this diary was brought and Mr. B. read out the entry about the above incident as it took place, along with the name and address of the lady who worked this miracle. Mr. Ramaswami Pillai, an old inmate of the Asramam condemned giving importance to such occurrences. He said, "I have seen more wonderful things, such as a person put inside a box and sawn asunder, and coming out whole. From such miracles all that I have learnt is that we should not trust our eyes, that we should never believe a thing to be real simply because our eyes say so." Bhagavan also added, "We see so many wonderful things done. The juggler puts a girl, tied fast, into a gunny bag and leaves it under a basket and the girl comes up from somewhere else when he calls her. There is such a thing as magic."

By this time it was time for our Tamil *parayana*. We began with the 29th stanza in *Ramana Deva Malai* (of Sivaprakasam Pillai) and by an odd coincidence it says, "Intellect or *buddhi* does not see reality on account of *maya*" and Bhagavan added in continuation of our discourse எல்லாம் மாயையின் செயலே (All is the work of *maya*), quoting Sivaprakasam Pillai's words.

31-1-46 Morning

About 8-30 a.m., *i.e.*, nearly half an hour after Dr. S. Rao had finished massaging Bhagavan's legs, Bhagavan said 'பிடிச்சுண்டிருக்கிறாப் போலிருக்குது, பார்த்தால் ஆளைக் காணோம்' *i.e.*, 'it looks as if he is massaging. But when I look for the man, there is none.'

About 11 a.m. a visitor asked, "Bhagavan told me this morning 'Unless one knows the reality (*yathartham*), one cannot get peace (*shanti*).' What is that reality?"

Bhagavan: That which always is, is the reality. It is peace. Peace is another name for it.

Visitor: How to reach it or how to get peace?

Bhagavan: As I said already, that which is, is peace. All that we need do is to keep quiet. Peace is our real nature. We spoil it.

What is required is that we cease to spoil it. We are not going to create peace anew. There is space in a hall, for instance. We fill up the place with various articles. If we want space, all that we need do is to remove all those articles, and we get space. Similarly if we remove all the rubbish, all the thoughts, from our minds, the peace will become manifest. That which is obstructing the peace has to be removed. Peace is the only reality.

Afternoon

Bhagavan was going through the new edition of *Ramana Lila.* He feels many errors have been allowed to creep in, in this edition. Some are due to the proofs not having been properly looked into, Mr. Venkatakrishnaiah having been at that time suffering from bad eyesight. But some others are due to insufficient care in verifying facts. Bhagavan was trying to correct these, *e.g.*, he corrected 15 years into 5 years, in connection with Bhagavan's horoscope given in the book. He found the direction and location of the river Papaharanadi not accurate. Such mistakes go against Bhagavan's grain and so he patiently goes through the whole book to discover them. It is too much of a strain for him, especially with his bad eyesight.

1-2-46 Morning

The radio news announced the death of the Maharaja of Cochin. Bhagavan said, "Is he gone? We read of his illness!" I said "He must have been old!" Bhagavan said, "Yes. Another old person may be getting on the throne now. The one that has passed away got on the throne only a few years ago. Appan Thambiran (he had visited Bhagavan and written about him), if he were alive now, would have got the kingship. They have a long list of princes, awaiting succession." I said, "They are generally not only old but very learned and religious — these Rajas of Cochin." Bhagavan said, "Yes. They are generally well-read in Sanskrit. Even when Travancore threw open its temples to Harijans, Cochin did not."

Balaram said, "When I was reading at College, the 42nd prince of Cochin was reading with me. They have such a long list of heirs in succession." Attendant Krishnaswami asked Bhagavan if Cochin was a big State. Thereupon we talked about Cochin being small, though Pudukottah was smaller. Somebody said that Pudukottah became a State because its original owner betrayed his master and helped the British. From this, the talk drifted to ஊமையன் (Oomaiyan) who was a terror to the English in those days, whom the English could not capture for a long time and who is said to have been finally captured with the help of the Pudukottah Paliagar. Bhagavan then said, "There is a fort at Dindigul. The front entrance used to be guarded and we boys were not allowed to enter in. We used to go to the farthest end of the wall, climb it, jump down into the fort and get out of the fort by a hole in the wall at the back of the fort, through which it was said Oomaiyan had escaped from the British. If we look at those walls now, we wonder how we climbed up and jumped down from them." Bhagavan continued to look at *Ramana Lila* and was discovering more mistakes.

Afternoon

Mr. G. Subba Rao read from *Ramana Lila* that Sankaracharya had told one of his disciples that Bhagavan was the third *avatar* of Subrahmanya, the first one having been Kumarila Bhattar and the second Jnana Sambandhar, and asked Bhagavan to whom it was Sankaracharya said so, Bhagavan did not know. But he said that Sankaracharya must be the one before the last, *i.e.*, the third back from the present one. Bhagavan also added, "That Sankaracharya came and met me at Skandasramam. He must have been repeating what he heard. It is only Nayana that started it. None said so before." Bhagavan came across in *Ramana Lila* Venkata Krishnayya's poetic description of Bhagavan's travel from Madura, that in the *vimanam* of his body he was traversing *daharakasha* or *chit akasa* and read it out to us. This reminded him of certain incidents in the past here and he said, "Once when we were at Skandasramam, in the month of *Thai*, we set out in a party of forty or fifty for going round the Hill one night. We all had a heavy meal before starting, with *puri*, etc., and tea on top. They had taken in addition *marundu* (*lehyam* with opium in it as an ingredient). By the time we came near here, a Namboodri, Atmananda Swami, began saying, 'I feel I am floating on *kshira sagara* and that a ship is taking me along that ocean'. Another said he felt that he was in the air flying in an aeroplane. Like that, Venkata Krishnayya says I was travelling in *daharakasa*!" Meanwhile Ramanatha Dikshitar came into the hall (he has been with Bhagavan since 1912) and Bhagavan said, on seeing him, "He must have been with us on that occasion. On another occasion, when we were at Virupakshi Cave, we had set out to go round the Hill and Chidambaram Subrahmanya Sastri was the leader of the party. When we came somewhere near here, he proposed that each one should lecture for an hour going round the Hill, on *Guru Bhakti* and Ramanathan's was the first turn. They had all taken *marundhu* (*i.e.*, ganja). R. began his lecture and elaborated his theme that Tiruvannamalai and Ramana, Chidambaram and Nataraja, and the body and the Self are the same and went on elaborating the theme and addressing ingenious arguments in support of the same with such fervour and spirit that he far exceeded his time limit. When he was asked to stop, he pleaded piteously for a little more time. So he was allowed to continue. Even after he had taken two hours he would not finish and he had to be stopped and another was asked to speak. It was wonderful the way R. spoke. None would have expected it of him. It was the next day he composed the song 'திருச்சுழி நாதனைக் கண்டேனே'. Mr. Balaram came across a passage in *Ramana Lila* in which it was mentioned that once at Virupakshi Cave Bhagavan alone was present and was working at putting up a small wall and that when some visitor came there and asked Bhagavan where was the Swami,

Bhagavan told him "Swami has gone out." Balaram asked Bhagavan "Is it so?" Bhagavan said "Yes". Reading further on, Balaram came across the statement that the man stayed a little and not finding any Swami returning went away, that he came again on the third day, that then too he stayed a little and finding none other than Bhagavan, was returning, that while returning he met Echamma and was told by her his Swami was none other than the one he saw at Virupakshi Cave that day and the previous occasion, that Echamma later asked Bhagavan whether it was proper for him to have misled the man like that and that Bhagavan replied to her, "Do you want me to go about with a bell round my neck announcing 'I am the Swami' or to have a label on my forehead that I am the Swami?"

This led Bhagavan to talk of his early days, how when he went about with only an old cod-piece and a small, tattered towel, it was naturally not easy for anyone to think of him as a Swami. He said, "When I was at Pachaiamman Koil I had a small towel which was tattered and torn, almost to rags, with threads having come out in most places. Once a cow-herd boy made fun of this torn rag, by telling me, 'The governor wants this towel'. I replied, 'Tell him I won't give it to him!' I never used to spread it out in public. I used to keep it rolled into a ball and wipe my body, hands or mouth as the occasion demanded with the towel so rolled up into a ball. I used to wash it and dry it in a place between two rocks, which place was never visited by any of those who were with me. Even my cod-piece would be tattered. When the top end used to become worn out, I would reverse the cod-piece and use it with the bottom end topmost. When going into the forest I would secretly mend my cod-piece with thread taken out of it with prickly pear thorn for needle. So, nobody knew or suspected the wretched state of my towel and cod-piece. One day somehow, one of those who used to be with me in those days went to the place where I used to dry my clothes and thus by chance discovered the state of my clothes.

They then wept that they had allowed such a state of things, that they had committed an inexcusable sacrilege (*apachara*) and so on. They had with them, in trunks, whole pieces of cloth and so many towels, etc., all meant by them to be used for me. Only they did not know how badly torn my towel and cod-piece were; otherwise they would have long ago substituted others for them." He added, "Our Muruganar has mentioned these facts in his songs and has described that I had Indra for my towel, (*i.e.*, a towel with thousand eyelets or holes) and a cod-piece stitched by means of a prickly pear spike. But one who does not know the facts may not be able to understand what exactly the poet meant." He also told us two stories from the life of Saint Sundaramurti. In one the saint was doing worship with climbing brinjal (தூதுவளை) leaves, while others took it he was preparing them for cooking. In the other, one Somayajulu got the saint's help through those leaves and secured the presence of Siva at his *yagna*.

2-2-46 Morning

A visitor told Bhagavan that he was working for Harijan uplift, that he and his co-workers in the cause had *darshan* of Mahatma Gandhi and got his blessings, that Mahatma Gandhi told them that if they could bring about marriages between Harijan girls and higher caste gentlemen, such marriages would have his blessings; and that he (visitor) would like to have Bhagavan's views in the matter. Bhagavan said, "If Mahatma Gandhi has said so, we will all hear what he has said. What more is there for us to do? He is a distinguished man and is working in that field. What have we to do with that?" Turning to us, Bhagavan added, "If I open my mouth, something will appear in the papers that so-and-so has also said such-and-such a thing. The next day there will be people to criticise it. Our business is to keep quiet. If we enter into all these, people will naturally ask, and justifiably, 'Why is he interfering in all these instead of keeping quiet?' Similarly if Mahatma Gandhi keeps quiet leaving aside all his activities, they will ask, 'Why is he keeping quiet instead of engaging in all these activities?' He must do what he has come for. We must do what we have come for."

One Ananda Swami, from Mount Abu, put questions and got the following answers:

Question: It is said in books that the *purusha* is *angushtha pramana*. What is it that is meant by it?

Answer: Evidently the books must be referring to the *upadhi* in which the *purusha* is manifesting. They cannot mean that the all-pervading *purusha* is *angushtha pramana*.

Question: Is that *purusha* in the heart?

Answer: If you mean the physical heart, it cannot be. But the books describe a heart which is an inverted lotus with a cavity inside and a flame in that cavity and all that. In such a psychic heart, the *purusha* may be said to abide and the flame may be of that *angushtha pramana*.

Question: Is seeing that light Self-realisation?

Answer: Abiding in it and being it, not seeing it, is Self-realisation.

Question: In *nirvikalpa samadhi* what happens to the *prana*?

Answer: It goes and merges where it came from.

Question: I wish to know if there will be breathing then.

Answer: It may not be then in the form of respiration, but in some *sukshma* form. They talk of *maha prana*.

Question: What is *sahaja samadhi*?

Answer: It is our *svabhava sthiti*. It is being in our natural state. *Nirvikalpa samadhi* also means merely giving up our *vikalpas*. *Samadhi* is our natural state, if we give up the *vikalpas*.

Question: What is the difference between *sushupti ananda* and *turiya ananda*?

Answer: There are not different *anandas*. There is only one *ananda* including the *ananda* enjoyed during the waking state, the *ananda*, of all kinds of beings from the lowest animal to the highest Brahma, the *ananda* of the Self. The bliss which is enjoyed unconsciously in sleep is enjoyed consciously in *turiya*. That is the difference. The *ananda* enjoyed during *jagrat* is *upadhi ananda*.

During the greater part of the afternoon Bhagavan was perusing a note book in which Venkatesa Sastriar had gathered together all the sayings of Ribhu found in the Upanishads.

3-2-46 Morning

The radio news announced that four to five lakhs of people had assembled to meet Mahatma Gandhi at Madura. Bhagavan said, "Where is the place to hold such a crowd? Perhaps, on the way to Alagar temple." This led Bhagavan to think of his old days in Madura and he said, "I had a relation, a sort of uncle, who was *manigar* in that temple. So I used to go there now and then, and we used to get all respect and attention there. They used to make very nice *pongal prasad* there, with a lot of ghee. Once they gave such *prasad* in a big brass plate and, as there was none else, I carried it all the way, nearly two miles, to that uncle's village. But I found the people in the house did not after all care so much for it, but gave away most of it to their servants. They were so used to it that it did not attract them. I used to go and play in the premises of that temple. There are various buildings round about the temple which, though neglected and in ruins now, were used by the Nayak Kings. Tirumal Nayak is said to have lived there too. In those days these Rajas used to fortify their hills and live there. See Ginjee for instance. The Ginjee fort was built on three hills. They are all in ruins. Padaiveedu nearby in this district was once a great city. Hampi was a great city and the capital of an empire. It is said that the town was built on the model of a Sri Chakra and that there had been some slight mistake somewhere, and that is why, though the empire flourished well for a time, it did not endure but failed. There is a rumour that a prophecy made by Vidyaranya, earlier a Dewan of Hampi empire and later a Sankaracharya, has declared that when again a descendant of that empire or a successor of his in the mutt builds a city on the model of Sri Chakra, a great empire will again flourish with that city as capital. Some people have even thought that the present Sankaracharya might be the person meant for such destiny. Our Nayana used to feel that as this town is by nature itself built on Sri Chakra model, by the gods themselves, if only we could build houses all round the hill and make a city of it, this will become the capital of a big empire. He used to be always thinking and speaking of *swaraj*, dreaming and planning for it and saying what he would do when *swaraj* is attained. People say there was a town in the old, old days somewhere here to the south of the hill. Who knows what will happen hereafter? Did we imagine that all these houses now here were going to be built?"

Bhagavan also said Alagar Temple was regarded by the Saivites as a temple of Muruga (Lord Subrahmanya), even as the Tirupati Temple, and that it was one of the six *padai veedus* (படை வீடு) of Muruga.

Afternoon

Bhagavan was reading the *sthala purana* of Tiruchuzhi, to see how the portion connecting saint Sundaramurti with the shrine is dealt with. He was explaining it here and there to us, and while reading various passages extolling the saint, Bhagavan could hardly proceed, being so choked with emotion. At least a dozen times he was so choked and he had to control himself and then proceed.

4-2-46

Last night Bhagavan read in Tiruchuzhi *sthala purana* that God appeared as Kalaiyar before Sundaramurti at Tiruchuzhi and asked him to come to Kanaperur. This word, *kalai* might mean either a bull or metaphorically a young and vigorous man. The book further said he appeared with a bouquet in his hand and weapon called *chuzhiyam* (trident). To clear the doubt Bhagavan said it would be better to look into the *sthala purana* of that Kanaperur if that could be had. Muruganar said that he had presented a copy of that book to our library. So it was at once picked out and given to Bhagavan, who went through the book. This afternoon again he was reading the book. The doubt could not be cleared, as almost the same words are used in this book also. He read out some portions to us and particularly the *Sundaramurti Padalam* in which the following incident, not generally known, is also given. It seems when Siva appeared as 'Kalaiyar' and asked Saint Sundarar, "Why have you not sung on us? We live at Kanaperur," the Saint began to sing even at Tiruchuzhi where he then was and went on singing towards Kanaperur. On the way he stopped at Tirupunaivasal. There the God and Goddess came to Sundaramurti as an old man and his wife and asked him for food, saying they were very hungry. He cooked some food in haste for them, but when it was ready the guests could not be found. Sundaramurti searched for them in the village, but could not trace them. When he returned home, he found the food got ready had also disappeared. Then Sundaramurti thought this the Lord's *lila.* And a voice said, "What are you doing here instead of coming to us at Kanaperur?" Sundaramurti replied, "What am I to do? You go and live in some forest. I hardly know the proper way to it." The voice added, "I shall be going on my bull in front of you. Follow the bull's footsteps." So Sundramurti followed them for some time. After a while the footsteps could not be found. Sundaramurti prayed again; and again the footsteps were seen and followed. After some distance the footsteps ceased and wherever he saw there were *lingams*. All was *linga maya, jyoti maya*. However, Sundaramurti advanced in one direction and then he espied the *vimanam* of the temple.

He and his party washed in the tank outside and wanted to enter in the temple and lo! the temple disappeared. Then Sundaramurti thought within himself, "Is it because I did not come here first that my Lord is displeased with me?" and began to pray. Thereupon the crests of the *vimanam* appeared one by one and the temple was there. Bhagavan narrated all this to us and turned to Saint Sundarar's *Thevaram* on this shrine to see whether the last mentioned sentiment and prayer were to be found there. They were not found. But Bhagavan read out the *Thevaram* and more than once, identifying himself with the *bhava* of those songs, was greatly moved and choked with emotion. But he did not lay aside the book as he sometimes does when overpowered by emotion, but controlled himself with great effort and finished the whole *Thevaram*. He particularly pointed out the lines in which the saint has said God is like nectar to those who meditate on him in reality in their hearts transcending all *bhava* (பாவஞ்தெம்) and also the lines where the saint calls God, his friend, lord and Master. He laid aside the book and soon after Muruganar entered the hall Bhagavan said, 'He comes now'; and I explained to Muruganar why Bhagavan said so. Soon after, Bhagavan began telling Muruganar almost the entire story I have recorded above.

This afternoon Mrs. Taleyarkhan said, "Bhagavan, I must report the experience I had at Tirukoilur. Though I have gone to Tirukoilur many times before, I had not so far seen the temples etc., visited by Bhagavan. So, I made it a point to visit them all this time, and purposely took our Viswanath with me to show me all the places. We first went to the Araiyani Nallur temple. It was about 8 a.m. when we reached the temple on 2-2-46. I found to my dismay the huge doors of the temple locked with a big lock.

There was not a person to be seen either inside or outside the temple. I did not know what to do. I was praying earnestly to Bhagavan that I must somehow see all the temples and the several places therein connected with Bhagavan's first journey. Viswanath told me, 'Let us go round the outer *prakara* and then see what is to be done'. So I started going round with him. But I was all along praying hard to Bhagavan in my heart that I should not be sent back disappointed and that I must fulfil the object of my visit. As we were coming round, I saw at one place some water and milk trickling down from inside the temple and I told Viswanath there must be somebody inside the temple. But Viswanath said it might be *abishekam* water trickling down. When I was turning round the fourth corner, what was my surprise to find the door slightly ajar, as if somebody was asking us to come in quietly on the sly. We finished the round and entered the temple. We found an old priest with a loveable face inside. He, however, did not speak even a word with us throughout our stay there. He did *arathi, archana*, everything for us and at our request lighted a lamp and showed us all the places as it was dark there. We came out and went round the temple again. By the time we finished our round, the doors had been again locked up and the old man gone. I feel it was only Bhagavan's grace that opened the doors and gave us *darshan* that day." Bhagavan asked Viswanath, "Did you enquire and find out who that old man was?" Viswanath replied, "No. I did not."

5-2-46

Bhagavan has been reading the *Kalaiyarkoil Puranam* and explaining to us various portions therein, both in the morning and in the afternoon. He was so absorbed in the songs and the story that he went on explaining to us this morning even after the papers arrived. Attendant Krishnaswami, who was chagrined that he had been denied his usual listening to the radio, remarked, 'To such stories, if Bhagavan takes them up, there will be no end at all'.

He thought he was rebuking us who were listening and thus in a way encouraging Bhagavan to speak on. He could not understand the pleasures of a literary excursion such as Bhagavan was having and which one likes to share with others. Bhagavan was explaining to us how the poet was showing his skill and how a single stanza might have cost the poet several days of anxious thought.

6-2-46 Morning

Last night Rajaratna Mudaliar, who was Deputy Collector here and was leaving for Cuddalore on transfer, came to Bhagavan to take leave. As requested by me, he had secured a copy of the songs, conversation, etc., used by the temple priests in connection with the ஊடல் (love quarrel) between the God and Goddess which is celebrated in the festival called here ஊடல் உற்சவம் and gave it to me. I left the same with Bhagavan last night for his perusal. When I entered the hall at about 7-45 a.m., Bhagavan was reading the above and explaining the same to those near him. Seeing me enter, Bhagavan said, 'You are coming only now?' After finishing the point he was explaining just then, he again for my benefit started reading and explaining from the beginning and read on to the end. We found the copy secured by Mr. Rajaratnam was not complete. I promised to find out whether there was anything with the temple priests not included in the copy sent to me.

Today, between 10 and 11 a.m., the foundation was laid for Bhagavan's new hall in front of the temple and Bhagavan attended the function. The *sthapathi* in charge (Sri Vaidyanatha Sthapathi) of the work made a short speech in which he said that it was his aim and endeavour to see the entire work finished in one year and that he wanted the co-operation and goodwill of all Bhagavan's devotees. A number of devotees also subscribed various sums. First a widow came and offered some money to *Sarvadhikari*. He took it and put it on a plate on the ground, saying 'This sum, the lady is offering as her contribution'. Thereupon various devotees began putting down various sums. I guess the amount offered on the spot could not have been less than Rs. 2,000. A radio singer, hailing from Tirukoilur, sang a few songs in praise of Bhagavan and the function ended with a feast for us, the inmates.

Afternoon

Bhagavan has read by now a great portion of the book of Kalaiyarkoil shrine and he is of opinion that 'Kalaiyar' means only a young and robust man and not a bull, *i.e.*, he appeared before Saint Sundara as a young man near Tiruchuzhi.

Night

After *parayana*, a person came and told Bhagavan, "we are going to our village tomorrow morning." Bhagavan said 'Yes' and the person left. Turning to the attendant, Bhagavan said "அவர்களுக்குக் கொடுத்தாச்சா?" (Have they been given?). The attendant went out, enquired, came back and reported, "They have not yet been given. But things have been reserved to be given to them." I was wondering what all this was about. Bhagavan told me, "There was one Annamalai Swami when I was at the Asramam on the hill (*i.e.*; Skandasramam). He died in *Thai* of 1922 and was buried near Eesanya *math.* This is his Guru *puja* or death anniversary. His relations come and celebrate it every year. They feed poor people there and leave some rice, etc., here. We give them our *prasadam* (*vadai, pongal*, etc.). It is usual to sing the songs composed by that Annamalai Swami on such Guru *puja* days, with our Tamil *parayana*. I don't know what they propose to do today." I said, "If that has been the custom, we shall certainly do the same today. Why should there be any doubt about it?" Meanwhile Balaram asked Bhagavan who that Annamalai Swami was. Bhagavan thereupon took out the life of Bhagavan brought out by Kamath with 111 illustrations and showed us a group photo in which that Annamalai Swami is standing at the right hand end of the picture. Bhagavan said, "Mother used to be very fond of him. He died in *Thai*. She passed away in *Vaikasi*." We all remarked, on seeing the picture, that Bhagavan was very thin and lean in it. Bhagavan said, "That is because I was then living on one meal a day. For something like a year I was eating only one meal a day. But this condition of mine in the picture is nothing. You should have seen me at Gurumurtham. I was only skin and bone, no flesh anywhere. All the bones were sticking out, collar bone, ribs, and the hip bones. There was no stomach to be seen. It was sticking to the back, having receded so far. So this condition in the picture is not really so bad." We asked Bhagavan when this picture was taken. He said it was about *Jayanti* time in 1921. From this the talk drifted to when Bhagavan was first photographed here. Thereupon he said, "It was in 1900 or 1901. The Government brought a photographer to take photos of some prisoners here. There were no photographers here then. This photographer was a disciple of Kumbakonam Mauna Swami and had, it seems, heard of me. So he took advantage of his trip here to visit me. He gave us a photo of his Kumbakonam Mauna Swami and took my photo. The first group photo taken was in 1906 or so. We were six in it. I, Palaniswami, Sivayya (he had not then become Mauna Swami of Courtallam), Pachai Pillai (who was Sanitary Inspector here then), Rangaswami Aiyangar (Best & Co.'s agent) and Overseer Sesha Iyer. No copy of this is available. The Aiyangar's family may have one. We have not been able to find out." At this stage Mrs. Taleyarkhan asked Bhagavan, "Is there no photo of Bhagavan as a child?" Bhagavan said, "In those days there were no photographers in places like Tiruchuzhi. But when I was about seven or eight years old a European photographer came there to take a group photo of the Sub-Magistrate and others at Tiruchuzhi. He was staying behind the hospital. After he had taken a group photo of the Sub-Magistrate, my uncle Nelliappa Aiyar wanted to have a photo of his taken. He liked to have me also by his side in this picture. So I was sent for from the school.

"I came in haste, just as I was, with my high forehead (*i.e.*, the top of my head projecting upward) clean-shaven recently, almost hiding the tuft behind, my *jibba* hanging loosely about me, with no buttons, and all unprepared generally for being snapped. By the time I arrived, my uncle was sitting in a chair in the hospital compound, where there were crotons for a good background and the photographer was busy adjusting his camera. I was made to stand to the left of my uncle, with my right hand on the left arm of my uncle's chair. A big book from the hospital was brought and I was asked to hold it in my armpit on the left side. So placed, I was to be snapped. But as ill-luck would have it, just as the photo was about to be taken, a fly sat on my face, and I raised my hand to chase away the fly, with the result that in the photo my right hand could be seen swaying in the air. We have not been able to get at this picture either. There was no other photo taken of me in my childhood or boyhood."

10-2-46

About 10-30 a.m. Mr. T.K. Doraiswamy Iyer (a Retired Professor who has settled down here for Bhagavan's sake) showed a letter he had received from Sir S. Radhakrishnan, in reply to his letter asking for an article for the Souvenir which it is proposed to bring out to celebrate the Golden Jubilee of Bhagavan's arrival in Tiruvannamalai. Sir S.R. has also been requested to get in touch with Mr. Evans Wentz and get a contribution from him also for the Souvenir. In the reply Sir S.R. had said he would do that also. Bhagavan showed Balaram this Evans Wentz in a group photo in *Self Realisation.* In this group Grant Duff is sitting to the left of Bhagavan and Evans Wentz to the right.

Bhagavan said that it was S.R. that sent Grant Duff here. In his introduction to *Five Hymns* Grant Duff confirms the above fact, though Sir S. Radhakrishnan's name is not mentioned.

Afternoon

I was reading Nallaswami Pillai's *Sivajnanabhodam* and came across a sentence challenging anybody to show in any *purana* that Siva took birth as *avatar* anywhere. I asked Bhagavan if it was not said that Siva was born as son to Vallala Maharaja in this place, and was even supposed to do annual ceremony every year to Vallala Maharaja. Bhagavan then explained that Siva was not born in any woman's womb even according to that story, that when Vallala's wife approached Siva, who had come as an old man, according to her husband's orders, she found the old man suddenly transformed into a male child; and that when she called her husband and both tried to take the child, the child disappeared and the God then assured Vallala that he himself would perform funeral rites and annual ceremonies for him. In this connection Bhagavan also narrated to me another story in *Tiruvilaiyadal Puranam* in which God appeared first as an old man, then changed into a young man, and finally into a child. The story is to be found in *Vriddha, Kumara, Bala Padalam*.

A visitor, an old devotee of Bhagavan, had brought with him a book called *Ramanopakhyanam* by one Thangavelu Nadar. I imagined from the title that the book dealt with Bhagavan's life and teachings. But Bhagavan told me it contained only the stanzas found in some *nadi* horoscope of Bhagavan, with the notes or commentary of a gentleman who was then editing a Tamil paper. He added that, besides this version, some other *nadi* versions of Bhagavan's horoscope have been traced and sent to the Asramam by different devotees. I thereupon remarked, "But it is said these so-called *nadi* horoscopes are not all quite correct on all points!" Bhagavan said, "Various people in various parts of the country claim to have various *nadis*. We don't know. This Thangavelu Nadar was originally at Kumbakonam. There used to be one at Tindivanam. When anybody went to him, he used to tell them, 'You must go and have *darshan* of Ramana Maharshi, at such and such a time. The same is indicated in the *nadi* horoscope'; and they used to come here and tell me about it. When I was at Skandasramam, Jadaswami came across some person who was said to be a great expert in reading one's palm and tracing one's horoscope from there. He seems to have read Jadaswami's horoscope in that way, and Jadaswami had apparently been greatly impressed. So, he brought the palmist to me and said, 'This is a great expert in this line. Even if we spend a great deal of money, we will not be able to get his services. All his readings are correct. It is fortunate he has come our way. I have brought him to you. Please show him your palm. He will tell all your future.' I declined. He tried to persuade me. But I never showed my palm and I told him, 'We have not understood the present. Why should we seek to know the future?' "

11-2-46 Morning

My old servant Divakaran came with me. As Bhagavan did not seem to recognise him, I reminded Bhagavan about him and told him he was now employed in Cochin, near his native village. This led to talk of Cochin State and Bhagavan said that Madhavi Amma (wife of Dr. P.C. Nambiar) had written that the present Maharaja was her daughter Janaki's father-in-law. I added, "Prabhavati (a princess of Devas, who used to be here and has now married one Mr. Sekharan of Dr. Pandalai's family) is connected with the Travancore State. So, we are now connected with both the States."

Bhagavan said, "Yes, yes. Even before this marriage, through Mrs. Pandalai, now through Prabhavati also."

Afternoon

On further reading of the *Kalaiyarkoil Puranam,* Bhagavan told us, "It was not at Tirupunaivasal that God and Goddess appeared to Saint Sundarar as an old man and his wife. I find it was at Tiruchuzhi itself. After having been asked by God to come to Kanaperur, it seems Saint Sundarar was thinking of going to Tirupunaivasal, possibly because he thought he had to go that way to reach Kanaperur. It was then that Sundarar met that old gentleman and his wife who mysteriously disappeared and also heard the Voice (*asariri*)." Bhagavan also sent for the book in the library which gives a map of all the places of pilgrimage, etc., and found that Tirupunaivasal is east of Kanaperur and situated on the sea coast. Bhagavan had asked Viswanath to add to his Tamil manuscripts of *Tiruchuzhi Thala Mahimai* an account of *Sundaramurti Padalam*. Mr. Viswanath had written out an account accordingly to be added to the manuscript. Bhagavan perused it and suggested some improvements.

12-2-46

A party of about fifty, mostly ladies, clad in ochre coloured saris and said to belong to the Satchidananda Asramam at Cocanada, arrived with their Guru, Rama Lakshmamma, and attended the morning *parayana*.

Afternoon

Nagamma read her Telugu version of Kalaiyarkoil story in *Sundaramurti Padalam*, and Bhagavan was listening and correcting where necessary. After it was read out, when Viswanath came in, Bhagavan suggested that a copy of the stanzas in the above *Padalam* must be made and kept in the *Tiruchuzhi Puranam* for reference. Bhagavan had already copied a few stanzas with the above object. Viswanath said he would complete it.

Evening

The Cocanada party again attended *parayana* in the hall and afterwards recited *Siva Stotra* and *Siva Mahima Stotra* in Sanskrit.

13-2-46 Morning

After *parayana*, Bhagavan was talking to a bearded gentleman past middle age and yet looking sturdy and strong. I went and sat by the side of the visitor. Bhagavan told me, "This is Gajanan, alias Daivarata, the answers to whose questions have been recorded in Chapter III of *Ramana Gita*. He was with us at Skandasramam in 1917." I thereupon said, "I know. The same who was in Nepal and whose photo and letter arrived immediately after Bhagavan was making enquiries about him once." For the benefit of those who might not know the incident, Bhagavan said, "Some years ago, when Nayana's son Mahadevan came here, I was enquiring about this Gajanan. We had not heard from him for about ten years. So I was making enquiries. When we were talking, the post arrived and with it a parcel of books. I perused the letters first and laid aside the parcel. When we were talking about this G., the parcel was by my side. After talking to Mahadevan, I opened the parcel and found G's letter and photo and books, and in the letter he had written that, though he was in Nepal, yet he was always at my feet. It looked as if, in answer to my question to Mahadevan as to where G. was, G. was saying, 'Here I am (*i.e.*, in the picture) at your very feet'."

The Cocanada party requested Bhagavan to give them *hastha diksha*, or to permit them to touch his feet. Bhagavan only replied as usual, 'Touch with your mind'.

At breakfast, Bhagavan enquired where G. was staying and what he was going to take. It was reported G. had gone for his bath. Bhagavan then said, "He would eat anything. If you give him a quantity of tender *margosa* leaves and a *chembu* of cow's urine, he would breakfast on them. He had lived on things like that."

About 10-30 a.m. G. was in the hall showing a picture of a Pasupati image in Nepal and explaining its esoteric significance.

A Swami in orange robes, called Jagadiswarananda, from Ujjain arrived this morning and a little after, the letter announcing his coming here, reached Bhagavan. The person was here before the letter.

In the night again G. was telling Bhagavan about Nepal. He said, among other things, "There are three important shrines in Nepal, all very sacred. The King is a very religious man and it is the custom and tradition there for the King not to do anything or go anywhere without first going and taking permission from the gods in these temples. In that State, cow-killing used to be punished with death sentence. Now the sentence is transportation for life. If a bull is beaten and blood appears, the offender will be punished with imprisonment for three months or so. The State has its own coins." Here G. showed some coins to Bhagavan. Mr. Balaram said, "He does *bhajan* with great spirit and enthusiasm. We should have it one day here." G. said, "Oh, yes. I can do even now. No fear, no shyness. So I can sing away. Can we get some tinkling beads (கஜ்ஜை) for my ankles, and some accompaniment?" Bhagavan also said, "He must have some *sruti* like harmonium, some accompaniment like *mridangam* or *ganjira* and some cymbals (jalra)." Then the talk drifted to Bhagavan and his party going round the hill in those days. Balaram asked if G. used to do these *bhajans* while resting on the way or during walking. Bhagavan replied, "Oh, he would do his *bhajan* while walking. He would jump from one side of the road to another. He was so full of life and enthusiasm." G. said, "I was much younger then. But I can do it even now." Discussing where and when we should arrange for such a *bhajan* by G. we found out that he would require a big space himself for moving about singing and that it would be better to arrange it in the dining hall.

14-2-46

In the morning post was received a letter written in French and Mr. Balaram translated it into English for Bhagavan. It is from the editors of the journal called *Spirituality*, which during the war penetrated all the prisoners' camps in Germany. They have published a book of about 600 pages called *Reconstruction of Man*. They say that their view is similar to Bhagavan's; they also hold that man in his egoless state, far from losing himself in a void, finds himself as he has always been in his profoundest depths. They say they belong to the Vedic brotherhood of Prajapatis. They hope to go to India next year and to visit Tiruvannamalai and Pondicherry.

In the afternoon a visitor sang some Tamil *Thevarams*, etc. After *parayana* in the evening, Bhagavan's old disciple Gajanan gave us a *bhajan* performance in the dining hall between 6-30 p.m. and 7-30 p.m. with Bhagavan seated at his usual place there. The *bhajan* was in North Indian style; and the way he ran and jumped about was remarkable for one who is at least fifty years old.

15-2-46

Mr. Ramaswami Iyengar of Kumbakonam, who was staying at Palakottu, passed away this morning at about 2 a.m.; and Kunjuswami informed Bhagavan of the same at once. R. passed away with Bhagavan's name on his lips.

Bhagavan made kind enquiries about Colombo Ramachandra's health, as he had been suffering from sciatica for about a week now, and was taken to the Doctor in the Government Hospital last evening. Among the letters received today was one from a lady, Kameswaramma, in which she asked for Bhagavan's opinion on the question whether the body can be kept alive eternally. While perusing the letter, Bhagavan made a few remarks and this led to questions from visitors. Bhagavan repeated his well-known views on the subject, more or less to the following effect: "As this lady writes, some have maintained that the body can be made immortal and they give recipes, medical and other, for perfecting this body and making it defy death. The Siddha school (as it is known in the south) has believed in such a doctrine. Venkaswami Rao in Kumbakonam started a school which believed the same. There is a Society in Pondicherry too. There is also the school which believes in transforming men into supermen by descent of Divine Power, as is mentioned in this letter. But all people, after writing long treatises on the indestructibility of their body, after giving medical recipes and yogic practices to perfect the body and keep it alive for ever, pass away one day!" Somebody raised this question, "What then about those who are spoken of as *chiranjivis* in our books?" Bhagavan replied, "But do they appear in physical bodies? They only appear to you in your *dhyana*." From this the talk drifted to whether they have individuality and Bhagavan said, "As long as you have individuality, you can see individuality in them, not afterwards!"

In the night Gajanan (Daivarata) said to Bhagavan, "When Nayana went to Gokarnam he went almost to every house and offered his superb *vidya* to everyone. But nobody cared for it then. But now, they come across a verse of his and they go into raptures over it, and exclaim 'What poetic gift!' and if they can get a picture of him they worship it as God. This seems to have been the way of the world always. There is a story about Maschendra Nath. It is said he went about saying, 'For two *pooran polies* (பூரண் போளி) I shall give you *Brahmam i.e., jnana*.' But nobody cared. At last Goraknath came along and when he heard this offer of M., he said he would bring the *polies*. He went into the city, got up a tall tree, hung from one of the branches head downwards, had a small fire lit up underneath, and made a *chela* or disciple sit by his side. The whole town swarmed around and wondered saying, 'What great *tapasya*! Some great Mahatma has come to our place!' People readily offered to do various services and present many things to the great *tapasvi*. The disciple explained that his Master would only accept a *bhiksha* in which a thousand persons should all be fed with the best *pooran polies.* This was readily arranged and Goraknath took two *polies* and ran up to Maschendra, telling the people, 'You feed the thousand persons. I shall go to the Ganges and offer the *polies* to Ganga.' G. told M., 'Here Sir, I have brought the two *polies.* Now give me *Brahmam*!' M. took the two *polies*, bit them here and there, threw the pieces to the birds, dogs and the river, and then both M. and G. disappeared. M. had given G. *Brahmam.*

"It seems to have been the way of the world always. Great men are rarely respected and rated at their true worth in their lives. Even Sankara was bitterly attacked during his lifetime as a *maya asura*. But now he is regarded not only here, but all over the world, as the greatest religious and philosophical thinker the world has produced!" Bhagavan said, "There is another similarity between Sankara and Maschendra Nath. It is said of Maschendra also that he was enjoying the company of a woman and forgot to return at the end of the period fixed by him, and that thereupon his disciple Goraknath went and sang and reminded him and brought him back, in the same way in which Sankara's disciples are said to have sung *Guru stuti* and brought back Sankara." Gajanan proceeded to relate that Goraknath was greatly revered in Nepal, from the King downward, and the State coin also bore the name of Goraknath. He said, "It seems, when Goraknath was alive, the then King of Nepal visited him. When G. was apprised of the King's arrival, he merely spat on the King. The King, to avert the spittle falling on his crown, drew back a little; the spittle fell on his feet. G. is said to have then told the King, 'You would not let the spittle fall on your head. If it had so fallen, you might have become the head of a big empire. However, as it fell on your feet, you would be the master of a small kingdom'."

The talk then drifted to miracles done by various saints. G. mentioned one Vasudeva Saraswati and said, "He has gone all over India. Bhagavan knows him. He was here too. He did various miracles. One morning he would bathe in the Krishna and at noon he would be found bathing in the Ganges at Benares and at a third place in the evening!" Then G. proceeded to speak of Samartha Rama Das and his miracles, and told the following story: "It seems one of his disciples, greatly devoted to him, used to grind the betel leaves and nut in his own mouth first and then offer it to Ramdas. Some co-disciples thought this sacrilegious and went and told Ramdas, 'Please ask him to bring the pestle and mortar with which he daily prepares betel leaves paste for you.' Ramdas thereupon asked those disciples, 'Yes, go and ask him to bring the mortar.' They accordingly went and told that disciple, 'Master wants us to bring from you the mortar in which you prepare betel leaf for him daily!' The disciple said, 'Wait. I shall give it to you presently.' So saying he took a sword, cut off his head and gave it to the other disciples! When the disciples took the head to the Master, the latter told them, 'Do you now see the *bhakti* of the man whom you misunderstood and maligned? Go and put his head back again on his trunk.' The disciples did as directed and the man came back to life." G. continued and said, "The sword 'Bhavani' was presented to Shivaji by Ramdas. Four men are required to handle that sword, handled by Shivaji. It is now preserved by the British Government."

16-2-46 Morning

G. took permission from Bhagavan to go and visit Skandasramam. Bhagavan said, "Yes" to him and, turning to us said, "What a difference between his state then and now! He was with us at Melasramam (Skandasramam) for more than six months, maybe even a year. He would take *bhiksha* in the town and eat the rice even without salt." Meanwhile another old disciple said to Bhagavan, "There was no room in those days close to the rock behind. Now I find a room with the rock for its western wall.

There used to be only a narrow passage there." Bhagavan said, "Yes. That room is new. During the latter part of my stay there, Vriddhachala Gurukkal of Tiruvannamalai made that room and installed Ambika there and used to do *puja* to the deity. He went in for *siddhis* and to show various feats such as getting sacred ash, sugar, coins. Sometimes he used to sit in *samadhi* for forty days. But latterly he was led astray by these *siddhis*."

At about 10 a.m. Bhagavan was enquiring about the deceased Ramaswami Iyengar and what was being done about the disposal of the body. It was reported that the body was going to be cremated here and that the bones would afterwards be taken and interred at Kumbakonam. Bhagavan then said, "That is all right. It seems that is what the deceased wished should be done." Bhagavan said, "He *i.e.*, R. Iyengar must be in one of the group photos. அப்போ ஜோராய் நின்று கொண்டிருந்தார் (He was standing gaily then)." So saying, he turned over the book with 111 illustrations and *Self-Realisation* but could not find the picture he had in mind. Thereupon he said, "It must be somewhere, in the earlier editions or among the pictures hung in the dining hall."

Evening

After *parayana*, Bhagavan introduced G. to Sanskrit Pandit Raju Sastri of this place and said, "He has written a work called *Pasupati Hridayam*." The book was shown to Sastri and G. read out a few verses from it. G. also told us that the Pasupati image in Nepal has five faces, four in the four directions and the fifth at the top; and that the image has two arms in each direction. Bhagavan told Sastri, "It seems there is a place called Uttara Gokarnam in Nepal, which is an important shrine. The Maharaja of Nepal is friendly to G. and wants him to stay there as a head-priest or something like that." G. said, "Yes, the Maharaja is very kind to me. He wants me there; as what, I do not know yet. He has some idea in his mind."

A party of forty ladies were ushered into the hall by the second son of Dandapani Swami of Palani. They were Kasiamma, present head of Subrahmanya Sastri's Asramam at Mettivaripalem. Guntur Dt., and some of her disciples. They sang a few songs before Bhagavan and then left.

17-2-46 Morning

Mr. P. D. Shroff arrived from Delhi this morning. He said to Bhagavan, "When I am away from you I feel so miserable. While I am at Delhi, far away, I feel such a pull, as though you are a cruel lover keeping yourself away. Then I must come here at any cost. But when I come here you are like an ordinary person. What is this?" Bhagavan said, "It is always like that. When one is separated, one wants to come."

Afternoon

A visitor asked Bhagavan, "How has *srishti* (creation) come about? Some say it is due to karma. Others say it is the Lord's *lila* or sport. What is the truth?"

Bhagavan: Various accounts are given in books. But is there creation? Only if there is creation, we have to explain how it came about. All that, we may not know. But that we exist now is certain. Why not know the 'I' and the present and then see if there is a creation?

Some young men who had come with an introduction from the Ramakrishna Mission at Madras asked Bhagavan, "Which is the proper path for us to follow?"

Bhagavan: When you speak of a path, where are you now? and where do you want to go? If these are known, then we can talk of the path. Know first where you are and what you are. There is nothing to be reached. You are always as you really are. But you don't realise it. That is all.

A little while after, one of the visitors asked Bhagavan, "I am now following the path of *japa*. Is that all right?"

Bhagavan: Yes. It is quite good. You can continue in that.

The gentleman who asked about creation said, "I never thought I was going to have the good fortune of visiting Bhagavan. But circumstances have brought me here and I find in his presence, without any effort on my part, I am having *santi*. Apparently, getting peace does not depend on our effort. It seems to come only as the result of grace!" Bhagavan was silent. Meanwhile, another visitor remarked, "No. Our effort is also necessary, though no one can do without grace." After some time, Bhagavan remarked, "*Mantra japa*, after a time, leads to a stage when you become *Mantra maya i.e.*, you become that whose name you have been repeating or chanting. First you repeat the *mantra* by mouth; later you do it mentally. First, you do this *dhyana* with breaks. Later, you do it without any break. At that stage you realise you do *dhyana* without any effort on your part, that *dhyana* is your real nature. Till then, effort is necessary."

In the evening Kasiamma's party again came to Bhagavan and after *parayana* sang a few *stotras*. Before leaving, Kasiamma approached Bhagavan and stood before him for a few minutes, during which Bhagavan was looking and yet not looking at her. (I mean, he gave her one of those abstract looks which are not unusual with him). Then the lady asked Bhagavan, "May I have from Bhagavan's lips some words on *svanubhava* or personal experience of Self-realisation?" Bhagavan kept quiet and after a few minutes K. and her party took leave and went away. After she went, Bhagavan remarked, "She was herself singing about *svanubhava* so far. Not that she does not know. She wants to hear about it from me."

18-2-46 Morning

Bhagavan was perusing a Telugu version of *Tiruchuzhi Sthala Puranam* made by Nagamma from Viswanath's Tamil story.

Afternoon

Old attendant and librarian T. S. Rajagopal came on a visit, Bhagavan told me, "He is on his inspection tour (R. recently has become an Inspector for *Madras Mail* with Trichy as Headquarters). He is inspecting us now. We are getting a copy of the *Mail* daily now. The local agent told us that under orders of the Inspector he was sending us a copy."

24-2-46 Morning

About 10-30 a.m. Mrs. Taleyarkhan came near Bhagavan, stood at his feet and asked, "May I say a few words, Bhagavan?" and continued, "I have a great friend, Mrs. W., wife of a prominent official in Los Angeles. In 1942, when I was here, I received a letter from her while I was sitting in this hall. It was a heart-rending letter in which she detailed how her husband fell in love with another woman, got a divorce decree and married the new woman. She was a most beautiful woman, Bhagavan, and they had already a girl about seventeen years old. She was a great society woman and it was impossible that any event of any social importance would take place without her being there. So she felt the grief immensely and wrote it all. I was moved terribly and keenly felt for her and prayed mentally to Bhagavan for her relief. I wrote back to her, sending her a small photo of Bhagavan, and told her, 'Don't be downcast. Your husband will come back to you. I am now with such and such a great personage. I am sending you a small picture of him. Have it on your table. I shall daily pray to him on your behalf. You too pray to him. You will see that you get relief.' But the friend — what do they know about Bhagavan and such things — was disconsolate. She wrote back, 'What you say is impossible. He won't come back.' I wrote again, 'Nothing is impossible with our Bhagavan. So just go on as I have advised you to do.' And now, Bhagavan, I have her letter by air-mail today that her husband has come back to her and she is going to set up a new home again. She writes, 'The impossible has happened. Your "gentleman" (meaning Bhagavan) has really worked a miracle. Now, I and my husband must come and see him. We want to fly and visit your Master, though the passage costs a lot. Please let me know whether there is a hotel there where we can come and stay'. I have always been praying to Bhagavan for this friend and I am glad Bhagavan has done this for her. I feel so grateful and was moved to tears when reading this letter here now."

I added, "What is there impossible for Bhagavan?" and told Bhagavan, "Only last evening Shroff was complaining to me about his having to go to Delhi. He said, 'It is the hopelessness of the situation that pains me most. There does not seem to be any chance of my coming here again. If I was certain that once in six months or even once a year, I could be visiting here, I would not feel the separation so much. It is the impossibility of it all that worries me'." And I told Shroff the same thing that Mrs. T. told her friend:

"There is nothing impossible at all where Bhagavan is concerned. You may get transferred to Madras. You may grow so rich suddenly as to possess a small aeroplane of your own. What is there that cannot happen by His grace?"

Mrs. Osborne told Bhagavan, "Kitty has written a letter and in it has sent her love to Bhagavan." Bhagavan, turning to me, said, "She has become shy now. When she was going she made her father come and tell me her message 'I hope Bhagavan won't forget me'. And I told her, 'You don't forget Bhagavan and Bhagavan won't forget you'."

25-2-46 Afternoon

Mrs. Taleyarkhan introduced a group, Miss Sen and some others (a Captain or Major Rao, who was going to marry this Miss Sen, and another lady from Indore) as friends of her sister Rita. Then I told Bhagavan that this Rita has had a miracle in her life and made Mrs. T. tell the story. Mrs. T. thereupon told Bhagavan the following: "Bhagavan, we got this Rita a seat in a medical college and hospital in London for training as a nurse, through the kind offices of Lady Willingdon who was then Vicerine here. The matron of the hospital there, however, disliked my sister from the beginning, because of her colour, and treated her as dirt. My sister patiently bore all this, and always prayed to St. Theresa in whom she had great faith. Her troubles came to a climax in this way. When it was about a month or so for her examination, she accidentally hurt her eye with the spray of an acid, when she was opening a bottle of the acid in the laboratory. The eye had to be kept in bandage for several days and it was not yet all right even close to the examination. But on the night before the examination, after she had gone to sleep, my sister had the following strange experience. She felt she heard a slight footstep and that someone opened the door and was coming gently towards her. She could even hear the rustle and swish of the dress as the visitor approached. The visitor came by the bedside and removed my sister's bandage. My sister opened her eyes and saw her favourite Saint Theresa standing by her with a scroll in her hand. The saint thereon unrolled the scroll and there my sister saw all the questions that were going to be asked in her examination next day. After my sister had ample time to go through the questions one by one and to remember them, the vision passed away, and my sister got up, woke up her friend in the next room, asked her to find from the books all the answers needed and to read them out to her. The next day my sister also attended the examination, found all the questions the same as revealed to her the previous night, answered them and not only passed her examination contrary to the expectations of her matron, but even won the gold medal for proficiency in that year."

When Mrs. T. concluded the above account, I said, "Miracles have not ceased to happen. They are happening even now to those who pray and have faith."

26-2-46 Morning

A visitor told Bhagavan, "Even in my dream I sometimes feel that I am dreaming, *i.e.*, I am conscious that it is a dream and that a fall for instance there cannot hurt me and so on. How is that?"

Bhagavan: How can that be? Even in a dream there must be hurt consequent on a fall. On the other hand, if you are aware it is a dream, you are no longer dreaming. At the best, it may be the transition stage when you are awaking from the dream state.

Another visitor told Bhagavan that some of his dream experiences stood very firmly rooted in his mind, while others were not remembered at all. Bhagavan remarked, "All that we see is a dream, whether we see it in the dream state or in the waking state. On account of some arbitrary standards about the duration of experience and so on, we call one experience dream experience and another waking experience. With reference to Reality, both the experiences are unreal. A man might have such an experience as getting *anugraha* (grace) in his dream and the effect and influence of it on his entire subsequent life may be so profound and so abiding that one cannot call it unreal, while calling real some trifling incident in the waking life, that just flits by, is casual, of no moment whatever and is soon forgotten. Once I had an experience, a vision or dream, whatever you may call it. I and some others including Chadwick had a walk on the hill. Returning, we were walking along a huge street with great buildings on either side. Showing the street and the buildings, I asked Chadwick and the others whether anybody could say that what we were seeing was a dream and they all replied, 'Which fool will say so?' and we walked along and entered the hall and the vision or dream ceased or I woke up. What are we to call this?"

Next the talk drifted to the Self being *pratyaksha* (self-evident) and Bhagavan then related how the song *Atma Vidya* was composed. He said, "Any *vidya* is for the purpose of knowing something. If it is so self-evident as to render the well-known classical example of *hastamalakam* or a gooseberry on the palm a false analogy, as Muruganar had put it, where was the need for *Atma Vidya*, whether you call it easy or not? What Muruganar meant to say was: 'In the classical example, a hand is necessary, a hand that will and can feel a fruit on it, a fruit, an eye that can see, a person that has already known what fruit it is, and so on and so forth. But for knowing the Self, nothing at all except the Self is needed.' In sleep for instance nothing at all exists for us except ourselves and we admit we existed during that sleep. On waking we say, 'I slept and none of us believes there are two 'I's, the one that slept and the one that is awake now. In the classical example all these must exist to make the fruit self-evident. All these depend on or derive from the Self and make the fruit self-evident. How much more self-evident must the Self itself be? Anyhow there it was, Muruganar had written the *pallavi* and *anupallavi* and wanted the *charanams*. He said he could not possibly complete the song, as somehow no more lines would come to him, and so requested me to complete it. Thereupon I wrote this song. First I wrote only one stanza or *charanam*, but Muruganar wanted at least four, thereupon I made three more. Finally I recollected, I had not made any mention of Annamalai and so made a fifth *charanam* also and made mention of Annamalai in it, as Ponnambalam is mentioned in the stanzas of the song in Nandanar story on which our song is modelled."

A squirrel came to Bhagavan and he was feeding it with cashew-nut pieces as usual. Turning to me, he said, "Shroff sent some cashew-nuts yesterday and said, 'They were intended for my dumb friends'." I said, "Probably Bhagavan would object to our calling these squirrels dumb." Bhagavan said, "They communicate with me. Sometimes I am in a nap. They come and draw attention to their presence by gently biting my finger tips. Besides, they have a lot of language of their own. There is one great thing about these squirrels. You may place any amount of food before them. They will just eat what they need and leave the rest behind. Not so the rat, for instance. It will take everything it finds and stock it in its hole."

I remarked, "Possibly it would be said that the squirrel is a less intelligent creature than the rat, because it does not plan or provide for the future but lives in the present." Bhagavan said, "Yes. Yes. We consider it intelligence to plan and live wretchedly like this. See how many animals and birds live in this world without planning and stocking. Are they all dying?"

Bhagavan then began speaking of monkeys and said, "They too don't build nests or stock things. They eat what they can find, and go and perch on trees when night falls. They are quite happy. I have known something about their organisation, their kings, laws, regulations. Everything is so perfect and well-organised. So much intelligence behind it all. I even know that *tapas* is not unknown to monkeys. A monkey whom we used to call 'Mottaipaiyan' was once oppressed and ill-treated by a gang. He went away into the forest for a few days, did *tapas*, acquired strength and returned. When he came and sat on a bough and shook it, all the rest of the monkeys, who had previously ill-treated him and of whom he was previously mortally afraid, were now quaking before him. Yes. I am clear that *tapas* is well known to monkeys."

27-2-46 Morning

With the post arrived a composition from the pen of Chinta Dikshitulu, in Telugu, entitled *In the first place, Who are you, Ramana*? After perusing the letters, Bhagavan asked Balaram to read it out in the hall and the same was done. The gist of the paper is: 'You ask everybody who puts a question 'Who are you that put this question?' But who are you? There is sufficient justification for one to regard you as Krishna, or as Skanda, or as the Goddess who became merged in Arunachala as Ardhanariswara or again as Dakshinamurti. In fact we can go on imagining as so many other gods also. Again, when you sit with your palms turned to the fire by your side, you look like giving *abhaya* (*i.e.*, protection from fear). Now, is it only to those in the hall you are giving *abhaya* or to all in the world? It must be the latter. For you have come into the world to give *abhaya* to all."

1-3-46 Morning

Mr. Osborne said, "Bhagavan, last evening Nuna (*i.e.* his daughter about four years old) told us, 'Dr. Syed is my best friend in the world.' Thereupon we asked her, 'What about Bhagavan? and she replied, 'Bhagavan is not in the world'."

Bhagavan was surprised at this remark of the child and involuntarily his finger rose to his nose and, holding it there, he said, "What a sage remark for a child to make! Even great men cannot understand what that remark means. They ought to have asked her, 'Where else is Bhagavan, if not in the world'?" Thereupon Mr. Osborne said, "Yes. We did ask her. She said, 'Bhagavan is out of the world'."

Dr. Syed asked Bhagavan, "Does not total or complete surrender require that one should not have left in him the desire even for liberation or God?"

Bhagavan: Complete surrender does require that you have no desire of your own, that God's desire alone is your desire and that you have no desire of your own.

Dr. Syed: Now that I am satisfied on that point, I want to know what are the steps by which I could achieve surrender.

Bhagavan: There are two ways; one is looking into the source of 'I' and merging into that source. The other is feeling "I am helpless by myself, God alone is all-powerful and except throwing myself completely on him, there is no other means of safety for me," and thus gradually developing the conviction that God alone exists and the ego does not count. Both methods lead to the same goal. Complete surrender is another name for *jnana* or liberation.

3-3-46 Morning

A visitor quoted verse 33 of Ch. 3 in *Bhagavad Gita* and asked Bhagavan, "Are we then to do nothing and simply allow the senses to go their own way?"

Bhagavan: It only means actions will go on, according to the *gunas* or *prakriti* of the man. They cannot be prevented. But, that is the very reason why man should acquire *jnana* and thus become unaffected by the consequences of such action. The verse says, "Acquire *jnana* and be unattached to the actions and their consequences."

Bhagavan said this after saying, "Let us see in what connection this verse occurs," and looking up the verse in question. Then I remembered that once before I asked Bhagavan about this very same verse, and then Bhagavan pointed out to me the very next verse in which we are directed not to yield to the senses. I mentioned this for the guidance of the visitor. Bhagavan had told me then that, if the two verses were taken together, it could not be contended that *Gita* teaches 'Don't restrain or attempt to restrain the senses, because what does restraint avail?'

Evening

A visitor asked Bhagavan, "When we get a dream, we emerge out of it without any effort on our part. If this life of ours is a dream, as it is said to be, then how is it that we have to make efforts and are called upon to make efforts to end this dream and wake into *jnana*?"

Bhagavan: We do not know about sleep or dream. But we know about the present state, the waking state. Let us try and understand it. Then all will become clear to us. Who is it that undergoes sleep, dream and waking states? You say we must get out of ignorance and wake into *jnana*. Who is it that has the ignorance, and ignorance of what? When you enquire into the source of 'I', all doubts will be set at rest.

5-3-46 Morning

Bhagavan seems to have said yesterday it would be good if one could find out what Nuna meant or felt when she said, 'Bhagavan is not in the world, but out of it.' So Mr. Osborne brought the following writing to day and handed it over to Bhagavan.

"I asked Nuna what she meant by 'Bhagavan is not in the world'. At first she was too shy to say anything. I said 'You think Dr. Syed is in the world, don't you?' Nuna said, 'Yes.' 'Where then is Bhagavan, if He is not in the world?' I asked. Nuna replied, 'In the Asramam and in heaven', and added after a pause, 'Bhagavan whom we cannot see is everywhere. If we are very good we can see Him. Everybody is Bhagavan, but not as good as Bhagavan'. How much is pure intuition and how much is what she understood and remembers from occasional talks, it is difficult to say. Sometimes there is no doubt that it is mere intuition. For instance, once at Kodaikanal when saying 'Good night' to her I asked her whether she had been praying and she said, 'Now I want to sleep, sleeping is praying'." After seeing the above Bhagavan and Balaram were both saying, 'Sleeping is praying is a very sane remark.' I could not understand, and so asked Bhagavan about it. He explained that they understood it to mean, sleeping or stilling the mind is real prayer. By 'sleep' should be understood, he told me, 'the sleepless sleep' we often hear mentioned in Tamil books, *e.g.* (தூங்காமல் தூங்கிச் சுகம் பெறுவ தெக்காலம்?) (When will I attain the bliss of sleeping, yet not sleeping).

Evening

When I entered the hall, Bhagavan was talking to Lakshmi, our Venkattoo's child, of whom I am very fond. I told Bhagavan, "There was a proposal some time back that Lakshmi should be left with her mother's sister at Erukoor. They seem to have thought the girl would be better off there, where they require a girl badly for petting and rearing, instead of here where she would be only one of several children. But I did not like the idea at all. When children born somewhere in Poland and other countries come here and grow up in the atmosphere of our Asramam, I could not reconcile myself to the idea of our Lakshmi born here being brought up elsewhere."

Bhagavan said, "The Thatha (the grandfather *viz.*, Pichu Aiyar) went to Erukoor; and do you think she would stay there after seeing her Thatha? If Thatha is there, then alone she would stay there." On this Balaram quoted from *Sakuntala* passages in which Sakuntala takes leave of the hermitage and Kanva Maharshi addresses the flowers and says, 'She who used to water you first before taking her food herself, she who would not pluck you however dearly she loved flowers and liked to wear them, she is now leaving you for her husband's house. Bless her.'

Balaram also quoted from some other book a passage which says, 'We, people of the world, have to make great efforts to draw the mind from the objects of sense or from the world and to fix it in the heart, on God. But you, Radha, in whose heart God is fully caught, you have to make effort to get away from God.'

On this Bhagavan remarked, "That is the stage of the *jnani*. He can't escape the Self or go away from it. Where else to go, as all that he knows is the Self which he himself is?"

Mr. Desai asked Bhagavan, "How is it that some saints, who must also have realised the Self, say that it is not desirable for one to merge in the Self, but one must have some slight individuality left to enjoy the bliss of the Self, just as the fly, to enjoy the honey, should not fall into the honey and be lost in it, but must sit on the edge and go on sipping the honey." Thereupon I told Mr. Desai, "Bhagavan has told us that the analogy is wrong and misleading. The honey is something inert and unconscious, a conscious being is required to taste it and enjoy it. On the other hand, the Self is consciousness and bliss itself and it is absurd to argue that when one becomes that, the Self, one will not be able to enjoy bliss and that one must remain separate to enjoy it." Mr. Desai asked, "Why then have some saints said so? That is our difficulty." I replied, "You must ask those saints. Bhagavan has given us his opinion quite unambiguously that it is not necessary to remain separate to enjoy complete bliss, and that, on the other hand, the bliss cannot be complete till the merger in the Self is complete."

6-3-46 Afternoon

When I entered the hall, Bhagavan was telling Balaram, "Different books and different schools have located the *kundalini* at different centres in the body. While the usual centre with which it is associated is *muladhara*, there are books which locate it in the heart, and other books which locate it in the brain." Thereupon I asked Bhagavan, "You say different people or schools differ on this matter. But as Mr. Desai asked Bhagavan yesterday, the difficulty we feel is this. If people who have mere book or theoretical knowledge say such contradictory things, we may simply brush them aside. But when they come from persons whom we regard as saints who have realised the Self, *i.e.*, those who have had direct or immediate knowledge of the Self, the doubt assails us, 'Why such difference of opinion among saints?' Yesterday I tried to silence Desai simply by saying, 'If others have given opinions different from Bhagavan's, you must ask them why they gave such opinions, not Bhagavan. Bhagavan has told us what is the correct opinion.' But now, I too want to know why different saints differ on such important points". Thereupon Bhagavan was pleased to say, "They may be Self-realised saints and they may know the truth. But they have to suit their teaching to those who ask for it and the differences in the teachings are to be explained by the differences in the *pakva* or fitness of those to whom such teachings are addressed."

Balaram was reading a collection of *Upanishads* and, coming across a passage dealing with *sahaja samadhi* or *sahaja sthiti*, asked me, "Did you not say that Mr. K. S. Ramaswami Sastri once told you that he did not believe in *sahaja* state and that *sahaja* state is not mentioned in the earlier books, but is a later innovation? I find it mentioned here in the *Varaha Upanishads* themselves." I said, "Yes. He thought so. He argued with me, 'How can one be in two planes at the same time? Either he sees the absolute and nothing else or sees the world and then does not see the absolute. And he said that the *sahaja sthiti* is not mentioned in the earlier books, but is found only in later works." Balaram said, "Where are these two planes for the *jnani*? He is only in one plane and so there is no point in Mr. Sastri's argument that one can't be in two planes at the same time." I said, "How can we say the *jnani* is not in two planes? He moves about with us like us in the world and sees the various objects we see. It is not as if he does not see them. For instance he walks along. He sees the path he is treading. Suppose there is a chair or table placed across that path. He sees it, avoids it and goes round. So, have we not to admit he sees the world and the objects there, while of course he sees the Self?" Bhagavan thereupon said, "You say the *jnani* sees the path, treads it, comes across obstacles, avoids them, etc. In whose eyesight is all this, in the *jnani's* or yours?" He continued, "He sees only the Self and all in the Self." Thereupon I asked Bhagavan, "Are there not illustrations given in our books to explain this *sahaja* state clearly to us?"

Bhagavan: Why not? There are. For instance you see a reflection in the mirror and the mirror. You know the mirror to be the reality and the picture in it a mere reflection. Is it necessary that to see the mirror we should cease to see the reflection in it? Or again take the screen illustration. There is a screen. On that screen first a figure appears. Before that figure on the same screen other pictures appear and the first figure goes on watching the other pictures. If you are the screen and know yourself to be the screen, is it necessary not to see the first figure and the subsequent pictures? When you don't know the screen you think the figure and pictures to be real. But when you know the screen and realise it is the only reality on which as substratum the shadows of the figure and pictures have been cast, you know these to be mere shadows. You may see the shadows, knowing them to be such and knowing yourself to be the screen which is the basis for them all.

9-3-46 Morning

Dr. Masalavala, retired Chief Medical Officer of Bhopal, who has been here for more than a month now and who is now also in temporary charge of the Asramam Hospital in the absence of Dr. Shiva Rao, put the following questions to Bhagavan and got the following answers:

Question: Bhagavan says, 'The influence of the *jnani* steals into the devotee in silence.' Bhagavan also says, 'Contact with great men, exalted souls, is one efficacious means of realising one's true being.'

Bhagavan: Yes. What is the contradiction? *Jnani*, great men, exalted souls — does he (Dr.) differentiate between these?

Thereupon I said, 'No'.

Bhagavan: Contact with them is good. They will work through silence. By speaking, their power is reduced. Silence is most powerful. Speech is always less powerful than silence. So mental contact is the best.

Question: Does this hold good even after the dissolution of the physical body of the *jnani* or is it true only so long as he is in flesh and blood?

Bhagavan: Guru is not the physical form. So the contact will remain even after the physical form of the Guru vanishes.

Question: Similarly, does the contact of a devotee with his Guru continue after the passing of the Guru or does it stop? It is possible that for a ripe soul his Self may act as his Guru after the going away of the Guru, but what is the unripe soul to do? Bhagavan has said that an outer Guru is also needed to push the mind of the devotee towards the Self. Can he come in contact with another adept? Is this contact to be necessarily physical or will a mental contact do? Which is better?

Bhagavan: As already explained, Guru not being physical form, his contact will continue after his form vanishes. If one *jnani* exists in the world, his influence will be felt by or benefit all people in the world and not simply his immediate disciples. All the people in the world are divided into his disciples, *bhaktas,* those who are indifferent to him and those who are even hostile to him and it is said in the following verse that all these classes will be benefited by the existence of the *jnani*. From *Vedanta Chudamani*:

நெறிமருவு சீடரோடு பத்தருதாசீனர் நிலையில் பாவி களென்று நால்வகை யோரிடத்து முறையினனுக்கிரகம் வந்துறு மருள்கொள் சீவன்முத்தனு லென்பவரவைமுறை யினெடுத் துரைப்பாம். Bhagavan quoted the next verse, *viz.*, தெரிவரிய ஜீவன்முக்தன்தனை நம்பும தனுற் சீடர்க்கு முத்தியு மன்பொடு வழிபாடதனைப் புரியு முயர்பத்தர்க்கு நல்வினையு மவன்றன் புனிதமுறு சரிதமது கண்ட யுதாசீனர்க்குரிய புண்ணிய லிருப்பு மவன்றன் வடிவினைக் கண்ணுறுதன் முதலானவற்றுல் பாவிகட்கு பாவ விரிவு முறுமென்பர். The gist is: 'Four classes of people are benefited by *jivanmuktas*. By his faith in the *jivanmukta*, the disciple attains *mukti,* the *bhakta* who worships his Guru attains merit, the indifferent who have seen the sacred life of the *jivanmukta* acquire desire for righteousness and even the sinners (*i.e.*, the hostile in the first verse) get rid of their sins by the mere fact of their having had *darshan* of such saints.' God, Guru and the Self are the same. After your *bhakti* to God has matured you, God comes in the shape of Guru and from outside pushes your mind inside, while being inside as Self he draws you there from within. Such a Guru is needed generally, though not for very rare and advanced souls. One can go to another Guru after his Guru passes away. But all Gurus are one, as none of them is the form. Always mental contact is the best.

Question: My practice has been a continuous *japa* of the names of God with the incoming breath and the name of Baba (*i.e.*, Upasani Baba or Sai Baba) with the outgoing breath. Simultaneously with this I see the form of Baba always. Even in Bhagavan, I see Baba. The external appearances are also much alike. Bhagavan is thin. Baba was a little stout. Now, should I continue this or change the method, as something from within says that if I stick to the name and form I shall never go above name and form? But I can't understand what further to do after giving up name and form. Will Bhagavan please enlighten me on the point?

Bhagavan: You may continue in your present method. When the *japa* becomes continuous, all other thoughts cease and one is in one's real nature, which is *japa* or *dhyana*. We turn our mind outwards on things of the world and are therefore not aware of our real nature being always *japa*. When by conscious effort or *japa* or *dhyana* as we call it, we prevent our mind from thinking of other things, then what remains is our real nature, which is *japa*.

So long as you think you are name and form, you can't escape name and form in *japa* also. When you realise you are not name and form, then name and form will drop off themselves. No other effort is necessary. *Japa* or *dhyana* will naturally and as a matter of course lead to it. What is now regarded as the means, *japa*, will then be found to be the goal. Name and God are not different. See the teaching of Nama Dev on the significance of God's name, extracted in the September, 1937, issue of the *Vision*. (This was read out in the hall).

Bhagavan also quoted the Bible, 'In the beginning was the Word and the Word was with God and the Word was God.'

Question: Is liberation to be achieved before the dissolution of the body or can it be had after death? What is the meaning of a verse like II, 72 or VIII, 6 of the *Gita*?

Bhagavan: Is there death for you? For whom is death? The body which dies, were you aware of it, did you have it, during sleep? The *body* was not, when you slept, but *you* existed even then. When you awoke, you got the body and even in the waking state *you* exist. You existed both in sleep and waking. But the body did not exist in sleep and exists only in waking. That which does not exist always, but exists at one time and not at another, cannot be real. You exist always and you alone are therefore real.

Liberation is another name for you. It is always here and now with you. It has not to be won or reached hereafter or somewhere. Christ has said, "The Kingdom of God is within you" here and now. You have no death. Thayumanavar has sung, 'சந்ததமும் வேதமொழி—ஜக மீதிருந்தாலும் மரணமுண் டென்பது சதாநிஷ்டர் நினைவதில்லை' (*i.e.*, even when living in the world those who are always in *nishta* do not think there is such a thing as death).

The *Gita* verse only means in the context of the whole *Gita* (Ch. II, for instance) that you must achieve liberation during your lifetime. Even if you fail to do it during your lifetime, you must think of God at least at the time of death, since one becomes what he thinks of at the time of death. But unless all your life you have been thinking of God, unless you have accustomed yourself to *dhyana* of God always during life, it would not at all be possible for you to think of God at the time of death.

14-3-46

I was away at Vellore from 11th afternoon to 13th night. During my absence one Mr. Sankara Dev from Dhulia was here and has left. He has been writing the life of Samartha Ramdas in Marathi, and one part of it has also been published. It seems there was one Ananta Mauni, a disciple of Ramdas, who is believed to have belonged originally to this place and to have gone with Ramdas in his South Indian tour. So the biographer was trying to gather all available information about this Ananta Mauni. Bhagavan was not able to give any information and so advised the visitor to go into the town with guides from the Asramam and try to gather information.

This morning Mr. Manickam, disciple of Sivaprakasam Pillai, arrived, bringing from Mr. S. Pillai two notebooks, containing full notes on *Reality in Forty Verses* in Tamil (Supplement not included), and the general meaning alone for Bhagavan's *Devikalottaram* and *Atmasakshatkaram*.

15-3-46

A visitor from Poona, who has been here for the last two or three days, asked some questions, and Bhagavan told him, "*Mukti* or liberation is our nature. It is another name for us. Our wanting *mukti* is a very funny thing. It is like a man who is in the shade, voluntarily leaving the shade, going into the sun, feeling the severity of the heat there, making great efforts to get back into the shade and then rejoicing, 'How sweet is the shade! I have after all reached the shade!' We all are doing exactly the same. We are not different from the reality. We imagine we are different, *i.e.*, we create the *bheda bhava* (the feeling of difference) and then undergo great *sadhana* to get rid of the *bheda bhava* and realise the oneness. Why imagine or create *bheda bhava* and then destroy it?"

Afternoon

Dr. Masalawala placed in Bhagavan's hands a letter he had received from his friend V.K. Ajgaonkar, a gentleman of about 35 (a follower of Jnaneswar Maharaj) who is said to have attained *jnana* in his 28th year. The letter said, "You call me *purna*. Who is not *purna* in this world?" Bhagavan agreed and continued in the vein in which he discoursed this morning, and said, "We limit ourselves first, then seek to become the unlimited that we always are. All effort is only for giving up the notion that we are limited." The letter further said, "The first verse in the *Isavasyopanishad* says the world is *purna*. It simply cannot be anything else, as its very existence is built on the *purna*." Bhagavan approved of this also, and said, "There is this typed letter, for instance. To see the world alone and not the *purna* or Self would be something like saying. 'I see the letters, but not the paper,' while it is the existence of the paper that makes the existence of the letters possible!" Dr. M. said, "In the letter we see the paper. But we are able to see only the world and we don't see God!" Bhagavan replied: "What happens in sleep? Where did the world go then? Then you alone or the Self alone existed."

The letter also said, "Jnaneswar Maharaj has said God will never forsake his *bhakta* who has undivided love for him." Bhagavan said, "Every saint, every book says so. I have been reading Ram Das's writings. Here, too, so many verses end, 'Ramachandra will never forsake his *bhakta*.'" So saying, Bhagavan read out a few of those verses.

The letter went on to say, "Ramana Maharshi is an exponent of *ajata* doctrine of *Advaita Vedanta*. Of course it is a bit difficult."

Bhagavan remarked on this, "Somebody has told him so. I do not teach only the *ajata* doctrine. I approve of all schools. The same truth has to be expressed in different ways to suit the capacity of the hearer. The *ajata* doctrine says, 'Nothing exists except the one reality. There is no birth or death, no projection or drawing in, no *sadhaka*, no *mumukshu*, no *mukta*, no bondage, no liberation. The one unity alone exists ever.' To such as find it difficult to grasp this truth and who ask, 'How can we ignore this solid world we see all around us?', the dream experience is pointed out and they are told, 'All that you see depends on the seer. Apart from the seer, there is no seen.' This is called the *drishti-srishti vada* or the argument that one first creates out of his mind and then sees what his mind itself has created. To such as cannot grasp even this and who further argue, 'The dream experience is so short, while the world always exists. The dream experience was limited to me. But the world is felt and seen not only by me, but by so many, and we cannot call such a world non-existent', the argument called *srishti-drishti vada* is addressed and they are told, 'God first created such and such a thing, out of such and such an element, and then something else, and so forth.' That alone will satisfy this class. Their mind is otherwise not satisfied and they ask themselves, 'How can all geography, all maps, all sciences, stars, planets and the rules governing or relating to them and all knowledge be totally untrue?' To such it is best to say, 'Yes. God created all this and so you see it.'" Dr.M. said, "But all these cannot be true; only one doctrine can be true." Bhagavan said, "All these are only to suit the capacity of the learner. The absolute can only be one."

The letter further said, "*Avyabhicharini bhakti* is the only necessary thing." As Dr.M. did not understand what *avyabhicharini bhakti* meant, Bhagavan explained that it only meant *bhakti* to God without any other thought occupying the mind. Bhagavan said, "This word, *ananya bhakti, ekagrata bhakti,* all mean the same thing." The letter continued, "In the mind two things do not exist at the same time. Either God or *samsar*. *Samsar* is already there. That is to be reduced little by little and God is to be entered in its stead." Bhagavan remarked on this. "God is there already, not *samsar*. Only you do not see it on account of the *samsar* rubbish you have filled your mind with. Remove the rubbish and you will see God. If a room is filled with various articles, the space in the room has not vanished anywhere. To have space we have not to create it, but only to remove the articles stocked in the room. Even so, God is there. If you turn the mind inward, instead of outward on things, then you see the mind merges in the one unity which alone exists."

Bhagavan also agreed with the writer when he said that to see God, Guru's grace is necessary, for which again God's *anugraha* is necessary, which in its turn, could be had only by *upasana*.

The letter conveyed the writer's *namaskar* to Bhagavan. Thereupon, Bhagavan said, "The mind merging in its source, the one unity, is the only true *namaskar*."

16-3-46

Ceylon Ramachandra sent me the five songs recently composed by him in Tamil on Bhagavan and his grace towards him, in saving him this time through all his serious illness, and sent word that I should read them before Bhagavan. So at about 10-30 a.m., I read out all the five songs, putting myself in R.'s place and trying to render the songs with their full *bhava*. The previous day, two of these songs alone were ready and had been shown to Bhagavan by Mrs. R. Mr. Viswanath had already written them out in the *stotra* book. Bhagavan made a few corrections and divided the feet (சீர்) properly, with the *sandhi* properly joined and not split as R. had written. In the evening, Mr. V. wrote down the remaining three verses also in the book of *stotras* kept in the hall.

17-3-46 Afternoon

Looking at the outgoing mail, Bhagavan remarked "Eknath's mother has passed away. Do you know?" Mr. R. Narayana Aiyar replied, "Yes. I saw in *The Mail* an announcement to that effect." Bhagavan then remarked, "She and her husband the late Dr. Nanjunda Rao came to me even when I was in Virupakshi Cave. After that too, they came once or twice. The last time, they came here with one Chakkarai Ammal, a lady who had learned something and had a following of her own and whom the doctor also regarded as a sort of Guru. They were, I think, returning from a pilgrimage to Benares and other places."

18-3-46

One Mr. Girdhari Lal, an old resident of Aurobindo's Ashram, came here last evening and is staying at the Asramam. He asked Bhagavan this morning. "It is said in the *puranas* that the *kaliyuga* consists of so many thousands of years, and that so much of it has passed and that so much yet remains, etc. May I know when this *yuga* is to end?"

Bhagavan: I don't consider time real. So I take no interest in such matters. We know nothing about the past or the *yugas* which were in the past. Nor do we know about the future. But we know the present exists. Let us know about it first. Then all other doubts will cease. After a pause he added, "Time and space always change. But there is something which is eternal and changeless. For example, the world and time, past or future, nothing exists for us during sleep. But *we* exist. Let us try to find out that which is changeless and which always exists. How will it benefit us to know that the *kaliyuga* started in such and such a year and that it would end so many years after now?"

Girdhari Lal: I know, from the standpoint of one whose level of consciousness is beyond time and space, such questions are useless. But to us, struggling souls, it may be important in this way. It is said that in the previous *yugas* e.g. *satya yuga*, man had not fallen to the low level in which he now is in this *kaliyuga* and that it was much easier for him then to attain liberation than now.

Bhagavan: On the other hand, it is said it is much easier to secure salvation in this *yuga* than in the *satya yuga*. Some days or hours of penance in this *yuga* would secure what several years of penance alone could have secured in those *yugas*. That is what the books say. Further, there is nothing to attain and no time within which to attain. You are always that. You have not got to attain anything. You have only to give up thinking you are limited, to give up thinking you are this *upadhi* or body.

Girdhari Lal: Then, why do these *puranas* give the exact duration of each *yuga* in so many years?

Bhagavan: There might be an allegorical meaning in the number of years mentioned for each *yuga*. Or, the immensity of the periods of time assigned to each *yuga* may be a mere device to draw man's attention to the fact that, though he should live up to his full span of a hundred years, his life would be such a trifling, insignificant fraction in the entire life of the universe, and that he should therefore take a proper view of his own humble place in the entire scheme and not go about with a swollen head, deeming himself as of great importance. Instead of saying, "What is man's life compared to eternity?" they have taught him to consider how short his span is. Further, it is said there is a regular cycle of such *yugas*. And who knows how many such cycles have come and gone. Again, each *yuga* is sub-divided into four *yugas*. There is no end to all such calculations; and different schools have their theory as to when the present *kaliyuga* is to end. When time itself does not exist, as for instance in sleep, what is the use of bothering oneself with all such questions?

20-3-46 Morning

After I left the dining hall about 11-15 a.m. Bhagavan sent for me there. I was surprised, because it is very unusual for him to send for me. When I went, he told me, "Poor Mr. Virabhadrayya (he was once Deputy Collector at Chittoor and was last at Bellary) is no more. When the letter was shown to me this morning, I looked for you in the hall, to tell you. But you were not there. The son has written. It seems there was a minor operation. We don't know what it was."

Again, in the afternoon, Bhagavan asked me if I was not writing to Mr. V.'s son. I replied: "The son may not even remember me. They may not expect any letter from me." I was just then reading *Dialogues from the Upanishads* by Swami Sivananda Saraswati, and almost the first story there is that of Nachiketas. So I reminded Bhagavan that, soon after Mr. V. came to Bhagavan for the first time from Chittoor, he wrote an article comparing Bhagavan to Nachiketas. He had a notion that Bhagavan was an incarnation of Nachiketas. Bhagavan said, "Yes. I remember the article. He wrote one or two more articles also besides that one."

Evening

Some gentlemen came and recited *Sama Veda* before Bhagavan. It was very pleasant and moving to hear.

21-3-46 Morning

Balaram came across a Sanskrit poem in which the hill called 'Anai Malai' (Elephant Hill) near Madura is mentioned. He mentioned it to Bhagavan and Bhagavan said, "Yes, there is such a hill near Madura. From a distance it looks like a big elephant lying down." The word 'Anaimalai' reminded Bhagavan of the 1st stanza in Tirujnana Sambandar's songs in which 'Anaimalai' is referred to and Bhagavan quoted the song. It begins 'மானின்

நேர் விழி' and Bhagavan explained, "The Madura King Pandyan was inclined towards Jainism. His wife was the daughter of the Chola King and was attached to *Saivism*. When she heard of the great saint Jnana Sambandar and his doings and of his camping at Vedaranyam, the Pandyan Queen, with the help of a minister who was also attached to *Saivism*, sent an invitation to the Saint to visit Madura and convert the Pandya to *Saivism*. The Saint came accordingly. But when the queen saw he was a mere boy of about ten or even less, she had serious misgivings whether he could be a match for all the big Jain leaders surrounding the King and whether by inviting this child she had put him in jeopardy. When the Saint noticed this, he sang these songs, addressed to the queen and assuring her, 'I am not in any way inferior to these Jains. The Lord is within me. Don't, therefore, be afraid.'

"The songs which follow mention the names of Jain leaders, referring to them in contempt and stating, 'I am not inferior to all these, as the Lord is within me.' It is amusing to read those songs."

Bhagavan added, "This was after the Saint came to Madura. When the invitation reached Vedaranyam, and Jnana Sambandar wanted to start for Madura, Appar (Tirunavukkarasar) who was with Sambandar said, 'Do not start today. The day is not auspicious for you. They, the Jains, are terrible and powerful persons.' Thereupon Jnana Sambandar sang the 'கோளறு பதிகம்' (*Kolaru Padhikam*), beginning 'வேயுறுதோளி பங்கன்' in which again he says, 'As the Lord is within me in my heart, no days, no planets, can affect me adversely and every day of the week is equally auspicious'."
In the afternoon I brought the *Thevaram* for reference and picked out the above two songs and Bhagavan read them, a few of them aloud. In the Madura poem Bhagavan referred to the last stanza and said, "When I explained the first stanza in the morning I gave the meaning as 'Because the Lord is within me' though the words only mean 'Because there is the Lord.' I was wondering whether

I was justified in my interpretation. I find in the last stanza it is clearly mentioned by the Saint himself that what he meant was 'Because the Lord is within me.' Besides, the same is clear from the whole of the 'கோளறு பதிகம்'. Look at the last verse in the Madura decad. With what authority he sings, 'No harm can approach those who sing these songs of the King of Shiyali and the master of Tamil.' Similarly in the last song of 'கோளறு பதிகம்' he says, 'By my order those who read these shall be saved'."

This evening also *Sama Veda* was recited.

22-3-46 Afternoon

Last night, Mr. Bose, his mother, Lady C. V. Raman and Swami Sambuddhananda of the Ramakrishna Mission, Bombay, arrived here. The Swami quoted a verse from *Bhagavad Gita* which says that one in a thousand succeeds and knows really the *tattva* or entity. For some time Bhagavan kept quiet. When the Swami wanted an answer, some of us could not help remarking, "What is your question? What answer do you expect?" Dr. Masalawala even pointedly asked, "What is the motive behind this question?" Thereupon, the Swami said, "I think our Bhagavan has attained Self-realisation. Such beings are walking *Upanishads*. So I want to hear, from his own lips, his experience of Self-realisation. Why are you all butting in and distracting us from the point and purpose of my question?"

After all this, Bhagavan said, "You say you think I have attained Self-realisation. I must know what you mean by Self-realisation. What idea do you have in your mind about it?" The Swami was not pleased with this counter-question, but added, after some time, "I mean the *atman* merging in the *paramatman*." Bhagavan then said, "We do not know about the *paramatman* or the Universal Soul, etc. We know we exist. Nobody doubts he exists, though he may doubt the existence of God. So, if one finds out about the truth or source of oneself, that is all that is required." The Swami thereupon said, "Bhagavan therefore says 'Know Thyself'." Bhagavan said. "Even that is not correct. For, if we talk of knowing the Self, there must be two Selves, one a knowing Self, another the Self which is known, and the process of knowing. The state we call realisation is simply being oneself, not knowing anything or becoming anything. If one has realised, he is that which alone is and which alone has always been. He cannot describe that state. He can only be that. Of course, we loosely talk of Self-realisation, for want of a better term. How to 'real-ise' or make real that which alone is real? What we are all doing is, we 'realised' or regard as real that which is unreal. This habit of ours has to be given up. All *sadhana* under all systems of thought is meant only for this end. When we give up regarding the unreal as real, then the reality alone will remain and we will be that."

The Swami replied, "This exposition is all right with reference to *Advaita*. But there are other schools which do not insist on the disappearance of *triputi* (the three factors of knowledge) as the condition for Self-realisation. There are schools which believe in the existence of two and even three eternal entities. There is the *bhakta*, for instance. That he may do *bhakti*, there must be a God." Bhagavan replied, "Whoever objects to one having a God to worship, so long as he requires such a separate God? Through *bhakti* he develops himself, and comes to feel that God alone exists and that he, the *bhakta*, does not count. He comes to a stage when he says, 'Not I, but Thou'; 'Not my will, but Thy will.' When that stage is reached, which is called complete surrender in the *bhakti marga*, one finds effacement of ego is attainment of Self. We need not quarrel whether there are two entities, or more, or only one. Even according to *Dvaitis* and according to the *bhakti marga*, complete surrender is prescribed. Do that first, and then see for yourself whether the one Self alone exists, or whether there are two or more entities."

Bhagavan further added, "Whatever may be said to suit the different capacities of different men, the truth is, the state of Self-realisation must be beyond *triputis*. The Self is not something of which *jnana* or *ajnana* can be predicated. It is beyond *ajnana* and *jnana*. The Self is the Self; that is all that can be said of it."

The Swami then asked whether a *jnani* could remain with his body after attaining Self-realisation. He said, "It is said that the impact of Self-realisation is so forceful that the weak physical body cannot bear it for more than twenty-one days at the longest." Bhagavan said, "What is your idea of a *jnani*? Is he the body or something different? If he is something apart from the body, how could he be affected by the body? The books talk of different kinds of *mukti, videha mukti* (without body), and *jivan mukti* (with body). There may be different stages in the *sadhana*. But in realisation there are no degrees."

The Swami then asked, "What is the best means for Self-realisation?"

Bhagavan: 'I exist' is the only permanent, self-evident experience of everyone. Nothing else is so self-evident (*pratyaksha*) as 'I am'. What people call 'self-evident' *viz.*, the experience they get through the senses, is far from self-evident. The Self alone is that. *Pratyaksha* is another name for the Self. So, to do Self-analysis and be 'I am' is the only thing to do. '*I am*' is reality. I am *this* or *that* is unreal. 'I am' is truth, another name for Self. 'I am God' is not true.

The Swami thereupon said, "The Upanishads themselves have said 'I am Brahman'." Bhagavan replied, "That is not how the text is to be understood. It simply means, "Brahman exists as 'I' and not 'I am Brahman'. It is not to be supposed that a man is advised to contemplate 'I am Brahman', 'I am Brahman'. Does a man keep on thinking 'I am a man' 'I am a man'? He is that, and except when a doubt arises as to whether he is an animal or a tree, there is no need for him to assert, 'I am a man.' Similarly the Self is Self, Brahman exists as 'I am', in every thing and every being."

The Swami remarked, "The *bhakta* requires a God to whom he can do *bhakti*. Is he to be taught that there is only the Self, not a worshipper and the worshipped?"

Bhagavan: Of course, God is required for *sadhana*. But the end of the *sadhana*, even in *bhakti marga*, is attained only after complete surrender. What does it mean, except that effacement of ego results in Self remaining as it always has been? Whatever path one may choose, the 'I' is inescapable, the 'I' that does the *nishkama karma*, the 'I' that pines for joining the Lord from whom it feels it has been separated, the 'I' that feels it has slipped from its real nature, and so on. The source of this 'I' must be found out. Then all questions will be solved. Whereas all paths are approved in the *Bhagavad Gita*, it says that the *jnani* is the best *karma yogi*, the best devotee or *bhakta*, the highest *yogi* and so on."

The Swami still persisted, "It is all right to say Self-analysis is the best thing to do. But in practice, we find a God is necessary for most people."

Bhagavan: God is of course necessary, for most people. They can go on with one, till they find out that they and God are not different.

The Swami continued, "In actual practice, *sadhakas*, even sincere ones, sometimes become dejected and lose faith in God. How to restore their faith? What should we do for them?"

Bhagavan: If one cannot believe in God, it does not matter. I suppose he believes in himself, in his own existence. Let him find out the source from which he came.

Swami: Such a man will only say the source from which he comes are his parents.

Bhagavan: He cannot be such an ignoramus, as you started by saying he was a *sadhaka* in this line already.

23-3-46 Afternoon

Bhagavan was perusing *Thirukovalur Puranam* and telling the story of Pari, the philanthropist, and about Avvai having got his daughters married to a king. Bhagavan was saying that in this book Pari is traced to Ceylon, whereas in other books a Pari is mentioned as having lived in these parts and having eclipsed by his liberality the three kings, Chera, Chola and Pandya.

24-3-46

I referred to Swami Sambuddhananda's last question, what to do with those who have lost faith in God and who, if asked to find out their source, may say, 'Our parents are the source from which we spring.'

Bhagavan: Fancy a man saying our source is our parents.

I asked, "But what about a pure materialist, who does not believe in God. How are we to deal with him?"

Bhagavan: He will come gradually, step by step, to find out the source of 'I'. First, adversity will make him feel that there is a power beyond his control, upsetting his plans. Then, he will begin with rituals, ceremonial worship, and through *japa, kirtan, dhyana*, go on to *vichara*.

I asked Bhagavan, "What is the fire that is called the Nachiketa fire in the *Kathopanishad?*"

Bhagavan: "I don't know what exactly it is. It must refer to some fire ritual. These terms are generally symbolical. Only today, I saw in the current number of the *Ramakrishna Vijayam* an article on the Five Fires." So saying, he took up the journal and read out to us almost the whole of the article. It refers to the *svarga loka*, the *megha mandala*, the earth, man and woman as the five fires, and gives allegorical interpretations for all the details.

25-3-46 Afternoon

I again asked Bhagavan about the Nachiketa fire. "I find from the *Kathopanishad* that there was already a fire sacrifice which was supposed to lead one to heaven. After Yama explained it to Nachiketas as the second boon, he voluntarily said, 'Hereafter this fire will be called the Nachiketa fire, after you.' But later, the Nachiketa fire is mentioned as three fires. I don't understand what this fire is and why it is called three fires." Thereupon, Bhagavan asked us to look up the commentary and we took out Krishna Prem's *Kathopanishad* and Bhagavan read out the portion concerned. He added, "Everything is allegorical. They gave out truths only in this way, never straight out in a simple and direct manner. The same fire has three branches or flames, and so is called one fire or three fires. But both the one fire and the three branches are allegorical, the fire standing for something and the branches for other things. The commentary says that the one central fire has to be kindled on the three planes, *bhu, bhuvar,* and *suvar*, or the physical, astral and mental planes."

Colombo Ramachandra had sent two more 'திருத்தாண்டகம்' (*Tiruttandagam*) stanzas composed by him. Bhagavan saw them this morning, passed them, and asked Muruganar to go through them, as well as the other six stanzas already composed by Ramachandra, and recorded in the *stotra* book. Muruganar perused all the eight and had no alterations or corrections to suggest. So, again with Bhagavan's permission, the two stanzas were recorded by Mr. Viswanath in the *stotra* book.

26-3-46

About 10-30 a.m. a gentleman from Jhansi, who it seems teaches music to a princess, arrived here recently in a state of great excitement and emotion, having made up his mind after reading about Bhagavan that he must somehow run up to him. He told Bhagavan last evening, "Bhagavan, I have come a long distance, travelling two days and two nights. I was not sure I would succeed in seeing Bhagavan. I did not even take leave from my employers. I was so mad about coming here that nothing else entered my mind. Now that I have arrived and seen Bhagavan, my mind is filled with bliss which I cannot express." And he sang a few songs. But emotion overpowered him and he could not proceed. Bhagavan was kindly looking at him for several minutes and showered his grace on the fortunate devotee.

26-3-46 Afternoon

A lady devotee Sitamma, a resident of Madura, read out and then gave to Bhagavan, a *kummi* poem composed by her in commemoration of the opening of Ramana Mandiram at Madura on the 10th of the Tamil month *Masi* in the year *Parthiva* when Bhagavan's portrait was carried in procession through that town. Chinna Swami told us that this lady came across the above procession without having had any previous notice about it, and was so overpowered with joy that she went into ecstasy and remained in a sort of trance for about 15 minutes.

27-3-46 Afternoon

Mr. Nanavati of Bombay asked Bhagavan the meaning of the word *madhvada* in the *Kathopanishad*. After consulting some books, it was found out that the expression means the ego or *jiva* which is the enjoyer of *madhu* or all the enjoyments of the world. In this connection Bhagavan said, "There are so many *vidyas* mentioned in the Upanishads. One of them is *madhu vidya*. Elaborate details and rules are given for each of these *vidyas*. But what is the use of all these *vidyas*? Still we must note that there are some whose minds are so built that they can take interest only in such *vidyas*. But the truth is, all karma of whatever kind will lead to fresh bondage. That is why it is said in 'ஒழிவில் ஒடுக்கம்'

(*Ozhivil odukkam*) that Guru who prescribes fresh karma or action of any sort *i.e.*, rituals or sacrifices to one who after trying various karmas comes to him for peace, is both Brahma and Yama to the disciple *i.e.*, he only creates fresh births and deaths. The following stanza which says this was quoted:

கிரியைக் கிளைத்துவந்து கேட்டவர்க்குச் சும்மா
திரியச் சுகம்விளைத்த சீமான்—குருவன்றிச்
சற்றே பதைப்புத் தரினுஞ் சகம்படைக்கக்
கற்றானுங் காலனுமாங் காண்.

28-3-46 Morning

Bhagavan's legs were being massaged by Dr. S. Rao, with a *taila*, prepared by Siva Das, which was being exhausted with today's use. So the Asramam was thinking of preparing a *taila* and to help them Bhagavan took up a book in Telugu containing recipes and, the moment he opened it, it opened at a page dealing with camphor liniment. The coincidence was remarkable. The recipe contained almost all the ingredients the Asramam intended to use and in addition *tulsi* leaf and something else. Bhagavan was very particular that the bottle in which Siva Das had sent his *taila* should be returned to him and gave instructions to that effect to attendant Krishnaswami. Again when Siva Das came to the hall later in the day, Bhagavan asked him and Krishnaswami whether the bottle had been returned and was satisfied only when he learned it had been done.

Afternoon

Bhagavan was looking into *Arunachala Sthalapuranam*, and reading the *Arunachala satakam*, where the story of Pari's daughters being got married by Avvai is briefly told, to compare it with the account given in *Thirukovalur Sthalapuranam*. The accounts tallied more or less. But Bhagavan told us that the Pari known as a great giver or philanthropist is supposed to have lived near Madura, Piranmalai etc., and to have been put to death by the machinations of the three kings, Chera, Chola and Pandya, who were envious of his reputation, whereas these two books mention Pari as having ruled in Ceylon.

29-3-46 Afternoon

A visitor wrote some questions in Tamil and presented them to Bhagavan. Bhagavan said, "He wants to know how to turn the mind from sense enjoyments and realise that bliss which is said to be so much above sense-enjoyments. There is only one way, making the mind merge in That which is not sense-enjoyment. As you concentrate on That, the sense attractions will fall of their own accord. Again, he asks, 'When can I attain that bliss?' He is daily enjoying that bliss in sleep. There, no sense object is present, and he still enjoys great bliss. We have not got to attain bliss. We are bliss. Bliss is another name for us. It is our nature. All that we have to do is to turn the mind, draw it from the sense objects every time it goes towards them, and fix it in the Self. He asks whether he will attain bliss after death. There is no need to die to attain bliss. Merging of the mind alone is necessary. Death is also another name for us. For what is death but giving up the body? Our real nature is to be without the body."

After a pause Bhagavan added, "The story of Indra and Ahalya in *Yoga Vasishta* strongly illustrates how, by the force of the mind being merged in one thing, all other things will cease to affect one. There Ahalya, the wife of a king, falls in love with a rake called Indra and they passionately love each other. The matter reached the king's ears and attains the magnitude of a great public scandal. The king then orders the couple to be put through various cruel tortures. But neither of them is affected by the tortures. Their faces do not even show a twitch of pain but are blissfully smiling at each other. The king, baffled by all this, asks them what the secret of their strength and resistance is. They said, 'What! don't you know? We are looking at each other, and so engrossed are we with each other, that our mind has no room in it for any other thoughts. So far as we are concerned, we two alone exist, each for the other, and nothing else exists. How then can we be affected by other things?' Such is the power of the merged mind."

Night

Muruganar brought a book by Raghava Iyengar, the famous Tamil scholar, and quoted authority to prove that, whatever *puranas* like *Thirukovalur Purana* may say, it has been established beyond doubt that Pari, the philanthropist known to Tamil literature, was one who lived and flourished near Piranmalai and not anyone who lived in Ceylon.

In the afternoon, Mr. Bose showed Bhagavan a letter he had received from Paul Brunton. In this, Brunton says he is going back to America and that he should have very much liked to meet Bhagavan during the last six years, but it was rendered impossible by the attitude of the Asramam and that therefore he had come to accept fate in this matter and was meeting Bhagavan only in the deep places of his heart where Bhagavan still is.

7-4-46 Night

A visitor said, "In the Pondicherry Aurobindo Ashram it is said that the final stage of spiritual progress is to become the *purushottama* and it would seem that activity is predicated of that *purushottama i.e.*, some *vritti* would seem to be associated with that state, whereas it is believed by other schools that cessation of all *vrittis* is liberation."

Bhagavan said, "You say, all schools advise you to give up all *vrittis* so that you can reach your final goal, whether it is becoming *purushottama* or something else. You must cease to be the three kinds of ordinary *purusha i.e.*, the *adhama, madhyama, uttama* and become that *purushottama*. This is accepted. Whether, when you transcend these three kinds and cease to be the ordinary *purusha*, there is any *vritti* still left is a matter with which you need not concern yourself now. Attain that state and see for yourself what that state is and whether there is any *vritti* in it. To speak even of *brahmakara vritti*, as we sometimes do, is not accurate. If we can talk of the river that has merged in the ocean as still a river and call it *samudrakara river*, we can talk of the final stage in spiritual growth as having *Brahmakara vritti*. When people from Sri Aurobindo's Ashram come here and ask about the differences between our school and theirs, I always tell them, 'There, complete surrender is advised and insisted upon before anything further could be hoped for or attained. So, do it first. I also advise it. After making such surrender, *i.e.*, complete surrender and not any partial or conditional surrender, you will be able to see for yourself whether there are two *purushas*, whether power comes from anywhere and gets into anywhere, etc.' For we know nothing about God or any source from which power comes and gets into us. All that is not known. But 'I exist' is known beyond all dispute by all men. So let us know who that 'I' is. If, after knowing it, there still remain any doubts such as are now raised, it will be time enough then to try and clear such doubts."

From this point, the talk drifted to the various schools of thought, one saying there is only reality, others saying there are three eternal entities such as *jagat, jiva* and *Ishwara,* or *pati, pasu* and *pasam.* In this connection, Bhagavan observed humorously, "It is not at all correct to say that *Advaitins* or the Shankara school deny the existence of the world or that they call it unreal. On the other hand, it is more real to them than to others. Their world will always exist, whereas the world of the other schools will have origin, growth and decay and as such cannot be real. Only, they say the world as world is not real, but that the world as Brahman is real. All is Brahman, nothing exists but Brahman, and the world as Brahman is real. In this way, they claim they give more reality to the world than the other schools do. For example, according to schools which believe in three entities, the *jagat* is only one-third of the reality whereas according to *Advaita,* the world as Brahman is reality, the world and reality are not different. Similarly, even to God or Brahman, the other schools give only one-third sovereignty. The other two entities necessarily limit the reality of God. So, when Shankara is called *mayavadi* it may be retorted, 'Shankara says *maya* does not exist. He who denies the existence of *maya* and calls it *mithya* or non-existent cannot be called a *mayavadi.* It is those who grant its existence and call its product, the world, a reality who should rightly be called *mayavadis.* One who denies Ishwara is not called *Ishwaravadi,* but only one who affirms the existence of *Ishwara.*'" Bhagavan went on to add, "All these are of course vain disputations. There can be no end to such disputations. The proper thing to do is to find out the 'I', about whose existence nobody has any doubt, and which alone persists when everything else vanishes, as during sleep, and then see if there is any room for such doubts or disputes."

8-4-46

Most of Bhagavan's time today was spent in listening to *Arunachala Mahatmyam*, compiled by Mr. Venkatrama Aiyar in English, with material culled from *Skanda Puranam* and other books.

9-4-46

Reading of the above work was continued and finished this morning.

In today's post were received two books in the Czech language, one being *The Life and Teachings of Ramana Maharshi* and the other a translation of Bhagavan's important works. First, we could not understand in what language the books were written.

But Mr. Osborne told us it was Czech. Bhagavan looked into the books and the pictures it contained of him and of the hill with the clouds above it.

Afternoon

Bhagavan found that the pages of one of the above books were uncut. So he took a penknife and cut some pages. Meanwhile, he discovered that the book had not even been stitched and bound properly. So he decided to send it to the local binder, who would also attend to the cutting, etc.

Mrs. Shroff brought a small ornamental box, apparently of silver, and a small plate of copper with some sweets in them, and offered them to Bhagavan as having been sent to him by her husband. Bhagavan asked the attendants to take the sweets and return the box and plate with one or two sweets to Mrs. S. But when they were returned, Mrs. S. said they were all offered to Bhagavan, not only the sweets. Thereupon, Bhagavan said, "What are we to do with them? Send them to the office and tell them Shroff has sent them." This put Bhagavan in a reminiscent mood and he said, "For many years, while I was on the Hill, we had nothing but one or two mud-pots — no vessel at all of any sort. After many years, one day, a woman brought me some eatables in a small vessel, very old and battered and patched up in many places, and when we took the eatables and returned the rotten old vessel, she insisted on our keeping the vessel too, saying, 'It might be of some use to people who come here for drinking water, etc. So please keep it here.' That was the beginning of our having any vessels at all. After that, gradually one vessel after another found its way into the Asramam, till now we have all sorts of things brought here, like this box and plate. What am I to do with such things?" Thereupon, I remarked, "Yes. What should Bhagavan do with these things? But when people come across any such fancy things and like them themselves, they like to offer them to one whom they love best. That is only natural."

10-4-46 Morning

Dr. Masalavala gave Bhagavan a letter addressed to him by a friend of his. Bhagavan perused it. Some portions of it were not cogent. With other portions there could be no quarrel. The letter said that all is contained in *asti* (*sat*), *bhati* (*chit*), *priya* (*ananda*), *nam* and *rup*, that the first three constitute reality, and the rest the fleeting and unreal; that *jnana* consists in seeing only the reality and not the *nam-rup,* that the first three constitute *aham* and the next two constitute *idam* (this). Bhagavan agreed and said, "'I' and 'this' between them exhaust everything." The letter also said that seeing Brahman alone in everything and everywhere is *jnanottara bhakti.* With reference to this, Bhagavan said, "This is a matter of mere words, whether you call the stage of seeing only Brahman, *jnanottara bhakti* or *bhakti-uttara jnana.* In reality, saying 'We must see Brahman in everything and everywhere' is also not quite correct. Only that stage is final, where there is no seeing, where there is no time or space. There will be no seer, seeing and an object to see. What exists then is only the infinite eye."

In the afternoon Mr. Narayanaswamy Aiyar's daughter, married to our Sundaresa Aiyar's son, sang a few songs and then related the following miracle:

"In Cawnpore, we are living on the third floor of a house and we are the only residents on that floor. We have a tap there, but water rarely rises up to that level and we have daily to go down several flights of stairs and climb up with all the water necessary for us. My husband used to do this work daily for me. It was too much for him. And I was too weak to be able to help him in this daily task. One day, when I was alone in the house and my husband was in his office, I was pondering over this hard situation of ours and how we were to find a solution for this. I had kept the empty vessel before the tap and was singing in a pensive mood. Then I began singing the song *Saranagati.* (This is a song well-known among

Bhagavan's devotees. It was composed by Mr. M.V. Ramaswami Aiyar and is sung by him and the members of his family whenever they want Bhagavan to interpose and avert evil from them or bring them good). It says, in brief, 'We take shelter under you and you are our sole refuge. Who else is there to whom we can turn? If you delay to come to our rescue, we can bear it no longer. So, come at once, end my misery, give me happiness!' Then the water began to trickle down the tap and kept on flowing more as I went on with the song. So I sang the song till all our vessels were filled with water. When my husband returned home, he was surprised to find so much water and could not conceive how I could have got all that water. Then I told him, 'I have discovered now a secret device for getting water. If I sing *Saranagati* I can get water.' My husband naturally could not believe it and so I tried the same device again in his presence and the water flowed from the tap. Ever since then, my water problem has ceased. I had only to sing *Saranagati*, and water will flow from the tap. I have tried other songs. But they don't give the same result. Afterwards, when I fell ill and father came to see me, I told him about this and he too could not believe it, till I again repeated the experiment before him and he saw it succeeded. He asked me to try other songs. I did. But none of them produced the same result." The girl told all this with great glee and there was such a ring of truth about the whole narration that I consider it would be absurd to doubt the truth of the experience.

In the night, Bhagavan asked attendant Vaikuntha Vasan whether the monkeys were properly fed in the noon and whether many monkeys turned up. It being 'Sri Rama Navami', Bhagavan had suggested, "This is their (monkeys') day. We must give them food". And accordingly about 11 a.m., when we were all having our food, Vaikuntha Vasan seems to have taken a good quantity of food, vegetables, *vadai, payasam, i.e.*, all that we were taking, all mixed up together, to the steps at the back of the Asramam for the monkeys. Bhagavan's question had reference to this.

Vaikunta Vasan replied, "When I went, there were only two or three monkeys. But after a time, all of them came and they were all well-fed. They did not quarrel with each other or bite each other." Bhagavan said, "They won't fight when there is enough for all. All trouble arises only when there is want. They would also raise a big cry as an indication of their joy, whenever they get plenty to eat. We have had such experiences when I was on the Hill. They used to be fed frequently there."

11-4-46 Morning

About 8 a.m., as Bhagavan was entering his 'cage' as he calls it, *i.e.*, the new railing round his sofa, he was staring hard at Dr. Srinivasa Rao who was standing near me to the south of Bhagavan's sofa. I was wondering why Bhagavan did so. But after a few minutes, Bhagavan explained, "It looked to me as if you were wearing shorts and I was wondering whether you were about to go out somewhere. Whenever Mudaliar gets into his pants, I know he is about to go out somewhere. So I thought you too were preparing to get out. But I see now you had only tucked up your *dhoti* in such a way that it looked as if you were in shorts." The Doctor said, "No, I have given up trousers now."

About 11 a.m. after the bell had been rung for lunch as usual, Bhagavan was trying to get up from his sofa. As usual, he was rubbing his legs, knees and massaging them gently before getting up; and turning to Mr. S. Doraiswamy Iyer (who arrived here last evening), told him, "Your friend *(i.e.*, Dr. S. Rao) is giving such great attention to this pain of mine that it refuses to leave me. Who will like to depart from a place where they received all hospitality and attention?" Mr. S.D. replied, "Apparently, Bhagavan is keeping this pain, only to benefit the doctor."

In the afternoon, as I entered the hall, Bhagavan was looking into the two Czech books recently received, and after looking at them and approving the binding done locally he returned them to me. I showed them to Mr. S. D. Then Bhagavan asked him if he had seen Zimmer's book in German on Bhagavan. Mr. S. D. replied he had not. So I went and got the book and showed it to Mr. S. D.

12-4-46 Morning

I told Bhagavan: "Last evening when I went into the town, a lady, who met me on the road, accosted me and asked me if I was doing well. I could not recognise her. She felt offended and told me she also claimed to be connected with Bhagavan. It seems her mother, one Unnamalai Ammal was giving milk regularly to Jadaswami when Bhagavan used to frequent Jadaswami's place, that then this Unnamalai Ammal would give milk to Bhagavan also, that her father used to fan Bhagavan, that she herself as a child of two or three had even clung to Bhagavan's back, that her name Rukmani was given to her by Bhagavan and that even now whenever she goes to the Asramam, Bhagavan enquires about her, and so on. I wonder if all this is true." Bhagavan said, "Yes. Yes. I knew the mother who was attending on Jadaswami. I have known this lady from her childhood. She comes here now too. They are a Komutti family. The father died long ago."

Afternoon

A visitor had given Bhagavan a piece of paper on which he had scribbled in pencil a number of questions. When I went into the hall about 3 p.m., Bhagavan was trying to decipher them and turning round to me said, "Here is a question paper."

Question 1: How to get rid of credulousness? The visitor's problem was that he starts with some ideal recommended to him, but when others come and recommend other ideals, he feels inclined to believe them and give up his old ideals.

Bhagavan: Yes. Yes. Our whole trouble is that we are credulous. We believe in everything except the reality. We must give up all our false beliefs, and that is the only thing we have to do. Then the reality will shine by itself.

Question 2: I start with great keenness towards some ideal. But gradually I get slack. What should I do to prevent it, and what is the reason for this happening?

Bhagavan: Just as there must have been a reason for your keenness at one time, there must be a reason for getting slack also later on.

Question 3: There are a number of spiritual teachers, teaching various paths. Whom should one take for one's Guru?

Bhagavan: Choose that one where you find you get *shanti* or peace.

Question 4: What is the best way of dealing with desires, with a view to getting rid of them — satisfying them or suppressing them?

Bhagavan: If a desire can be got rid of by satisfying it, there will be no harm in satisfying such a desire. But desires generally are not eradicated by satisfaction. Trying to root them out that way is like pouring spirits to quench fire. At the same time, the proper remedy is not forcible suppression, since such repression is bound to react sooner or later into forceful surging up with undesirable consequences. The proper way to get rid of a desire is to find out "Who gets the desire? What is its source?" When this is found, the desire is rooted out and it will never again emerge or grow. Small desires such as the desire to eat, drink and sleep and attend to calls of nature, though these may also be classed among desires, you can safely satisfy. They will not implant *vasanas* in your mind, necessitating further birth. Those activities are just necessary to carry on life and are not likely to develop or leave behind *vasanas* or tendencies. As a general rule, therefore, there is no harm in satisfying a desire where the satisfaction will not lead to further desires by creating *vasanas* in the mind.

Question 5: What is the meaning of '*Om*'?

Bhagavan: 'Om' is everything. It is another name for Brahmam.

I was looking into the January issue of *Vision* and came across a story about Kulasekhara Alwar. Having heard during a *kalakshepam* that Ravana had taken away Sita, Kulasekhara identified himself so much with the situation in the story that he thought it was his duty as a worshipper of Rama at once to hasten to Lanka and release Sita, that he ran up and had entered the sea to cross over to Lanka, that then Rama appeared with Sita and Lakshmana showered His grace on him. I remembered another version, that Kulasekhara started on a campaign with his army to succour Rama, that meanwhile the Bhagavatar doing the *kalakshepam,* sensing the situation, passed on at once to Rama emerging victoriously from the battle, killing all his enemies, etc. Bhagavan also thought the version I had in mind was the correct one and that the matter referred to Rama's battle with Khara and Dushana and not with Ravana for Sita. Bhagavan looked up a history of the Alwars and told us that both incidents are found in Kulasekhara's life. This led me to make the following remark, "Some Maratha Saint also did a similar thing. He leaped up to the roof, I think." Thereupon, Dr. S. Rao asked Bhagavan, "I don't know that story. What is that story?" Thereupon Bhagavan said, "Ekanath was writing the Ramayana and when he came to the portion in which he was graphically describing that Hanuman jumped across the ocean to Lanka, he so identified himself with his hero Hanuman, that unconsciously he leaped into the air and landed on the roof of his neighbour. This neighbour had always a poor opinion of Ekanath, taking him for a humbug and religious hypocrite. He heard a thud on his roof and, coming out to see what it was, discovered Ekanath lying down on the roof with the cadjan leaf in one hand and his iron stile in the other, and the cadjan leaf had verses describing how Hanuman leapt across the sea. This incident proved to the neighbour what a genuine *bhakta* Ekanath was and he became his disciple."

After a pause, Bhagavan also related, "God appeared in a dream to Ekanath and asked him to go and repair the tomb of Jnaneswar. When Ekanath went there accordingly, he found a contractor ready to do all the work and take payment at the end. The contractor opened a big account, in which all expenses were entered, with the names of all the workmen and wages paid to them. Everything went on systematically and when the work of repairs having been completed, the accounts had to be looked into and the contractor paid his dues, the contractor and his big account book totally disappeared. Then alone Ekanath came to know God was his contractor and did the work. Such things have happened."

13-4-46

Today is Tamil New Year Day. The *panchangam* for the New Year was read out by our Sastriar in Bhagavan's presence in the afternoon.

14-4-46 Afternoon

Attendant Sivananda was reading out the Tamil *Siva Sahasranama* found at the end of *Tiru Arul Mozhi*. When I entered the hall about 3 p.m. Bhagavan was trying to correct S. as the latter went on reading. So I ran up to my room and brought my copy of the same book and gave it to Bhagavan, so that it would be easier for him to follow S. and correct him. Bhagavan said, "No. It is impossible to correct him. He makes so many mistakes." Thereupon I offered to help S. and the reading went on for some time. In the course of this reading I found out how much it goes against Bhagavan's grain if poems are not read out according to 'சீர்' (prosodic feet) and in the proper way in which each kind of verse is to be read, or if mistakes are made. After some time S. himself thought he would stop reading and did so.

Nagamma returned the Telugu journal *Bharati* and Bhagavan asked me if I had read Chinta Dikshitulu's *Asal Neevu Evaru* (*In reality who are you*?) which appeared in that journal. I said, "Yes". Bhagavan suggested that an English translation of it might be useful. I was under the impression that Mauni had already translated it into English. For, I remembered that Balaram in the hall translated 'Asal' as 'In reality' and that later Mauni translated it as 'In the first instance' and I preferred the latter. So I ran up to Mauni and asked if he had not made an English translation. He said he had only translated the title of the article. So, I told Bhagavan I would myself translate it. Meanwhile, we requested Viswanath to translate it into Tamil with the help of Subba Rao.

15-4-46 Morning

About 8 a.m. Nagamma came into the hall and prostrated herself before Bhagavan, after having gone round the hall a few times. Bhagavan said, "Ah! you too have started going round. Have you learnt it from Ravanamma? She used to go round and round, till I spoke to her about it the other day. If one goes round like that, everybody who comes here thinks 'Apparently the proper thing here is to go round' and starts going round. Thus all people go round. After all, the proper *pradakshina* is going round the Self, or, more accurately, to realise that we are the Self and that within us all the countless spheres revolve, going round and round, as described in the following stanza of *Ribhu Gita* (3rd Chapter, 39th Verse).

பூரணவா நந்தான்மா வகமென் றெண்ணல்
புகழ்புட்பாஞ் சலியாகு மநந்த கோடி

காரியமாம் பிரமாண்ட மென்னி டத்தே
கற்பிதமாய்ச் சுழலுமெனந் தியானந் தானே

நேரதுவாய் வலம்வரலா மென்று மென்னை
நிகிலருமே வந்திப்பார் நானெப் போது
மாரையுமே வந்திக்கே னென்னுந் தியான
மான்மமகா லிங்கத்தினை வணங்கலாமே.

An English translation of this stanza is as follows:

Reflecting "I am the all-blissful Self"
Is worship as with words and flowers.
True circumambulation is the thought,
"In me the million universes roll",
He who knows all beings bow to him
And he to none,
He bows before the Mahalinga-Self.

"Some go on doing a number of *namaskarams, e.g.* that Janaki, she goes on striking her head down countless times along with *namaskarams*. She goes round a number of times. At each window she falls down and does a number of *namaskarams.* However much I tell her, she won't leave off such practices." Somebody here interjected, "It seems she is known to Bhagavan since her childhood." Bhagavan said, "Yes, yes," and continued, "There are others who come and fall before me while I am moving. They lie prostrate for some minutes. I cannot stand for them on account of my physical infirmity. So I walk on, telling myself, 'Only if we do *namaskarams* we will be benefited. After all, true *namaskaram* is only the giving up the 'I'-sense, or killing the ego'."

I said, "Bhagavan himself advises us to go round the Hill, for instance. I know Bhagavan is also not against going round the image in a temple. There are people here who have the faith that going round Bhagavan is as good as going round the temple-image or the Hill. How can we object to that?" Bhagavan said, "I don't say such things should not be done. But the best going round is going round yourself, or the *bhava* expressed in the verse quoted. The other *pradakshinams* are not condemned. The *jnani,* though he knows that meditation on the Self is the best worship, will join in all the other kinds of worship for the good of others and as an example to them. In fact, he may observe all the other ways even more correctly and steadfastly than those who follow only those paths and know nothing of *jnana*. That is referred to in the following verse, also occurring in *Ribhu Gita*.

தந்தைமுதன் மரணத்திற் பந்து வின்றித்
தளர்தனயன் றிரவியமே தந்த ழைத்து
வந்தசன மழுகின்ற நீதி யன்னோன்
வழங்குதனப் பொருட்டன்றி யுண்மை யன்றே
யந்தவித மாசிரியன் சிட னுக்கிங்
கத்துவிதம் புகலுங்காற் றுதவித மோதல்;
மைந்தவிதி லையமிலை யதனுற் றெற்த
மறந்தென்று மத்துவித வடிவே யாவாய்.

The gist is, "If the Guru refers to *dvaita* when teaching *advaita* to the disciple, it is not to be regarded as his real teaching any more than one should regard as real the grief of one who weeps because he is paid to do so."

When Bhagavan quoted the first verse above extracted, I went and brought the book for his reference. He took it in his hand and opened it. The book opened exactly where the passage is found. Such a thing has happened many others times too.

In the afternoon I was reading a recent issue of *Prabuddha Bharata.* There I found that one disciple asked Shivananda, a direct disciple of Sri Ramakrishna Paramahamsa, "It is said Paramahamsa once said, 'Those who have come here will have no more births.' Did you hear him say so? What does it mean? Will only those who came to him and saw in the flesh and worshipped him be saved, or even those who have only heard about him and worshipped him?" It is said Shivananda replied, "The above remark of Paramahamsa is found in all the books, and it means that both classes of people will be saved, provided however they have surrendered unto him."

I pointed out, "All that Paramahamsa said was, 'Those who have come here will have salvation.' Why do these people make this addition, 'provided they surrender unto him?' If a man makes complete surrender to God, Self or Guru he is of course saved. That is well known. To a man who is able to make complete surrender, *sat sang* is superfluous." Bhagavan said, "When Paramahamsa said 'People who come here' the words really imply 'People who have come and surrendered themselves here'." I said, "If he meant it, would he not have said so? I believe there are people, to approach whom, is to obtain salvation, whether we are able to surrender completely or not. Did not all the crowd that went to attend Saint Sambandar's marriage, including the pipers and drummers, get salvation? The drummer and piper had no idea of making complete surrender." Bhagavan remained silent. Then he said, "It is said Sundarar got a *vimana* and went to heaven and that he invited others to join him, but that none came forward. But in Tukaram's life it is said that he went to heaven with his body and that he took twenty-one people with him." To look up this last reference, I brought *Bhakta Vijayam* in Tamil and Bhagavan read how Tukaram, before going to heaven with his body, invited everyone to go with him and, after seven days, he went with twenty-two people to Heaven.

In this connection, I told Bhagavan, "It has come down as a sort of tradition, and I have also heard it said, that Bhagavan once told some disciples that those who are here (*i.e.*, with Bhagavan) need not worry about their salvation, even as upper class passengers, having informed the guard, may quietly go to sleep in their berths and will be awakened and detrained at their destination by the guard. I have not been able to find out when, where and to whom Bhagavan said words to the above effect." Bhagavan said nothing in reply. But so far as I am concerned, the fact that he did not deny it in words or by facial expression is enough to convince me that Bhagavan must have, in some unguarded moment, uttered these words (of great hope to lazy men like me).

16-4-46

In the evening, after *parayana,* Muruganar brought a Tamil book and gave it to Bhagavan saying that the author had sent two copies of the book through Padananda. Thereupon Bhagavan asked M., "When did Padananda arrive?" and he replied, "Last night". On enquiry, Muruganar told me it was a book by Tiruttani Chengalroya Pillai, comparing the two famous poet-saints Tirumoolar and Arunagirinathar. Bhagavan said, "It is a short book and can be read out now either by you or Viswanath." V. was sitting in the front row before Bhagavan. I looked at all the rows behind, standing near the first row, and told Bhagavan, "V. is not here." Then Bhagavan showed V. to me and laughed saying, "Why, he is here." I said, "Then, let us ask him to read it. I have not got my glasses with me." Bhagavan remarked, "I see that is why you could not see Viswanathan." Then V. read out the pamphlet and we all heard it. Some Telugu visitor got up and requested Bhagavan that the matter should be translated or summarised in Telugu. But such translation seemed neither necessary nor feasible. The book did not strike any of us as worth all the trouble it must doubtless have entailed.

17-4-46

Yesterday morning itself, Viswanathan had given to Bhagavan a Tamil rendering of *Asal, Neevu Evaru, Ramana Bhagavan*? Bhagavan asked me yesterday afternoon if I had done the English translation. I had to say 'No'. So I sat down last night and revised the English translation which one Mr. Sitarama Rao had done for us and left with me. I fair-copied the revised draft and gave it to Bhagavan at 10-30 a.m. today. Soon after he began to peruse it, the second *tapal* arrived and he had to attend to it. After finishing it, though it was then five minutes to eleven, Bhagavan took up the English translation for perusal and went on with it till the bell rang for lunch at 11 a.m.

Afternoon

Bhagavan continued reading the English translation and finished it after suggesting about half a dozen corrections.

18-4-46 Afternoon

Mr. Nanavati of Bombay asked Bhagavan, "In the fifth stanza of *Arunachala Pancharatna* reference is made to seeing 'Your form in everything'. What is the form referred to?" Bhagavan said, "The stanza says that one should completely surrender one's mind, turn it inwards and see 'you' the Self within and then see the Self in 'you' in everything. It is only after seeing the Self within that one will be able to see the Self in everything. One must first realise there is nothing but the Self and that he is that Self, and then only he can see everything as the form of the Self. That is the meaning of saying, 'See the Self in everything and everything in the Self', as is stated in the *Gita* and other books. It is the same truth that is taught in stanza 4 of the *Reality in Forty Verses*. If you have the idea that you are something with form, that you are limited by this body, and that being within this body you have to see through these eyes, God and the world also will appear to you as form. If you realise you are without form, that you are unlimited, that you alone exist, that you are the eye, the infinite eye, what is there to be seen apart from the infinite eye? Apart from the eye, there is nothing to be seen. There must be a seer for an object to be seen, and there must be space, time, etc. But if the Self alone exists, it is both seer and seen, and above seeing or being seen."

19-4-46 Morning

After Krishnaswami had been massaging for seven or eight minutes, Bhagavan said, "You have been massaging me. It seemed to me as if I was not being massaged." And turning to me, he said, "Sometimes, when they are not massaging me, I feel as if I was being massaged. What to say?"

Somasundaram Pillai of Cuddalore returned after a visit to Tiruchuzhi, Madura, and other places, and was telling Bhagavan that the day he was at Madura it happened to be *Punarvasu Nakshatra,* and that devotees gathered in the Ramana Mandiram there, had *bhajan,* etc., and that there was milk and *vadai* for *naivedyam* which was afterwards distributed to all those who were present at the function. Just as he was saying this, Santhamma entered the hall, with milk for *naivedyam* and distribution, because she had just entered her new house. Bhagavan said, "You say milk was offered as *naivedyam,* and distributed to you. Here comes milk for the same purpose." S. continued to tell Bhagavan about his trip and Bhagavan asked, "Did you enquire in Tiruchuzhi, whether on *Masi Makam,* which was only a little before you went there, water rose in the temple tank as it used to do in my boyhood?" S. replied, "No. I took it for granted that even now the water rises and so did not make any enquiries." Then Bhagavan said that the water of the temple tank is reputed to cure many skin diseases and added, "That is certain. We have seen as boys that when we bathed in the tank our silver bangles all turned black, and we had to rub them well with mud before going back home, lest our parents should blame us for bathing in the tank. The water contains sulphur."

20-4-46 Afternoon

A Muslim visitor put some questions and got the following answers:

Question: This body dies. But there is another imperishable body. What is it?

Answer: 'Imperishable body' is a contradiction in terms. The term *sariram* means that which will perish. Of course, there is something imperishable, something which exists even after the body dies.

Question: It is said the Lord's light resides in the eye.

Answer: The eye does not see. That which gives light to it is the reality, whether we call it Lord's light or anything else.

Question: The Lord has created all this, has He not? What was created first? It is said light or sound was created first.

Answer: All these things, which you say have been created have to be seen by you before you say they exist. There must be a seer. If you find out who that seer is, then you will know about creation and which was created first. Of course various theories as to what came into existence first from God are given out. Most, including scientists, agree that all has come from light and sound.

Question: Can we call anything created, like this piece of wood, for example, God? It is said it is very wrong to do so.

Answer: Even this piece of wood, does it exist apart from God? Can we confine God to any time or place, since He is everywhere and in everything? We should not see anything as apart from God. That is all.

22-4-46 Afternoon

Nagamma told Bhagavan the two latest poems in Telugu by Naganariya *Skandasrama Santarsanam* and *Ghooha jnani* had not yet been read out in the hall and that *Athai* (*i.e.*, Bhagavan's sister) and others wanted to hear them, and took permission from Bhagavan and read out the same.

Later, Mr. Rajagopala Sarma, Sanskrit Pandit in Maharajah's College at Pudukottah, came and introduced himself to Bhagavan, saying that he was well known to our Lakshmana Sarma, and that, though he had often heard about Bhagavan, he had got the privilege of seeing Bhagavan only now, for the first time. Then he read out three slokas composed by him in praise of Bhagavan, and also explained the same to us in Tamil. In these slokas the Pandit compares Bhagavan to the moon but finds him superior in some respect. Here is a gist of the slokas: "Like the moon, you bring coolness and pleasantness to all. If there is a difference between you and the moon, it is in your favour. The moon brings sorrow to separated lovers. But you give pleasure to all without exception by your kind grace. The moon has its dark fortnight. But you are ever shining.

"The moon is eagerly awaited by the *chakora* bird which feeds on the nectar flowing from the moon. So are all the *bhaktas* gathered here, eagerly awaiting, and being benefited by the nectar of your presence and speech.

"The flower *kuvalaya* blossoms on the moon rising. The hearts of the entire *kuvalaya* (the world), or the hearts of all men, blossom on seeing you.

"Moonlight disperses the gloom of the night which hides the objects in the world. Thy light dispels the darkness of *ajnana* which hides the reality from us.

"The moon is worn by Siva on the crown of His head. All creation or Brahma bears you on His head.

"The moon was born in the Milky Ocean. You are born in the ocean of Vedanta."

24-4-46 Afternoon

When Chinta Dikshitulu's *Ramana Gopalan* first came here, Mr. D.S. Sastri sent us an English translation of the article. It was read out before Bhagavan and we thought at the time a few corrections were needed. Mauni took the translation for the above correction. But it seems to have lain long with him, without being attended to. So, Nagamma brought it back three or four days ago and gave it to me and asked me to do the revision. Bhagavan asked me this afternoon if I had finished the work. I replied, "I had the Telugu read out to me by Nagamma only last evening and started writing the revised translation this morning. When I came to the sentence in which *thaga, thaga* occurs I wanted to see how our Viswanath had rendered it in Tamil. I got the Tamil rendering only at 11 a.m. I am going on with the work and shall finish it soon." Then we discussed the words *mutte, thaga thaga, eppatiki appudu,* etc., occurring in the original article. I finished the revision and gave it to Bhagavan. He asked me to keep it along with the other translations. I gave them to Nagamma and requested her to bind all together for future reference. Nagamma asked Bhagavan for the three slokas in Sanskrit by the Pudukottah Pandit and offered to write them down in the *stotra* notebook. We found they had already been copied by Viswanath. Bhagavan took up the slokas and read them out. I took advantage of this, to read my summary of the first of these *slokas* as given in this diary and see if Bhagavan thought it fairly correct. Bhagavan gave me the compliment of remarking, "How did you manage to remember all this and write them down in your notebook?" I had omitted reference in my account to Bhagavan having been born in the ocean of Vedanta, while the moon was born in the milky ocean. During this reading I added this also.

While I was at Nagamma's place on the 23rd evening, to get the Telugu *Ramana Gopalan* read out to me, she said in the course of conversation, "You are filling up book after book. But I have written only little." (This was with reference to accounts of significant utterances by Bhagavan about which she has been writing letters regularly to her brother at Madras, and keeping copies herself). I told Bhagavan now, "Nagamma says I am writing all sorts of rubbish and filling up book after book; and that she will record only important events or statements."

This I said somewhat in jest. Poor Nagamma came out "Can you utter lies like these, even in Bhagavan's presence?" I replied laughing, "They are not exactly lies."

Evening

Throughout the day the *Sarvadhikari* has been inviting all *bhaktas* to have a look at a clay model of Bhagavan which the Madras sculptor engaged to make Bhagavan's statue, has prepared here. After *parayana,* Mr. Narayanaswami Iyer, retired drawing master, came to Bhagavan and expressed his opinion that the model was not satisfactory. He wanted Bhagavan's opinion. Bhagavan only said, "Don't ask me. How can one know one's own face? How can I judge this clay model?" Poor N. Iyer was disappointed. Bhagavan added after a while, "Each person has a different opinion. Rangaswami says the nose is too big, and the sculptor actually measures it and shows it is correct. But R. says, the nose looks too big. What are we to do? Supposing someone produces the most exact possible resemblance, I wonder whether even then if all those who look at the result will give the same unanimous verdict."

Mr. N. Iyer again came when we were all starting with Bhagavan for the night meal, and pleaded that he must give his opinion to please his *bhaktas.* He said he would produce two big mirrors and that Bhagavan could first study his own face standing between the two mirrors and then judge the clay model and give his frank opinion. Bhagavan stoutly refused to do any such thing.

25-4-46 Morning

When Bhagavan returned from his stroll about 7-30 a.m. and entered the hall, he said, "As I was getting up the steps to get into the Asramam compound I was saying, 'How is it Dr. T.N.K. has not arrived? If he came by the morning train, he should have arrived by now.' Before I closed my mouth, I find T.N.K. before me. I wonder if it was his being here that made me think of him. I think of him and there he is before me." Then Bhagavan told T.N.K., "It must have been a great inconvenience for you to rush up like this now. These people wouldn't listen to me. They wired to you. They wired to the *sthapati.* The *sthapati* replied he could not come now. They have now sent a man to fetch him. I don't know if the *sthapati* is going to come after all. All this is quite unnecessary. But they won't heed me."

When discussing some days ago the meaning of *dakshina parsam* occurring in *Asal Neevu Evaru*, Bhagavan wanted to know if the image of Dakshinamurti in the Madras museum has its head turned to the right, looking at the heart-centre there. Bhagavan then remarked, "If we write to Dr. T.N.K., he will at once take a photo of the image and send it." Nagamma reminded Bhagavan of this in the hall this morning, soon after Dr. T.N.K. left the hall. So, soon after, I brought Dr. T.N.K. again into the hall and Bhagavan asked him to take and send a photo of the image or images of Dakshinamurti in the museum. Bhagavan also enquired if the museum authorities would object. Dr. T.N.K. replied they would not, and that they might even have photos of the image or images already with them. He also wanted to have for reference with him, the sentence in the article describing the image of Dakshinamurti. So I gave him the extract, with a translation in Tamil.

A visitor asked Bhagavan, "When I try to be without all thoughts, I pass into sleep. What should I do about it?"

Bhagavan: Once you go to sleep, you can do nothing in that state. But while you are awake, try to keep away all thoughts. Why think about sleep? Even that is a thought, is it not? If you are able to be without any thought while you are awake, that is enough. When you pass into sleep, that state, in which you were before falling asleep, will continue and again, when you wake up, you will continue from where you had left off when you fell into slumber. So long as there are thoughts of activity, so long would there be sleep also. Thought and sleep are counterparts of one and the same thing.

Bhagavan quoted the *Gita* and said, "We should not sleep very much or go without it altogether, but sleep only moderately. To prevent too much sleep, we must try and have no thoughts or *chalana* (movement of the mind), we must eat only *sattvic* food and that only in moderate measure, and not indulge in too much physical activity. The more we control thought, activity and food the more shall we be able to control sleep. But moderation ought to be the rule, as explained in the *Gita*, for the *sadhak* on the path. Sleep is the first obstacle, as explained in the books, for all *sadhaks.* The second obstacle is said to be *vikshepa* or the sense objects of the world which divert one's attention. The third is said to be *kashaya* or thoughts in the mind about previous experiences with sense objects. The fourth, *ananda,* is also called an obstacle, because in that state a feeling of separation from the source of *ananda*, enabling the enjoyer to say 'I am enjoying *ananda*' is present. Even this has to be surmounted and the final stage of *samadhana* or *samadhi* has to be reached, where one becomes *ananda* or one with the reality and the duality of enjoyer and enjoyment ceases in the ocean of *sat-chit-ananda* or the Self."

26-4-46 Morning

Bhagavan asked me if I had seen Colombo Ramachandra's letter received by the Asramam yesterday. I said, "No." Thereupon he told me, "R. has written enclosing Gunaratna's letter. He says that this is the first time any saint's life is written in the Sinhalese language. It seems, if they try to bring out the book in time for the Jubilee occasion here, it may have to be greatly abridged.

I don't know what they are going to do. The *Ashtakam*, which R. wrote when here, has also been given for publication, and he will be getting the printed copies in a day or two."

I told Bhagavan, "Yes. Even when here, R. already sent it to the press, while he had written only five of the poems. He wanted it as a folder with Bhagavan's picture on the first page. But he had asked me not to mention it to Bhagavan just then."

Meanwhile, Mr. Somasundaram Pillai said that in R.'s letter it is stated that the Ramakrishna Mission, after coming to know of what we have done about the Tiruchuzhi house, are taking steps to secure the house where the Paramahamsa was born, and make it a place of pilgrimage and worship.

Then Bhagavan said, "The *bhattar* at Tiruchuzhi might have been expecting Ramachandra at Tiruchuzhi on his way back from here to Colombo. Does he know of R. having gone back?"

Somasundaram Pillai: I told him all about R. and how I had to escort him as far as Dhanushkodi.

Bhagavan: It seems the *bhattar* has been invited to Vadapuri to attend some special function there, in celebration of Saint Manikkavachagar.

Then we began talking of Vadavoor, which Bhagavan said was only about twenty miles from Madura, and also of Perundurai; there is much controversy among research scholars whether Perundurai of *Tiruvachakam* is the place called Avudayarkoil where there is a temple, and a tradition that Saint Manikkavachakar built it, or whether it is some place farther west. Bhagavan said, "All sorts of theories are put forward, with ingenious and far-fetched arguments both for and against."

Later, the Mauni wanted for reference the poems composed and left here by Dilip Kumar Roy of Aurobindo Ashram, when he was here last, and also the poem by Mr. Chadwick in which he had addressed Bhagavan, "You will not let me go." I searched in the files and could get only D.K. Roy's. Then I got from Mr. Chadwick a copy of his poems which, we found, had been composed in 1941. I gave both Roy's and Chadwick's poems to Mauni.

Evening

After *parayana,* when the monkeys were getting their usual parting gifts of fruit of the day, Bhagavan recounted his old experiences with monkeys at Skandasramam, and how his favourite Nondippaiyan (the lame one) hurt him twice. After the monkeys were supplied, there was one plantain left, and Bhagavan said "Give it to these children" pointing to four of them who were there and adding, "these are tail-less monkeys."

27-4-46 Morning

The priest of a temple at Dwaraka, returning from Aurobindo's Ashram, visited Bhagavan and asked him in Sanskrit, "I wish to get *sakshatkara* of Sri Krishna. What should I do to get it?" This question was put while Bhagavan was reading a rather long letter from Lt. Shroff, which his wife had brought. The letter closed with the sentiment: "Do what you will to me. Send me health or sickness, riches or poverty." Bhagavan said with reference to the priest's question, "I did not want to disturb his faith, but wanted to tell him 'Just leave it to Sri Krishna, — even this *sakshatkara* of Krishna.' And this letter of Shroff contains the same thing."

After saying this, Bhagavan added, "What is your idea of Sri Krishna and what do you mean by *sakshatkara*?" On this, the priest replied, "I mean the Sri Krishna who lived in Brindavan and I want to see him as the Gopis saw him."

Bhagavan replied, "You see, you think he is a human being or one with a human form, the son of so and so, etc., whereas he himself has said, 'I am in the Heart of all beings, I am the beginning, the middle and the end of all forms of life.' He must be within you, as within all. He is your *Atman* or the *atman* of your *Atman*. So if you see this entity or have *sakshatkara* of it, you will have *sakshatkara* of Krishna. *Atma Sakshatkara* and *sakshatkara* of Krishna cannot be different. However, to go your own way, surrender completely to Krishna and leave it to Him to grant the *sakshatkara* you want."

29-4-46 Afternoon

Mr Nanavati asked Bhagavan, "What is the heart referred to in the verse in *Upadesa Saram* where it is said 'Abiding in the heart is the best *karma, yoga, bhakti* and *jnana*'?"

Bhagavan: That which is the source of all, that in which all live, and that into which all finally merge, is the heart referred to.

Nanavati: How can we conceive of such a heart?

Bhagavan: Why should you conceive of anything? You have only to see wherefrom the 'I' springs.

Nanavati: I suppose mere *mauna* in speech is no good; but we must have *mauna* of the mind.

Bhagavan: Of course. If we have real *mauna,* that state in which the mind is merged into its source and has no more separate existence, then all other kinds of *mauna* will come of their own accord, *i.e.*, the *mauna* of words, of action and of the mind or *chitta.*

Bhagavan also quoted in this connection, the following from Thayumanavar.

"சித்த மவுனஞ் செயல்வாக் கெலாமவுனஞ்
சுத்த மவுனமென்பால் தோன்றிற் பராபரமே"

[If I get pure *mauna* (quiescence), I shall have *mauna* of *chitta,* mind, word and deed]. Bhagavan added, "Such *mauna* is not inertness but great activity. It is the most powerful speech."

Mr. Ramasubba Iyer was taking out a book from the Asramam Library. Bhagavan asked him what book it was. He said he was taking a copy of *Nannool*, because he wanted to learn 'யாப்பியல்' or prosody. Bhagavan thereupon advised him to take another book dealing with prosody called 'யாப்பிலக்கணம்' or, 'அணியிலக்கணம்', as *Nannool* gives only a brief treatment of prosody. Bhagavan then fell into a discourse on various metres and told us something about Tamil prosody and how there are six parts in Tamil poetry — எழுத்து, அசை, சீர், தளை, அடி & தொடை. Bhagavan continued, "*Venba* is very difficult to make, even more difficult than the *arya vrittams* in Sanskrit, as Kavyakantha himself had to admit once to me. *Venba* is described as a 'tiger' even to pandits. It will overcome even great poets. Of course, all this is only spoiling one's peace of mind. When great effort is put forth to do all sorts of literary gymnastics, what is the result but loss of peace of mind? Sometimes, the first 'சீர்' in all the four lines will appear to be the same word or words. But, when with great skill the words are split up differently in each line, the meanings would be found to be different." From this the talk drifted to how by training the mind people achieve such wonderful things as *satavadhana* (attending to a hundred things at the same time) and Bhagavan described how Nayana (Kavyakantha Ganapati Sastri) used to do *satavadhana* in Bhagavan's presence, how it was really wonderful, how Nayana used to say that, what he was exhibiting was only a thousandth part of the powers of memory and mind he had developed, and how Nayana once composed three hundred stanzas of his *Uma Sahasram* between eight and twelve one night dictating different chapters to different writers at the same time.

2-5-46 Morning

A visitor asked, "I have been visiting various shrines in a pilgrimage, and worshipping various images. What exactly is God's true form?"

Bhagavan: The only thing to know is that there is an entity who is in all these forms, but who is not these forms. We see the One in the many. We see the One as many, the Formless in the forms.

In the afternoon, T.P.R. asked Bhagavan where the ஊர்ந்து குடிச்சான் சுனை (the name of a spring) is on the Hill and Bhagavan described the locality and said it was first shown to him by a woodcutter. Bhagavan continued, "In those days I used to go all by myself. For answering calls of nature I used to stroll along, taking no water with me, but going wherever water may be available. It was on one such occasion, on one morning, that I came across the banyan tree of which I have spoken often.

"As I was walking in the bed of a hill-stream, I saw a big banyan tree on a boulder, with big leaves, and crossing the stream I wanted to get to the other bund and view from there this big tree. When I accidentally put my left foot near a bush on the way to the other bank, the hornets clustered round my left leg up to the knee and went on stinging. They never did anything to my right leg. I left the left leg there for some time, so that the hornets could inflict full punishment on the leg which had encroached on their domain. After a time, the hornets withdrew and I walked on. The leg got swollen very much and I walked with difficulty and reached 'Ezhu Sunai' (Seven Springs) about 2 a.m., and Jadaswami, who was camping there then, gave me some buttermilk mixed with jaggery which was all that he could provide by way of food. This is what actually happened. But afterwards, people have gone and written that I had purposely set out to explore and find out the banyan tree described in the *purana* as the one on the northern peak of the Hill, where Arunachala is said to be residing as a *siddha.* I never had any such idea. When I saw for the first time a remarkable banyan tree on a huge and precipitous boulder, I was prompted by curiosity to have a look at it. Meanwhile, the hornets stung me and I forgot all about the tree."

In the afternoon, an European walked into the hall, sat in a corner and walked away after a few minutes. Bhagavan turned to me and asked me if I didn't know him. I told Bhagavan I had seen him here before, but I had forgotten his name. He is a friend of Mr. McIver. Bhagavan said, "His name is Evelyn. His wife — don't you know he married that Parsi girl who used to come and stay with Mrs. Taleyarkhan — has written to Viswanathan to look after her husband, saying he had come out of the hospital and that he is better now."

5-5-46 Afternoon

Mr. Kasturi Chetti brought news that Ganapati Sastri had passed away that morning, and that hernia was the cause. Talking about G. Sastri, Bhagavan said he was a great friend of Grant Duff, that he was a great lover of books, and that he would promptly buy (not necessarily read) all good books that came out and keep them in his library.

Bhagavan said, "Some rare books, which could not be got elsewhere, were available with him." Mr. T.P.R. said Bhagavan was once waylaid and taken to G.'s house to see the library he had collected. Bhagavan said, "It was he who got the *Ramana Gita* written in Nagari characters. Nayana wrote it down in Telugu characters."

Evening

About two days ago, four books in French were received from Swami Siddheswarananda in Paris. In the letter the Swami wrote, "I hope the French devotee Mrs. Sen is still there. I meet her friends here. If she is there, she may be able to tell Bhagavan about the references in those books to Bhagavan." So Bhagavan asked me to give those books to Mrs. Sen for perusal. This evening she came and said, "In these books reference is made to Bhagavan as a perfect *sthita prajna,* though some other words in French are used for *sthita prajna.*" Thereupon,

Bhagavan read out to her the verses in *Vivekachudamani* (from the English translation) which describes a *sthita prajna*. Bhagavan also told us how the *Bhagavad Gita* describes the same man as *sthita prajna* in Chapter II, later on in dealing with *bhakti*, as *bhagavat bhakta*, later still as *gunatita* (or beyond *gunas*). This Bhagavan said when I read in *Vivekachudamani* the verses that follow those that describe a *sthita prajna*. These deal with the *jivanmukta* (one liberated while yet alive). A *sthita prajna* is described as one who has attained steady illumination in *Vivekachudamani*. I asked Bhagavan if these terms were not intended to denote the same class. It was then that Bhagavan referred to the Gita passages.

5-5-46

In answer to a visitor, Bhagavan said, "Find out to whom is *Viyoga*. That is yoga. Yoga is common to all paths. Yoga is really nothing but ceasing to think that you are different from the Self or Reality. All the yogas — karma, *jnana, bhakti* and *raja* — are just different paths to suit different natures with different modes of evolution and to get them out of the long cherished notion that they are different from the Self. There is no question of union or yoga in the sense of going and joining something that is somewhere away from us or different from us, because you never were or could be separate from the Self."

In the afternoon I showed Bhagavan the passage in today's *Sunday Times* where Dr. T.M.P. Mahadevan, in his radio talk, quotes Sri Shankara's reference to his own experience as proof of the existence of the *jivanmukta* and about the controversies concerning various kinds of *mukti*. He read out passages from a Tamil book called அத்வைத உண்மை (*The Truth of Advaita*) in which all doubts about the state of the *jivanmukta* are raised and answered. Then he said:

"Various illustrations are given in books to enable us to understand how the *jnani* can live and act without the mind, although living and acting require the use of the mind. The potter's wheel goes on turning round even after the potter has ceased to turn it because the pot is finished. In the same way, the electric fan goes on revolving for some minutes after we switch off the current. The *prarabdha* which created the body will make it go through whatever activities it was meant for. But the *jnani* goes through all these activities without the notion that he is the doer of them. It is hard to understand how this is possible. The illustration generally given is that the *jnani* performs actions in some such way as a child that is roused from sleep to eat, eats but does not remember next morning that it ate. It has to be remembered that all these explanations are not for the *jnani*. He knows and has no doubts. He knows that he is not the body and is not doing anything even though his body may be engaged in some activity. These explanations are for the onlookers who think of the *jnani* as one with a body and cannot help identifying him with his body.

"There are various controversies or schools of thought as to whether a *jnani* can continue to live in his physical body after realization. Some hold that one who dies cannot be a *jnani*, because his body must vanish into air, or some such thing. They put forward all sorts of funny notions. If a man must at once leave his body when he realises the Self, I wonder how any knowledge of the Self or the state of realisation can come down to other men. And that would mean that all those who have given us the fruits of their Self-realisation in books cannot be considered *jnanis* because they went on living after realisation. And if it is held that a man cannot be considered a *jnani* so long as he performs actions in the world (and action is impossible without the mind), then not only the great Sages who carried on various kinds of work after attaining *jnana* must not be considered *jnanis*, but the gods also, and *Ishwara* Himself, since He continues looking after the world. The fact is that any amount of action can be performed, and performed quite well, by the *jnani* without his identifying himself with it in any way or ever imagining that he is the doer. Some power acts through his body and uses his body to get the work done."

Bhagavan has said the same on previous occasions also. He continued to speak about *mukti* and said, "*Mukti* is not anything to be attained. It is our real nature. We are always That. It is only so long as one feels that he is in bondage that he has to try to get released from bondage. When a man feels that he is in bondage he tries to find out for whom is the bondage and by that enquiry discovers that there is no bondage for him but only for the mind, and that the mind itself disappears or proves non-existent when turned inwards instead of outwards towards sense-objects; it merges into its source, the Self, and ceases to exist as a separate entity. In that state there is no feeling either of bondage or liberation. So long as one speaks of *mukti* he is not free from the sense of bondage."

The visitor who had asked about yoga in the morning now pursued his questions further.

Visitor: I did not quite grasp all that Bhagavan said this morning. What am I to do when the mind strays in various directions during *dhyana*?

Bhagavan: Simply draw the mind back each time it strays and fix it in *dhyana*. There is no other way. (Bhagavan also quoted Chapter VI, Verse 26 from the *Bhagavad Gita* which says the same thing).

Visitor: Then is there no use in *pranayama* (breath control)? Should I not practise it?

Bhagavan: Pranayama is also a help. It is one of the various methods that are intended to help us attain *ekagratha* or one-pointedness of mind. *Pranayama* can also help to control the wandering mind and attain this one-pointedness and therefore it can be used. But one should not stop there. After obtaining control of the mind through *pranayama* one should not rest content with any experiences which may accrue therefrom but should harness the controlled mind to the question 'Who am I?' till the mind merges in the Self.

The visitor further asked whether in his meditation he could use forms and images of God and *mantras*.

Bhagavan: Yes, of course. All these things can help, or why should they be recommended in the books? Various things are prescribed to suit various natures. Each person must choose what seems easiest and appeals to him most.

6-5-46

At about 10 o'clock this morning, in the presence of Bhagavan, the corner-stone was laid for the New Hall that Bhagavan is to sit in, in front of the temple of the Mother. The foundation was laid on January 25th, 1945, and is now ready to be built upon.

In the afternoon a visitor, Lakshmi Narayana Sastri from Vizianagaram, read out portions of his book for Bhagavan's approval and blessing. It is a Telugu verse rendering of Kavyakantha Ganapati Sastri's Sanskrit book *Uma Sahasram* with commentary.

7-5-46

In the afternoon L.N. Sastri again read out portions of his book. Bhagavan asked how much was already translated and he replied only about one century. He also read out a few poems that he himself had composed in praise of Bhagavan under the title *Atma Nivedanam* and prayed for Bhagavan's blessings. He told Bhagavan that he had applied to the publishers of the Sanskrit original that he was translating, for permission to publish his translation, but the permission had not yet come. Bhagavan said: "It will come; there will be no difficulty."

I could not judge these poems, as they are in Telugu, but Nagamma tells me they are very good and L.N. Sastri is a poet of some standing.

8-5-46

In the afternoon there was the following talk with a young *sadhu* from North India:

Sadhu: I want to know who I am. The Arya Samajists say that I am the *jivatma* and that if I purify the mind and *buddhi* I can see God. I don't know what to do. If Bhagavan thinks fit, will Bhagavan please tell me what to do?

Bhagavan: You have used a number of terms. What do you mean by *jivatma*, mind, *buddhi* and God? And where is God and where are you that you should want to go and see God?

Sadhu: I don't know what all these terms mean.

Bhagavan: Then never mind what the Arya Samajists tell you. You don't know about God and other things, but you do know that you exist. You can have no doubt about that. So find out who you are.

Sadhu: That is what I want to know. How can I find out?

Bhagavan: Keep all other thoughts away and try to find out in what place in your body the 'I' arises.

Sadhu: But I am unable to think about this.

Bhagavan: Why? If you can think about other things you can think about 'I' and where in your body it arises. If you mean that other thoughts distract you, the only way is to draw your mind back each time it strays and fix it on the 'I'. As each thought arises, ask yourself: "To whom is this thought?" The answer will be, "to me"; then hold on to that "me".

Sadhu: Am I to keep on repeating "Who am I?" so as to make a *mantra* of it?

Bhagavan: No. 'Who am I?' is not a *mantra.* It means that you must find out where in you arises the I-thought which is the source of all other thoughts. But if you find this *vichara marga* too hard for you, you can go on repeating "I, I" and that will lead you to the same goal. There is no harm in using 'I' as a *mantra.* It is the first name of God.

God is everywhere, but it is difficult to conceive Him in that aspect, so the books have said, "God is everywhere. He is also within you. You are Brahman." So remind yourself: "I am Brahman". The repetition of 'I' will eventually lead you to realise "I am Brahman".

* * * *

A young man called Krishna Jivrajani from Karachi said, "When I reach the thoughtless stage in my *sadhana* I enjoy a certain pleasure, but sometimes I also experience a vague fear which I cannot properly describe."

Bhagavan: You may experience anything, but you should never rest content with that. Whether you feel pleasure or fear, ask yourself who feels the pleasure or the fear and so carry on the *sadhana* until pleasure and fear are both transcended and all duality ceases and the Reality alone remains.

There is nothing wrong in such things happening or being experienced, but you must never stop at that. For instance, you must never rest content with the pleasure of *laya* experienced when thought is quelled but must press on until all duality ceases.

* * * *

L.N. Sastri has now written out a fair copy of his verses to Bhagavan. He read it out to Bhagavan and gave it to Bhagavan. He then said: "I have stayed here for three days. If Bhagavan gives me leave I shall go tonight; if not I shall stay two days more." As usual in such cases, Bhagavan made no reply. He took leave of Bhagavan in the evening and departed.

9-5-46

Nagamma asked me to get her the Asramam book in which Telugu poems are written so that she could copy in it those of L.N. Sastri. I took it out and gave it to her. Then I told Bhagavan: "It seems that this L.N. Sastri is a great poet. Nagamma is all praise for his poems and tells me he is about the best Telugu poet who has come to Bhagavan for the past five or six years." G. Subba Rao said: "Yes, I agree, he is a great poet."

Bhagavan said, "He is a pandit in the Raja's College at Vizianagaram. Nobody would take him for such a great poet. He looks a very ordinary man. He wants to become an ஆசுகவி (one who can compose extempore poems on any given subject). But all this is only activity of the mind. The more you exercise the mind and the more success you have in composing verses or doing *satavadanam* (giving attention to many things at a time) the less peace you have. What use is it to acquire such accomplishments if you don't acquire peace? But if you tell such people this, it does not appeal to them. They can't keep quiet. They must be composing songs. As Nayana used to say: 'In going forward one can run any distance at any speed, but when it is a question of going backward, that is turning inwards, even one step is hard to take.'

"Somehow it never occurs to me to write any book or compose poems. All the songs I have made were made at the request of someone or other in connection with some particular event. Even the *Reality in Forty Verses*, of which so many commentaries and translations now exist, was not planned as a book but consists of verses composed at different times and afterwards arranged as a book by Muruganar and others. The only poems that came to me spontaneously and compelled me, as it were, to compose them, without anyone urging me to do so, are the *Eight Verses to Arunachala* and the *Eleven Verses to Arunachala*. The first day the opening words of the *Eleven Verses* suddenly came to me one morning, and even if I tried to suppress them, saying, 'What have I to do with these words?' they would not be suppressed till I composed a song beginning with them, and all the words flowed easily without any effort. In the same way the second stanza was made the next day and the succeeding ones the following days, one each day. Only the tenth and eleventh were composed the same day. The next day I started out to go round the hill. Palaniswami was walking behind me, and after we had gone some way, Ayyaswami seems to have called him back and given him a pencil and paper saying, 'For some days now Swami has been composing poems every day. He may do so today as well, so you had better take this paper and pencil with you.' I learnt about this only when I noticed that Palani was not with me for a while but came and joined me later. That day, before I returned to Skandasramam, I wrote six of the eight stanzas in the *Ashtakam.* Either that evening or the next day Narayana Reddi came. He was at that time living in Vellore as an agent of Singer & Co. and he used to come from time to time. Ayyaswami and Palni told him about the poems and he said, 'Give them to me at once and I will go and print them.' He had already published some books about me. When he insisted on taking the poems, I told him he could do so and could publish the first eleven as பதிகம் (*padikam*) and the rest, which were in a different metre, as அஷ்டகம் (*ashtakam*). To make up the அஷ்டகம் I at once composed two more stanzas and he took all the 19 stanzas with him to get them published."

In this connection I told Bhagavan, "I hear Narayana Reddi is now at Tindivanam and that he stays confined in one room."

Bhagavan said, "That is all right. The mind must have peace; that is all that matters."

In the evening the girl Ramana Sundari came and told Bhagavan she was going to attend the marriage of her mother's uncle.

I asked Bhagavan if he remembered how, the last time she came back here, she ran up to Bhagavan and caught hold of Bhagavan's hands and said: "I have had to wait so long to see Bhagavan!"

Bhagavan said, "Yes, she rushed up to me when the others of her party were still far behind and took both my hands and pressed them to her heart and said: 'It is two years since I have seen Bhagavan!' Actually, I don't think it was two years; I think it was about a year; but apparently she felt so."

I said, "She was so overcome with emotion that she disregarded the Asramam rules about going right up to Bhagavan or touching him."

Ramaswami Pillai thereupon put in, "These rules don't apply in such cases."

This talk of exceptional cases reminded me of one instance, about which I now reminded Bhagavan. Some years ago a Brahmin lad of about 17 came here. I don't know what trouble he had at home, but one morning he said to Bhagavan: "I pray that what I have in mind may come to pass." And Bhagavan replied: "Yes, it will come to pass."

The lad came and told me about it but I did not believe him because Bhagavan had never, to my knowledge, made such a promise to any devotee, and this lad was coming to Bhagavan for the first time. But the next day he repeated the same request before taking leave and I actually heard Bhagavan say: "Yes, it will come to pass."

On hearing this, G. Subba Rao said: "I have had the good fortune to have a similar experience myself. Once when I was in trouble and asked Bhagavan about it Bhagavan actually said: 'Don't fear.' That was many years ago."

10-5-46

In the afternoon Krishna Jivrajani said to Bhagavan, "During *sadhana* I feel that something in me is going up. Is that right or should it go down?"

Bhagavan: Never mind whether anything goes up or down. Does it exist without you? Never forget that. Whatever experience may come remember who has the experience and thus cling to 'I' or the Self.

Jivrajani: Bhagavan has said one must dive deep into oneself like pearl divers with breath and speech controlled and discover the Self or attain the Self. So does Bhagavan advise me to practise breath-control?

Bhagavan: Breath-control is a help in controlling the mind and is advised for such as find they cannot control the mind without some such aid. For those who can control their mind and concentrate, it is not necessary. It can be used at the beginning until one is able to control the mind, but then it should be given up. Since mind and *prana* rise from the same source, control of one gives control of the other also.

Jivrajani: Is it good to strain to achieve breath-control?

Bhagavan: No, straining is not good. Only a little *pranayama* should be done at the beginning — as much as is possible without undue strain.

Jivrajani: I have never been able to understand Bhagavan's explanation as to how *ajnana* comes about.

I put in, "Bhagavan has said, 'Find out to whom is the *ajnana* and then the doubt will be dispelled'."

Bhagavan: Ignorance of what ?

Jivrajani: Bhagavan has said that when the ego is submerged or killed something else arises within us as 'I-I'. Will Bhagavan please tell me more about that?

Bhagavan: Everyone has to find that out by his own experience. It cannot be described. In the same way, you say, "something goes up"; can you describe that?

Jivrajani: It is only by developing the intellect that intuition can be attained; in fact perfection of intellect is intuition, is that not so?

Bhagavan: How can that be? The merging of the intellect in the source from which it arose gives birth to intuition, as you call it. The intellect is of use only to see outside things, the outside world. Perfection of the intellect would lead only to seeing the outside world well. But the intellect is of no use at all for seeing within, for turning inwards towards the Self. For that, it has to be killed or extinguished, or in other words it has to merge in the source from which it sprang.

Jivrajani: Has closing the eyes during meditation any efficacy?

Bhagavan: The eyes can be closed or open as one finds convenient. It is not the eyes that see. There is one who sees through the eyes. If he is turned inwards and is not looking through the eyes they can be open and yet nothing will be seen. If we keep our eyes closed it is the same to us whether the windows of this room are open or shut.

Jivrajani: Suppose there is some disturbance during meditation, such as mosquito bites, should one persist in meditation and try to bear the bites and ignore the interruption or drive the mosquitoes away and then continue the meditation?

Bhagavan: You must do as you find most convenient. You will not attain *mukti* simply because you refrain from driving away the mosquitoes, nor be denied *mukti* simply because you drive them away. The thing is to attain one-pointedness and then to attain *mano-nasa.* Whether you do this by putting up with the mosquito bites or driving the mosquitoes away is left to you. If you are completely absorbed in your meditation you will not know that the mosquitoes are biting you. Till you attain that stage why should you not drive them away?

11-5-46

L.N. Sastri, who had taken leave of Bhagavan on the 8th, returned today. After he left the Asramam I was talking to Bhagavan about him and said that his poems seemed good but that it was a pity he did not tell us their meaning, as the Pudukottai Pundit had, and Bhagavan said: "He also would have explained them if you had asked him." So today I asked him, and at about 3 o'clock in the afternoon he gave the gist of the poems as follows:

"You, Bhagavan have realized the Self, turning away from the world and going inwards into yourself. You have come into the world for its benefit and uplift. I am always going out, attracted by the world and its objects; nor is there anything strange in this, since God has given me the senses and sense organs, between which and the things of the world he has created a natural and irresistible attraction. It is not possible to escape from this without the aid of a Guru who has himself escaped. I have been in search of a Guru, and today it has at last been my lot to come face to face with one, and I feel that today all my misery is ended. I have read books about the Self but had no actual experience. It is for you, endowed, as the great ones have said, with the nature and power of Lord Subrahmanya, as the embodiment of tenderness and mercy, come here for the uplift and enlightenment of the world, to take me up and bless me and save me, as I surrender myself completely to you."

When he had finished this explanation of his verses, he asked us to give him some subject on which he would try to compose verses extempore. We all said: "Why then, on Bhagavan. What other subject need we suggest?" So he composed a few verses on Bhagavan very fast and fluently. An advocate from Guntur who was there jotted them down, but in some places he could not keep pace with the poet and had to leave blanks.

In the evening M.V. Ramaswami Aiyar's son brought two printed copies of *Adhyatma Ramayanam* and gave them to Bhagavan, and Bhagavan immediately began going through them.

M. V. R. Aiyar composed this work about a year ago but it has only just been printed.

14-5-46

At 11 o'clock this morning, the Asramam lunch-time, Bose's mother brought various dishes that she had specially prepared for Bhagavan and was serving them herself. She has brought food like this a number of times during recent weeks, and it means a good deal of cooking, since Bhagavan will not take anything unless there is enough for all to partake of it alike. Bhagavan asked me to tell her not to take all this trouble and to say that it was work enough to prepare food for her family and it was unnecessary to send things for so many people. He said: "Let her cook and eat her food at home, dedicating some of it to me, saying 'this is for Bhagavan'. They think I have special liking for one thing or another, but really I have not. All food is the same to me. I would gladly mix up all the different things served and take it all together, but those who have prepared the food and think, 'Bhagavan will like this' or 'Bhagavan will like that' would be disappointed, so I don't. Time was when I took pleasure in variety, but after realizing unity all that disappeared."

15-5-46

In answer to a visitor Bhagavan made the following remarks:

"You can have, or rather you will yourself be, the highest imaginable kind of happiness. All other kinds of happiness which you have spoken of as 'pleasure', 'joy', 'happiness', 'bliss' are only reflections of the *ananda* which, in your true nature, you are.

"You need not bother about the lights which you say you see around things and people. Whether lights are seen or sounds are heard or whatever may happen, never let go the enquiry 'Who am I?' Keep on asking inwardly: 'Who sees these lights or hears these sounds?'

"What do you mean by taking *sannyasa*? Do you think it means leaving your home or wearing robes of a certain colour? Wherever you go, even if you fly up into the air, will your mind not go with you? Or can you leave it behind you and go without it?"

Another visitor asked Bhagavan for a benedictory foreword to a book he had written, called *The Destiny of Freedom* or something of that sort. He said that someone else had already agreed to write an introduction but he would be grateful if Bhagavan would write a few words conveying his message and blessing. Bhagavan explained to him that he had never done such a thing and therefore should not be expected to now. The visitor persisted, and I went to some trouble to convince him that all his persuasion would be in vain. Then he began saying that the world badly needs a spiritual message and that the youth of India and of the world are not properly brought up, since religion is not instilled into them, and so forth. I had to tell him that Bhagavan holds that before a man tries to reform the world he should first know himself, and then he can go about reforming the world if he still feels the inclination. I believe the visitor was still for continuing his argument but fortunately it was time for the *parayanam* and he was effectively stopped by our starting to chant.

23-5-46

I had been away for several days and this morning was standing at the doorway to the dining hall when Bhagavan entered, so I thought he saw me, but apparently he did not recognise me, so bad has his eyesight become. And yet he will not use his spectacles. At breakfast I was sitting in the first place in the row on his right and he recognised me and asked when I had arrived. I replied, "Last night, but it was after 9-30 when I arrived."

G.V. Subbaramayya had come while I was away and he was making a Telugu translation of a parody Bhagavan had composed of a stanza by Avvai. Avvai's stanza goes: "Oh, pain-giving stomach, you will not go without food even for one day, nor will you take enough for two days at a time. You have no idea of the trouble I have on your account. It is impossible to get on with you."

Bhagavan immediately replied with a parody giving the stomach's complaint against the ego: "Oh ego! You will not give even an hour's rest to me, your stomach. Day after day, every hour, you keep on eating. You have no idea how I suffer; it is impossible to get on with you."

Then Bhagavan explained, "In the month of *Chittrai* in 1931, on full moon day, we had all eaten heavily and everyone was complaining of uneasiness in the stomach, so someone, I think the late Somasundaram, quoted this stanza of Avvai's. Then I said that the stomach had more cause to complain against us than we against it. It can be expected to work but it should be given some rest too and after taking rest it can work again. But we never give it a rest. It might not mind even having no rest if we gave it more food to digest only when it had finished digesting what we had already given, but we do not even do that; we load it with more food while it is still digesting the previous meal. So it has just cause for complaint. That is why I composed a stanza like that."

Then Bhagavan asked whether I had been shown the photograph of the Dakshinamurti image at Madras Museum that had been received at the Asramam during my absence. I said that I had not but that the Parsi boy, Framji's son, had told me about it. So Bhagavan asked T.P.R. to show it to me. I found it had the head turned to the right but the eyes looking rather to the left. When I mentioned this Bhagavan said: "Head and face are all the same; perhaps that is why he wrote — 'with face turned to the right'." Bhagavan was referring to a phrase in the letter that accompanied the photograph. Someone remarked that the gaze seemed to be turned rather inwards than to the left and I must admit that it is so.

When I entered the hall in the afternoon Bhagavan was already explaining in answer to some questions put by Mr. Poonja, a Punjabi:

"I ask you to see where the 'I' arises in your body, but it is really not quite correct to say that the 'I' rises from and merges in the heart in the right side of the chest. The heart is another name for the Reality and it is neither inside nor outside the body; there can be no in or out for it, since it alone is. I do not mean by 'heart' any physiological organ or any plexus of nerves or anything like that, but so long as one identifies oneself with the body and thinks he is in the body he is advised to see where in the body the 'I'-thought rises and merges again. It must be the heart at the right side of the chest since every man, of whatever race and religion and in whatever language he may be saying 'I', points to the right side of the chest to indicate himself. This is so all over the world, so that must be the place. And by keenly watching the daily emergence of the 'I'-thought on waking and its subsiding in sleep, one can see that it is in the heart on the right side."

In the course of the day, G.V. Subbaramayya asked Bhagavan how Ganapati Sastri wrote his *Ramana Gita*, whether he took notes on the conversations and then wrote them out. Bhagavan replied, "Remembering such talks was child's play to him. He could listen to a long and learned lecture on some intricate subject and then at the end reproduce the gist of it accurately in the form of *sutras*, not omitting anything of importance that had been said. Once he and Arunachala Sastri, who was also a learned man, had a discussion. Ganapati Sastri took up the position of *drishti srishti,* that we create and then see, that is to say that the world has no objective reality apart from our minds, while Arunachala Sastri took up the opposite view of *srishti drishti*, that creation exists objectively before we see it. Arunachala Sastri argued first and upheld his standpoint with a great display of logic and learning and many quotations. Then Ganapati Sastri wrote down in the form of *sutras* all that he had maintained and asked him whether the *sutras* gave a faithful summary of everything he had said. He agreed that they did, so Ganapati Sastri said: "Then now you will have my criticism and condemnation of it". He then expounded very ably the *advaitic* point of view, that the world is an illusion as world but real as Brahman, that it does not exist as world but exists and is real as Brahman. In the same way he could record any discussion he heard; so remarkable was his power of memory, that he must have reproduced the *Ramana Gita* in that way. It would have been mere child's play for him."

24-5-46

Crowds of devotees have already arrived for tomorrow's *Mahapuja*.* All is bustle and joy with devotees meeting again under Bhagavan's gracious watchful care. One of the arrivals was Mrs. Ranga Aiyar, the wife of Bhagavan's boyhood friend at Tiruchuzhi. She brought two ladies with her and introduced them to Bhagavan. Bhagavan asked her, "Has Ranga come?" and she said, "No".

In the afternoon she sang. After singing three songs from *Ramana Stuthi Panchakam* she sang a song from *Ramanamritam*. Bhagavan called G.V.S. and told him, "This is from the songs composed by Ranga Aiyar's son celebrating my 'marriage'." G.V.S. came and told me this and I told him that the author was the old lady's son and that she was Ranga Aiyar's wife.

25-5-46

*Mahapuja** was celebrated in a grand scale as usual.

---

* Death Anniversary of the Mother of Bhagavan.

26-5-46

When today's mail came Bhagavan read a postcard and said, "Pichumani Aiyar of Madurai writes that Meenakshi is no more. Only this morning or yesterday I thought of her and now I get this news."

G.V.S. read out to Bhagavan two stanzas that he had composed on the occasion of his last visit. Their gist was, "On seeing your kindness to all sorts of animals, to squirrels, peacocks, dogs, cows and monkeys, how can one remain unaffected? One's very bones melt at it. All sorts of birds and beasts approach you, receive your glance and touch, and so attain salvation. Vouchsafe the same to this human animal and save it also."

In the afternoon Ramaswami Aiyar of Manamadura, a relative of Bhagavan, came and sat in the hall and Bhagavan said to him: "Do you know, Meenakshi is no more. We received this news from Pichu this morning. Only this morning or yesterday I thought of her as my last paternal aunt still surviving, and now she too has passed away."

After some further talk Bhagavan said, "Once before, when your wife was ill, I dreamed that I went and sat beside her bed and touched her and she opened her eyes and asked, 'Who is touching me?' and when she saw it was I, she said, 'Is it you? Then you can'. I do not know whether she had any corresponding dream."

G.V.S. Replied, "I asked about this and learned that Mrs. Ranga Aiyar had a corresponding dream that Bhagavan came and sat beside her and touched her."

In this connection, G.V.S. Said, "I was once present when Bhagavan's aunt came here — the one who fed him when he left for Tiruvannamalai — Bhagavan was specially gracious to her. I could not help wondering why Bhagavan was so gracious towards his aunt when he is said to have been harsh towards his mother. Is it because Bhagavan wanted to help rid her of the natural feeling that Bhagavan was her son?"

Bhagavan kept quiet, and I too said that he must have behaved so deliberately in order to train her to see in him a *jnani* and not her son. He still did not answer but we gathered from his attitude that our surmise was correct. And then after some time Bhagavan said: "I used to say something harsh to her and she would cry, and then I would say, 'Go on, cry! The more you cry the better pleased I am'."

27-5-46

Nagamma's niece, a girl of about 9, wanted to know why Bhagavan would never leave Tiruvannamalai and go to visit his devotees. She put the question through G.V.S. but Bhagavan kept silent. However, she importuned G.V.S. to get a reply. Finally Bhagavan said: "You wanted to see me, so you came here, and as I am always here you were able to see me; but if I kept moving about you might not find me here. Many people come here and if I was absent they would have to go away disappointed. And even if I left here how do you know I should ever reach your house, when there are so many people in Tiruvannamalai and other towns on the way who would invite me to their houses. If I agreed to go to your house I should have to agree to go to their houses too, and I might never reach yours. And besides, all this crowd of people you see here would go with me. Even here I can't go anywhere or the whole crowd follow, like that time when I went to Skandasramam." He added, jokingly, "I am kept in confinement. This is my gaol."

28-5-46

In the afternoon Mrs. Ranga Aiyar sang almost the whole of the book *Ramanamritam* composed by her son about the 'marriage' of Bhagavan to *jnana.* Bhagavan listened very graciously. One of the songs referred to an incident in his fifth or sixth year when, for something that he had done, his father said: "Take away his cloth and drive him out." I asked Bhagavan about this and it led him to talk about those early years and about a group photograph of his father and others that was taken in the hospital compound and another that was taken later of himself with his uncle. He said that it was from a copy of the group with his father, recovered from Ranga Aiyar's house, that we got the photograph of his father that hangs in the dining hall, but that the other photograph, the one with Bhagavan in it, had been lost.

In the evening, when Bhagavan was going out, Nagamma's niece was standing in his way and Bhagavan said, laughing, "If you want to take me you will have to tie me up and put me in a cart; that is the only way."

29-5-46

Bose: When the *Upanishads* say that all is Brahman, how can we say, like Shankara, that this world is *mithya* or illusory?

Bhagavan: Shankara also said that this world is Brahman or the Self. What he objected to is one's imagining that the Self is limited by the names and forms that constitute the world. He only said that the world does not exist apart from Brahman. Brahman or the Self is like the screen and the world is like the pictures on it. You can see the picture only so long as there is a screen. But when the seer himself becomes the screen only the Self remains. *Kaivalya Navaneeta* has asked and answered six questions about *maya*. They are instructive.

The first question is: What is *maya*? And the answer is: It is *anirvachaniya* or indescribable.

The second question is: To whom does it come? And the answer is: To the mind or ego who feels that he is a separate entity, who thinks: 'I do this' or 'this is mine'.

The third question is: Where does it come from and how did it originate? And the answer is: Nobody can say.

The fourth question is: How did it arise? And the answer is: Through non-*vichara*, through failure to ask: who am I?

The fifth question is: If the Self and *maya* both exist does not this invalidate the theory of *Advaita*? The answer is: It need not, since *maya* is dependent on the Self as the picture is on the screen. The picture is not real in the sense that the screen is real.

The sixth question is: If the Self and *maya* are one, could it not be argued that the Self is of the nature of *maya*, that is illusory? And the answer is: No; the Self can be capable of producing illusion without being illusory. A conjuror may create for our entertainment the illusion of people, animals and things, and we see all of them as clearly as we see him; but after the performance he alone remains and all the visions he had created have disappeared. He is not a part of the illusion but is real and solid.

30-5-46

Today again Bose reverted to the subject of *maya* and asked Bhagavan, "What is *Hiranyagarbha*?"

Bhagavan replied, "*Hiranyagarbha* is only another name for the *sukshma sarira* or *Ishwara*. The books use the following illustration to help explain creation. The Self is like the canvas for a painting. First a paste is smeared over it to close up the small holes that are in any cloth. This paste can be compared to the *antaryami* in all creation. Then the artist makes an outline on the canvas, and this can be compared to the *sukshma sarira* of all creation, for instance the light and sound, *nada, bindu*, out of which all things arise. Then the artist paints his picture with colours etc., in this outline, and this can be compared to the gross forms that constitute the world."

In the afternoon, T.P. Ramachandra Aiyar remarked: "Chadwick has a picture of Bhagavan in a recumbent posture where Bhagavan looks a mere skeleton. I don't think anyone else has such a picture."

I said: It must have been taken at the time when Bhagavan was purposely under-eating.

Bhagavan said: Yes, for some time when I was at Skandasramam I used to take only one meal a day at 11 a.m. and nothing else. At that time I got very thin.

In connection with this, G.V.S. asked Bhagavan about his early days and whether he ever went about accepting alms. Then Bhagavan related how it was T.P. Ramachandra Aiyar's father who first took him by mere force to his house and fed him, and how the first time he begged for food was from Chinna Gurukal's wife. He went on to tell how after that he freely begged in almost all the streets of Tiruvannamalai. He said: "You cannot conceive of the majesty and dignity I felt while so begging. The first day, when I begged from Gurukal's wife, I felt bashful about it as a result of habits of upbringing, but after that there was absolutely no feeling of abasement. I felt like a king and more than a king. I have sometimes received stale gruel at some house and taken it without salt or any other flavouring, in the open street, before great pandits and other important men who used to come and prostrate themselves before me at my Asramam, then wiped my hands on my head and passed on supremely happy and in a state of mind in which even emperors were mere straw in my sight. You can't imagine it. It is because there is such a path that we find tales in history of kings giving up their thrones and taking to this path."

In illustration of this, Bhagavan told us a story of a king who renounced his throne and went begging, first outside the limits of his State, then in his own State, then in its capital city, and finally in the royal palace itself, and thus at last got rid of his ego-sense. After some time, when he was wandering as an ascetic in another State, he was chosen to be its king and accepted because now that he had completely lost the sense of 'I' he could act any part in life as a mere witness and the cares of kingship no longer worried him. When his own former State heard of it, they also asked him to resume his kingship, and he did so, because however many kingdoms he might rule over, he realized now that he was not the doer but simply an instrument in God's hands.

Actually, Bhagavan did not finish the story, because when he was in the middle of it Mrs. Ranga Aiyar began to sing and he broke off and told us apologetically, "She is leaving tonight and wants to finish all her songs before she goes." I asked him for the rest of the story next day.

31-5-46

Mr. Phillips, an Englishman who used to be a missionary and is now a teacher and who has been about 20 years in Hyderabad, came this morning. He said: "I lost my son in the war. What is the way for his salvation?"

Bhagavan was silent for a while and then replied. "Your worry is due to thinking. Anxiety is a creation of the mind. Your real nature is peace. Peace has not got to be achieved; it is our nature. To find consolation, you may reflect: 'God gave, God has taken away; He knows best'. But the true remedy is to enquire into your true nature. It is because you feel that your son does not exist that you feel grief. If you knew that he existed you would not feel grief. That means that the source of the grief is mental and not an actual reality. There is a story given in some books how two boys went on a pilgrimage and after some days news came back that one of them was dead. However, the wrong one was reported dead, and the result was that the mother who had lost her son went about as cheerful as ever, while the one who had still got her son was weeping and lamenting. So it is not any object or condition that causes grief but only our thought about it. Your son came from the Self and was absorbed back into the Self. Before he was born, where was he apart from the Self? He is our Self in reality. In deep sleep the thought of 'I' or 'child' or 'death' does not occur to you, and you are the same person who existed in sleep. If you enquire in this way and find out your real nature, you will know your son's real nature also. He always exists. It is only you who think he is lost. You create a son in your mind, and think that he is lost, but in the Self he always exists."

K.M. Jivrajani: What is the nature of life after physical death?

Bhagavan: Find out about your present life. Why do you worry about life after death? If you realize the present you will know everything.

In the afternoon, Bhagavan saw a relative of his, a young man called Sesha Aiyar, in the hall. He said: "Seeing you reminds me of something that happened in Dindigul when I was a boy. Your uncle Periappa Seshaiyar was living there then. There was some function in the house and all went to it and then in the night went to the temple. I was left alone in the house. I was sitting reading in the front room, but after a while I locked the front door and fastened the windows and went to sleep. When they returned from the temple no amount of shouting or banging at the door or window could wake me. At last they managed to open the door with a key from the opposite house and then they tried to wake me up by beating me. All the boys beat me to their heart's content, and your uncle did too, but without effect. I knew nothing about it till they told me next morning."

I asked, "How old was Bhagavan then?"

Bhagavan said, "About eleven." Then he continued: "The same sort of thing happened to me in Madurai too. The boys didn't dare touch me when I was awake, but if they had any grudge against me they would come when I was asleep and carry me wherever they liked and beat me as much as they liked and then put me back to bed, and I would know nothing about it until they told me in the morning."

I said, "It would seem that even in those days Bhagavan's sleep was not ordinary sleep but some state like *samadhi*."

Bhagavan: I don't know what state it was, but that is the fact. Some who have written about my life have called it somnambulism.

I: It was certainly not somnambulism; that is walking in one's sleep. This was more like *samadhi* or absorption in the Self.

In the evening Bose asked, "Is it good to do *japa* and *puja* and so on when we know that enquiry into the Self is the real thing?"

Bhagavan: All are good. They will lead to this eventually. *Japa* is our real nature. When we realize the Self then *japa* goes on without effort. What is the means at one stage becomes the goal at another. When effortless, constant *japa* goes on, it is realisation.

Bose: Why did Bhagavan regard Arunachala as Father?

Bhagavan did not reply but sat smiling.

Bose: Perhaps for the benefit of others?

Bhagavan: Yes; so long as there is the feeling 'I', it must have a source from whence it came.

1-6-46

When Bhagavan returned from his morning walk at about 7-45, the attendant Sivananda offered to massage his legs. Bhagavan forbade him and said: "If I let them they go on massaging for a long time. This morning too, at *parayana*, I did not let them. They begin with the *parayana* and don't stop till it is finished, and sometimes I am unaware of it."

G.V. Subbaramayya: Bhagavan once told me that Bhagavan is aware of the beginning of *parayana* and knows nothing more till the end of it.

Bhagavan: Yes, it often happens that I hear the beginning and then the end and have been absorbed so that I have lost count of time in between, and then I have wondered whether they had left out whole passages to get to the end so soon.

After a moment, Bhagavan continued: "Similarly, those people go on massaging and I am sometimes not at all aware that I am being massaged. So now I am not going to let them. I will do it myself." So saying, Bhagavan took the liniment and rubbed it over his knees.

In the afternoon Bhagavan explained in answer to Mr. H.C. Khanna of Kanpur:

Why should your occupation or duties in life interfere with your spiritual effort? For instance, there is a difference between your activities at home and in the office. In your office activities you are detached and so long as you do your duty you do not care what happens or whether it results in gain or loss to the employer. But your duties at home are performed with attachment and you are all the time anxious as to whether they will bring advantage or disadvantage to you and your family. But it is possible to perform all the activities of life with detachment and regard only the Self as real. It is wrong to suppose that if one is fixed in the Self one's duties in life will not be properly performed. It is like an actor. He dresses and acts and even feels the part he is playing, but he knows really that he is not that character but someone else in real life. In the same way, why should the body-consciousness or the feeling 'I-am-the-body' disturb you, once you know for certain that you are not the body but the Self? Nothing that the body does should shake you from abidance in the Self. Such abidance will never interfere with the proper and effective discharge of whatever duties the body has, any more than the actor's being aware of his real status in life interferes with his acting a part on the stage.

You ask whether you can tell yourself: "I am not the body but the Self". Of course, whenever you feel tempted to identify yourself with the body (as you may often have to, owing to old *vasanas*) it may be a help to remind yourself that you are not the body but the Self. But you should not make such repetition a *mantram*, constantly saying: "I am not the body but the Self". By proper enquiry into the Self, the notion 'I am this body' will gradually vanish and in time the faith that you are the Self will become unshakeable.

K.M. Jivrajani: In the early stages would it not be a help to man to seek solitude and give up his outer duties in life?

Bhagavan: Renunciation is always in the mind, not in going to forests or solitary places or giving up one's duties. The main thing is to see that the mind does not turn outward but inward. It does not really rest with a man whether he goes to this place or that or whether he gives up his duties or not. All that happens according to destiny. All the activities that the body is to go through are determined when it first comes into existence. It does not rest with you to accept or reject them. The only freedom you have is to turn your mind inward and renounce activities there.

K.M. Jivrajani: But is it not possible for something to be a help, especially to a beginner? Like a fence round a young tree. For instance, don't our books say that it is helpful to go on pilgrimage to sacred shrines or to get *sat sang*.

Bhagavan: Who said they are not helpful? Only such things do not rest with you, as turning your mind inward does. Many people desire the pilgrimage or *sat sang* that you mention, but do they all get it?

K.M. Jivrajani: Why is it that turning inward alone is left to us and not any outer things?

I answered: Nobody can answer that. That is the Divine scheme.

Bhagavan: If you want to go to fundamentals, you must enquire who you are and find out who it is who has freedom or destiny. Who are you and why did you get this body that has these limitations?

3-6-46

G.V. Subbaramayya: Did Subramania Bharati ever come to Bhagavan?

Bhagavan: I think he did once. It was when we were on the hill. One evening when only Sivayya (the late Mauni Swami of Kutralam), who is dead now, was with me, someone came and sat for nearly an hour before me and then went away without saying a word. Later, when I saw pictures of Bharati I thought it must have been he.

G.V. Subbaramayya: Was it Sivayya who beat a monkey and the monkey was so grieved that it went and drowned itself?

Bhagavan: No, it was someone else. And the monkey was not even beaten, it was only scolded. Even that was more than it could stand and it went and drowned itself very soon after. It was a dog that was beaten. He was a very strange dog. All day he would lie quiet in a place among the rocks, higher up than our Asramam, and where it was not easy to see him, and he would only go out at night. Seeing something black going out and coming back at night, we looked during the day time and found that it was a dog. He continued in this way for many days, so we took pity on him and began giving him food. But even then he would not come near us. We used to put some food a little distance away from us and he would come and eat it and then go away. If we went near he would run away. And then one day, when a number of us had been out and were returning, this dog ran up to us, and he came straight to me out of all the crowd and jumped up on me and tried to make friends with me. After that he stayed with us and he would go and lie in the lap of any devotee. Some of the orthodox ones didn't like it, and one day Iswara Swami beat him for interfering when a devotee was doing *puja*. This was more than the dog could stand and he immediately disappeared. We don't know what happened to him. We searched for him but could never find out.

After this, the talk turned to some of the famous or notable persons who had visited Bhagavan. Speaking of the late Maharaja of Mysore, Bhagavan said: "He came and stayed quietly and then went away."

Some of us asked whether he did not ask any questions, and Bhagavan said, "No, no, nothing of that sort."

I said, "I have heard that he asked for Bhagavan's blessing to be able to rule his subjects to their best advantage, or something like that."

Bhagavan: Yes, he asked for blessing on his work. He said, "I can't serve you, as those here are privileged to, but still I crave your grace," or something like that. Apart from that he did not discuss anything with me.

Somebody wanted to know what happened when Rajendra Prasad was here.

Bhagavan: He also was quiet all the days he was here.

K.S. Seshagiri Aiyar: I was here at the time. Bajaj did all the talking. He talked for Rajendra also. I remember him saying: "Rajendra gave up a very lucrative practice to work for his country; why should such a man be plagued with a distressing complaint like asthma?" And Bhagavan was silent for a while and then replied: "This body itself is a disease, so that is a disease of a disease."

Bhagavan: When Satyamurti came he also was silent and never spoke at all. When Srinivasa Sastri came he asked me some questions but when I put him counter-questions he would not answer them. He wanted to go his own way. I wanted to take him inward but he wouldn't, and he wanted to pull me outward.

In the afternoon K.S.S. (Ramanadasa) narrated the following incident:

When Bhagavan was living at Skandasramam I was once alone with him, sitting on the steps leading up to the Asramam when a man came to the gate with his family and stopped there and called out to me. When I went there he asked me to go and ask the Swami whether they could approach him and receive his *darshan.* I was surprised and said, "Why do you ask permission?" And he said, "We are untouchables."

I started to go back to Bhagavan, but then it occurred to me that even to ask Bhagavan would be an injustice to him, so I told the man that caste had no meaning with Bhagavan and that they would be welcome. The whole party came and prostrated before Bhagavan, and I well remember how for about ten minutes his gracious look dwelt on that untouchable and his family; and how many rich and notable people have I seen fall at his feet without being vouchsafed such grace.

* * * *

Bhagavan was going through the latest edition of *Ramana Lila* and pointing out to G.V.S. some errors that had crept into it, and in the course of the talk he referred to one Kathirvelu who was his class-mate at Tiruchuzhi and in whose notebook he had, at Kathirvelu's request, written down his name, class and school in English and added 'Madras Presidency' in Tamil and had also numbered the pages in his own hand. The classmate never came here, but after his death his son sent the notebook together with another one in which Kathirvelu had written various things, including essays on religious subjects. Bhagavan wanted to show us the notebooks, especially the one in which he had written a few lines, but we couldn't find it, so Bhagavan himself got up from his couch and came to the shelf and picked it out for us. The Tamil handwriting even then was like print, and so was the numbering of the pages.

6-6-46

In the afternoon G.V.S. asked, "What is the difference between *manasa japa* and *dhyana*?"

Bhagavan: They are the same. In both, the mind is concentrated on one thing, the *mantra* or the Self. *Mantra, japa, dhyana* — are only different names. So long as they require effort we call them by these names, but when the Self is realized this goes on without any effort and what was the means becomes the goal.

8-6-46

T.P.R., G.V.S. and some others went in a party today to Gurumoortham, the mango orchard nearby, Ayyankulam, Arunagirinatha Temple, the Pathalalingam Temple, the Vahana Mantap, the *iluppai* tree within the Big Temple — all the places where Bhagavan stayed in his early days. When they got back in the evening Bhagavan asked them about their expedition and they said it was very enjoyable and that at Ayyankulam and on the way back from there they sang in ecstasy, Viswamoorthi taking the lead in singing and in rousing them to ecstasy.

Bhagavan said that the marks left on the wall at Gurumoortham by his leaning against it and also the first writing in charcoal for Nayanar could still be discerned if the whitewash were scraped off. They said that the whole place was now filled with bundles of tobacco so that they could not even see the corner where Bhagavan used to sit.

9-6-46

In the afternoon T.P. Ramachandra Aiyar made Viswamoorthi sing two of the songs he had sung at Gurumoortham the previous day. After that Viswamoorthi sang his Kannada life of Bhagavan in which each line ends with 'Sri Ramana', and T.P.R. and I joined in the 'Sri Ramana' as a chorus. T.P.R. then told Bhagavan that the previous day Venkatesa Sastri had roused them to sing this song with fervour, and they not only sang but danced and went into ecstasy. Bhagavan said, "Is that so? They did not tell me that yesterday: I thought you simply sang."

10-6-46

Dr. Haridas, a disciple of Swami Madhava Theertha and a relative of Mahatma Gandhi by marriage, asked Bhagavan, "If *ajnana* is also Brahman, why is Brahman not visible but only *ajnana* or the world?"

Bhagavan: Brahman is not to be seen or known. It is beyond the *triputis* (triads) of seer, seen and seeing or knower, knowledge and knowing. The Reality remains ever as it is; that there is *ajnana* or the world is due to our *moham* or illusion. Neither knowledge nor ignorance is real; what is beyond this, as all other pairs of opposites, is the Reality. It is neither light nor darkness but beyond both, though we sometimes have to speak of it as light and of ignorance as its shadow.

G.V.S.: It is said that the Self cannot be realized by reading books but only by *anubhava* (personal experience).

Bhagavan: What is *anubhava*? It is only going beyond the pairs of opposites or the *triputis*.

In the evening Bhagavan said with reference to a question somebody had asked: "During sleep there is both the Self and *ajnana* — *ajnana* because we knew nothing and the Self because we existed, and when we wake we say, 'I slept well', although we knew nothing. If one asks how the Self and *ajnana* can exist together, any more than light and darkness, the answer is that to one who realises, the Self is all light and there is no such thing as darkness at all, but to one who has not realised we say that there can be *ajnana* in the Self like the seeming shadows on the moon."

13-6-46

Visitor: I do *japa* with an image of Lord Subrahmanya with Valli and Daivayanai on either side, but as soon as I close my eyes the image of Subrahmanya as the Palani Andavar, that is as a beggar with a staff, appears before my mind's eye. I don't know what that means. Should I change the image I have before me for *japa*?

Bhagavan did not reply.

I said to Bhagavan: It is strange that when a man does *japa* before an image another image though of the same God should appear before his mind's eye.

Then the visitor added: There is one more thing I must add. I used to do *japa* before a Palani Andavar image; but my mother said that such an image is not auspicious in a household and that I should change it for one of Lord Subrahmanya with Valli and Daivayanai.

I said: Now it is understandable. That is probably the explanation.

But still Bhagavan made no reply.

An ascetic claiming to be a native of Bagdad, naked, keeping silent and holding his right arm permanently aloft in the air, has been staying in Palakothu since the 11th. He claims to have been with Sai Baba for 25 years. If this is true he must be at least 65 now, though he looks only 30 or 35. He met Bhagavan this morning when Bhagavan was returning from his morning walk and asked for Bhagavan's blessing. I went to see him out of curiosity. He sent the following question to Bhagavan through Ramasubba Aiyar: "What is my future?"

First Bhagavan said, "Why does he bother about the future and not the present?" Later he added: "Tell him his future will be as his present is."

I told Bhagavan that I was not impressed with him. When I told Bhagavan that his finger nails were five or six inches long, Bhagavan said, "That means nothing. When I was at Gurumoortham I found that in less than a year the nails grow an inch long. Matted locks also grow very long in a few years. Ordinary hair does not grow so long. I remember when Udhandi Nayanar had matted hair only five or six inches long and twenty-five years later it was fifteen feet long. So however long and imposing nails and matted hair may be they are no sign of great age."

I recalled how Bhagavan had once told us that in those early days people used to look at his nails and say: "He is ever so old; he has been like this for years." And Bhagavan said, "Yes, yes."

15-6-46

When I entered the hall in the evening Bhagavan was saying, "Everything we see is changing, always changing. There must be something unchanging as the basis and source of all this."

G.V.S.: What justification have we for imagining that the source of all this must be unchanging?

Bhagavan: It is not mere thinking or imagining that the 'I' is unchanging. It is a fact of which everyone is aware. The 'I' exists in sleep when all the changing things do not exist. It exists in dream and in waking. The 'I' remains changeless in all these states while other things come and go.

Dr. S. Mani, Assistant Director of Public Health at Madras, a frequent visitor, asked Bhagavan "But why should these things, that is the world, appear?"

Bhagavan: To whom does it appear? You see and so the world exists. Does it exist independently of the seer? Does it come and tell you, "I exist"? What proof is there of its existence except that you say you see or perceive it?

Another visitor said to Bhagavan: I want to have *darshan* of God. What should I do?

Bhagavan: First we must know what you mean by 'I' and 'God' and by '*darshan* of God'.

The visitor dropped the matter and said no more.

16-6-46

G.V.S.: Is it stated in any book that for ultimate and final Self-realization one must ultimately come to the Heart even after reaching *sahasrara,* and that the Heart is at the right side?

Bhagavan: No. I have not come across this in any book. But in a Malayalam book on medicine I came across a stanza locating the heart on the right side and I have translated it into Tamil in the *Supplement to the Forty Verses.*

We know nothing about the other centres. We cannot be sure what we arrive at in concentrating on them and realizing them. But as the 'I' arises from the Heart it must sink back and merge there for Self-realization.

Later in the day G.V.S. said, "It is said that by repeating his own name a number of times Tennyson used to get into a state in which the world completely disappeared and he realised that it was all illusion." And a discussion ensued as to where the quotation came from and whether we could find it.

17-6-46

When Bhagavan returned from his morning walk on the Hill, a Bangalore photographer took a photograph of him in *Padmasanam* posture for inclusion in the *Golden Jubilee Souvenir* that is to be brought out in September.

Sri Gunaji, a retired advocate who is now a naturopath at Belgaum, has been here for some days, massaging Bhagavan's legs for rheumatism, and today he sang a song he had composed in Hindi. He gave its meaning in English as: "I ask nothing of Thee, Lord; but if Thou art disposed to grant me any favour, then take away this ego-sense, kill all my thoughts, destroy the world and let my mind be dissolved in the ocean of Self."

Bhagavan said, laughing, "You are not asking me to give but to take." And then he added, "There is nothing to give. If all this goes, that is the ego and the world created by it, the Reality remains. That is all. Nothing new is brought in. If the false goes the true remains."

In continuation of yesterday's conversation about Tennyson, the relevant passage was found in a footnote to the English translation of *Upadesa Saram*. It was not in a poem but in a letter to B.P. Blood. Bhagavan asked me to read it out, so I did: " . . . .a kind of waking trance I have frequently had, quite up from boyhood, when I have been all alone. This has generally come upon me through repeating my own name two or three times to myself, silently, till all at once, as it were out of the intensity of consciousness of individuality, the individuality itself seemed to dissolve and fade away into boundless being: and this not a confused state but the clearest of the clearest, the surest of the surest, the weirdest of the weirdest, utterly beyond words, where death was an almost laughable impossibility, the loss of personality (if so it were) seeming no extinction but the only true life."

Bhagavan said, "That state is called abidance in the Self. It is described in a number of songs."

He took up *Thayumanavar* and it opened at the very page where was the poem he was looking for. He read out the poem, 'கூடுதலுடன் பிறிதலற்று' which is the 8th stanza in 'சின்மயானந்த குருவே'. Bhagavan also quoted the 2nd stanza in 'ஆசையெனும்' the 5th in 'பரிபூரணானந்தம்' of Thayumanavar which all refer to this 'நிலை' of 'சகஜநிஷ்டை' (state of *sahaja nishta).*

18-6-46

G.V.S. translated the *Pancharatna* (the last of the *Five Hymns*) of Bhagavan in English verse and showed it to Bhagavan. Bhagavan said, "The third stanza deals with the *sat* aspect, the fourth with the *chit* and the fifth with the *ananda*. The *jnani* becomes one with the *sat* or Reality, like the river merging in the ocean; the yogi sees the light of *chit;* the *bhakta* or *karma-yogin* is immersed in the ocean of *ananda*."

19-6-46

G.V.S. slightly altered his translation of the *Pancharatna* and showed it to Bhagavan. In the talk that followed, Bhagavan said, "This is how the *Pancharatna* was composed: I had somehow composed the first stanza in a slightly different form, when Ganapati Sastri saw it and altered it a little and said it had become, *Arya Geetha* and asked me to write four more similar stanzas saying that he would use them as *mangalam* for his works. That was in 1917. Later, in 1922, Aiyasami Pillai was getting up an edition of the first four songs of the present *Arunachala Stuti Panchakam* and I was asked to translate the *Pancharatna* also into Tamil to go with them, and I did."

A newcomer called Gajendra Mehta asked Bhagavan about the state of the soul after death. He has just returned from Africa. He has been writing to Bhagavan for four years but this is the first time he has come here.

Bhagavan: If you know the present you will know the future. It is strange that people don't want to know about the present, about whose existence nobody can have any doubt, but are always eager to know about the past or the future, both of which are unknown. What is birth and what is death? And who has birth or death? Why go to birth and death to understand what you daily experience in sleeping and waking? When you sleep, this body and the world do not exist for you, and these questions do not worry you, and yet you exist, the same you that exists now while waking. It is only when you wake up that you have a body and see the world. If you understand waking and sleep properly you will understand life and death. Only waking and sleeping happen daily, so people don't notice the wonder of it but only want to know about birth and death.

G. Mehta: Is there a rebirth?

Bhagavan: If there is birth there must be not only one rebirth but a whole succession of births. Why and how did you get this birth? For the same reason and in the same manner you must have succeeding births. But if you ask who has the birth and whether birth and death are for you or for somebody distinct from you, then you realize the truth and the truth burns up all karma and frees you from all births. The books graphically describe how all *sanchita karma,* which would take countless lives to exhaust, is burnt up by one little spark of *jnana*, just as a mountain of gunpowder will be blown up by a single spark of fire. It is the ego that is the cause of all the world and of the countless sciences whose researches are so great as to baffle description, and if the ego is dissolved by enquiry all this immediately crumbles and the Reality or Self alone remains.

G. Mehta had also asked a personal question: Whether he should remain abroad or return to India, but to that Bhagavan said: "Don't worry what you should do. Things will happen as they are destined to happen."

In the evening the Senior Maharani of Baroda arrived to stay for a few days with Mrs. Taleyarkhan.

20-6-46

G. Mehta: If I am not the body am I responsible for the consequences of my good and bad actions?

Bhagavan: If you are not the body and do not have the idea 'I-am-the-doer' the consequences of your good or bad actions will not affect you. Why do you say about the actions the body performs "I do this" or "I did that"? As long as you identify yourself with the body like that you are affected by the consequences of the actions and you have merit and demerit.

G. Mehta: Then I am not responsible for the consequences of good or bad actions?

Bhagavan: If you are not, why do you bother about the question?

G. Mehta: Then does that mean that if one has not the sense of 'I do this' or 'I am the doer' one need not do anything at all?

Bhagavan: The question of doing only arises if you are the body.

This Mehta tells me that he has been in Africa for the past 20 years, visiting India from time to time. He comes from Ahmedabad. For the last six years he has not been able to come owing to the war. Early this year he received a letter from the Asramam that he would be able to come this year and it turned out so in spite of great difficulties.

Sri Krishniah Chowdhuri arrived today. Bhagavan told me: "It seems he is writing my life in Telugu and has finished two chapters. He said he would read them to me this afternoon."

He came at three and read till about a quarter past four and then said he would finish tomorrow. It was written in the life that Bhagavan went to Tiruchuzhi on receiving news of his father's death, but Bhagavan said that in fact he went there four or five days before his father's death. He got news that his father was dangerously ill and went to Tiruchuzhi at once and his father died only four or five days later. The error arose as this was not clear in the Telugu *Ramana Lila* on which Chowdhuri was basing his life.

24-6-46

Lokamma sang Muruganar's benediction from *Sarana Pallandu*; when she finished Bhagavan said, "The last song she sang can be translated for them," meaning the Maharani of Baroda and Mrs. Taleyarkhan. I accordingly gave the meaning of it: "May all those devotees with great love also live long, who, coming to Ramana, get their desires fulfilled and, planting his feet in their heart, set all their troubles at rest and attain peace."

Explaining why he wanted me to translate it, Bhagavan said, "Yesterday Mrs. Taleyarkhan asked me to have the best poem about me by Muruganar read out in the hall and translated for her and the Maharani. Sundaresa Aiyar suggested the benediction in Tamil, but I thought that 'வண்டுவிடுதூது'* and the reply of the bee in particular would be more appropriate, so we read them out and translated them. And now Lokamma sang the benediction, and when she sang the last stanza it occurred to me that they would like to hear it and it might be a consolation to them."

Just then Muruganar walked in after an absence of two or three months and prostrated himself to Bhagavan. Bhagavan remarked: "We were talking about him and his '*Benediction*' and here he comes."

* A song in which the bee is sent as a messenger.

I asked him which of the poems in his *Ramana Sannidhi Murai* he liked best, but he could not say. I told him that I liked *Arunai Ramanesan* best and proceeded to sing 'தஞ்சமெனத் தாள் சேர்ந்தார்' from it, and Bhagavan asked me to translate that also for the Maharani, so I did. The gist of it is that Ramana bears upon his head, because it is his fate, the burdens of all those who throw themselves at his feet and regard him as their sole refuge, that peace comes naturally to all those who live with him, that whatever dangers may threaten his devotees they need have no fear, and that Bhagavan had saved him, Muruganar, bidding him not to fear.

In the afternoon, when Muruganar came into the hall, Bhagavan explained to him why the last song in *The Benediction* was translated and also added, "When I was coming back from my walk the Maharani met me and requested, 'When next I come here I should like to come with my husband to your feet.' He is now in England and they had news that he is not well, so I thought it would be comforting to them to hear that last stanza in the *Benediction* translated." Muruganar did not remember it, so Bhagavan took out the book and read it to him.

In the evening Mrs. Taleyarkhan told Bhagavan, "When the Maharani left she was very sorry to have to go. She told me that the five days she spent here have been the happiest days in her life."

26-6-46

T.P.R. told Bhagavan that he took only *kanji* (gruel) for lunch, as he had dysentery. Bhagavan spoke highly of the efficacy of a gruel made of rice, dried ginger, coriander and rock salt *(induppu)* and added: "It seems they are going to give us all *kanji* (gruel) tomorrow morning. I am told Sama Thatha is going to prepare it. Somebody must have asked him to. People do not realize how wholesome *kanji* is and how tasty." Bhagavan was then reminded of old Keerai Patti, who used to gather all kinds of green vegetables and cook them somehow, although she was half-blind. It seems Bhagavan would thoroughly enjoy it. "In those days we would make *kanji* (gruel) and one *aviyal* with all the vegetables we had on hand. None of the fine dishes they make here now can equal the simple fare we enjoyed then. People do not realize the enjoyment of such a meal." Bhagavan went on to say, "People don't know how a poor man appreciates his food, simple though it often is. He comes home terribly hungry after a day's hard work in the field or elsewhere, and then when he sits down for his meal, down goes one huge fistful after another until it looks as though he would swallow the plate as well. Your rich man sits down to a meal with all sorts of delicacies served on fine plates before him and nibbles or sips at one thing after another but relishes nothing and has no sort of satisfaction from all the luxury spread before him. Even after we came down here we still used to make *kanji.* At first there were a lot of men working on the premises, clearing it of cactus and levelling it, and we used to prepare a midday meal for them in addition to their wages. For them and us together we used to prepare only two dishes; a huge pot of *kanji* and another of all the vegetables we happened to have on hand. You can imagine the quantity when I tell you that the ladle we stirred it with was the branch of a tree. In those days I used to do all the grinding for the cooking. Once I made *uppuma* out of 'கீரைத்தண்டு' (*keeraithandu).* Somebody had brought a whole sack of 'கீரைத்தண்டு' and we cut the whole lot up into small bits. There were seven or eight measures of it. I added one measure of 'ரவை' (*ravai*) to it and boiled the whole lot well and made *uppuma* out of it. Everyone enjoyed it as *uppuma* made of *ravai,* but when I told them how it was really made, they were not so pleased. People always like something expensive."

When the Mauni brought the mail today he was limping with a pain in his right thigh. Bhagavan advised him to rub some liniment on it and told the attendant to give him some. Bhagavan's small bottle for constant use was empty, so Bhagavan told the attendant to take the big bottle from the cupboard. Bhagavan told Vaikunta Vasar to take a small bottle of it to Mauni and see that he used it. When the large bottle was taken out of the cupboard Bhagavan noticed that it was not full, so he turned to Khanna, who had bought it for him, and said: "It looks as though you bought this for yourself or your children and then gave it to me when you saw what a state I am in. And perhaps the *Chavanaprash* you gave me was also bought for you or your children."

Khanna assured Bhagavan that the liniment was not needed for himself or his family but had been bought specially for Bhagavan, and he explained that the reason why the bottle was not full was that he had bought it in several smaller bottles and transferred it to this large one.

A little later he handed Bhagavan a piece of paper on which he had written something. After reading it, Bhagavan said: "It is a complaint. He says: 'I have been coming to you and this time I have remained nearly a month at your feet and I find no improvement at all in my condition. My *vasanas* are as strong as ever. When I go back my friends will laugh at me and ask what good my stay here has done me'."

Then, turning to Khanna, Bhagavan said, "Why distress your mind by thinking that *jnana* has not come or that the *vasanas* have not disappeared? Don't give room for thoughts. In the last stanza of *Sukavari* by Thayumanavar, the Saint says much the same as is written on this paper." And Bhagavan made me read the stanza and translate it into English for the benefit of those who do not know Tamil. It goes: "The mind mocks me and though I tell you ten thousand times you are indifferent, so how am I to attain peace and bliss?"

Then I said to Khanna, "You are not the only one who complains to Bhagavan like this. I have more than once complained in the same way, and I still do, for I find no improvement in myself."

Khanna replied, "It is not only that I find no improvement but I think I have grown worse. The *vasanas* are stronger now. I can't understand it."

Bhagavan again quoted the last three stanzas of *Mandalathin* of Thayumanavar, where the mind is coaxed as the most generous and disinterested of givers, to go back to its birthplace or source and thus give the devotee peace and bliss, and he asked me to read out a translation of it that I once made.

Khanna then asked, "The illumination plus mind is *jivatma* and the illumination alone is *paramatma*; is that right?"

Bhagavan assented and then pointed to his towel and said, "We call this a white cloth, but the cloth and its whiteness cannot be separated, and it is the same with the illumination and the mind that unite to form the ego." Then he added: "The following illustration that is often given in books will also help you. The lamp in the theatre is the *Parabrahman* or the illumination, as you put it. It illumines itself and the stage and actors. We see the stage and the actors by its light, but its light still continues when there is no more play. Another illustration is an iron rod that is compared to the mind. Fire joins it and it becomes red-hot. It glows and can burn things, like fire, but still it has a definite shape, unlike fire. If we hammer it, it is the rod that receives the blows, not the fire. The rod is the *jivatma* and the fire the Self or *Paramatma*."

27-6-46

In the afternoon, T.V.K. Aiyar, who had with him our library copy of *Tiruvoimozhi* with commentary, asked Bhagavan whether we had any better commentary than that. Bhagavan replied that we had not and added, "All sorts of learned commentaries are written on the *Nalayira Prabandam* in the conventional *Vaishnavite* language, twisting the texts that are clearly *Advaitic* into some laboured *Dvaitic* meaning. In the old days some *Vaishnavites* used to come to me, and when they were wearing the 'U' mark they would put it on me also, and when they were wearing the 'Y' mark they would put that on me, and then they would prostrate themselves before me. I used to let them do what they liked with me."

T.V.K. then told Bhagavan, "Recently a man of the *thengalai* school who is well versed in the esoteric meaning of *Vaishnavite* literature initiated me and gave me *samasanam* and *sama asrayam* and taught me their esoteric meaning. He gives discourses and does good work among the poor, but he would not admit *vadakalais* to his discourses; according to the *Vaishnavite* teaching one must do *kainkaryam* or service to God."

Bhagavan replied rather sarcastically: "So God can't get on without their services? On the contrary, God asks: 'Who are you to do service to Me?' He is always saying: 'I am within you; who are you?' One must try to realize that and not speak of service. Submission or surrender is the basic teaching of *Vaishnavism*, but it does not consist in paying a Guru a fee for initiation and telling him that you have surrendered. As often as one tries to surrender, the ego raises its head and one has to try to suppress it. Surrender is not an easy thing. Killing the ego is not an easy thing. It is only when God Himself by His grace draws the mind inwards that complete surrender can be achieved. But such grace comes only to those who have already, in this or previous lives, gone through all the struggles and *sadhanas* preparatory to the extinction of the mind and killing of the ego."

Bhagavan added, "In the old days these *Vaishnavites* used to come and advise me to undergo a *samasanam* but I used to keep silent."

Bhagavan continued to speak of the *Dvaitism* of the *Vaishnavites* and quoted the Nammalvar song beginning 'யானே என்னை அறியகிலாதே' the gist of which is: "not knowing myself, I went about saying 'I' and 'mine'. Then I discovered that 'I' was 'You' and 'mine' was 'Yours', oh God." He said: "This is clear *Advaita,* but these *Vaishnavites* would give it some interpretation to make it accord with their feeling of duality. They hold that they must exist and God must exist, but how is that possible? It seems that they must all remain for ever doing service in *Vaikunta*, but how many of them are to do service and where would there be room for all these *Vaishnavites*?"

Bhagavan said this laughing, and then, after a pause, he added, "On the other hand, *Advaita* does not mean that a man must always sit in *samadhi* and never engage in action. Many things are necessary to keep up the life of the body, and action can never be avoided. Nor is *bhakti* ruled out in *Advaita.* Shankara is rightly regarded as the foremost exponent of *Advaita,* and yet look at the number of shrines he visited (action), and the devotional songs he wrote."

Bhagavan then gave further quotations from the eighth decad of *Tiruvoimozhi* to show that some of *Vaishnavite* Alwars had clearly endorsed *Advaita.* He particularly emphasised the third stanza where it says: "I was lost in Him or in That" and the fifth, which is very like the *Thiruvachagam* stanza that says the ego got attenuated more and more and was extinguished in the Self.

Later a visitor asked whether Bhagavan had ever thought of making a tour all round India or would consider such a proposal.

Bhagavan: I have never had any such idea, though several devotees have proposed it. Rajeswarananda once said he would arrange for a special train to take me all over India. But what is the use of my going anywhere? I am not able to see anything.

(I took this to refer to Bhagavan's seeing only the Self in everything). They say I must go and give *darshan* to all the people in those parts who may not be able to come here, but even if I went, who would take any notice of a beggar going about clad only in a loin-cloth? Or should I go with a label on my forehead or a card hung round my neck saying: 'Here goes a Maharshi'? Or I should have to take a big retinue who would go about proclaiming: 'Here comes our great Ramana Maharshi'. Besides, out of all the millions of people, to how many should I be able to give *darshan*?

Again at about seven o'clock in the evening, when I went into the hall, Bhagavan returned to the subject, saying: "People come here to give *darshan* to me, so why should I go to give *darshan* to them? If I yielded to the importunity of some devotee and went to some place when he asked me I should have to go to every place that every other devotee asked me to and there would be no end to my trouble."

28-6-46

In the afternoon Khanna's wife appealed to Bhagavan in writing: "I am not learned in the scriptures and I find the method of Self-enquiry too hard for me. I am a woman with seven children and a lot of household cares, and it leaves me little time for meditation. I request Bhagavan to give me some simpler and easier method."

Bhagavan: No learning or knowledge of scriptures is necessary to know the Self, as no man requires a mirror to see himself. All knowledge is required only to be given up eventually as not-Self. Nor is household work or cares with children necessarily an obstacle. If you can do nothing more, at least continue saying 'I, I' to yourself mentally all the time, as advised in *Who am I?*, whatever work you may be doing and whether you are sitting, standing or walking. 'I' is the name of God. It is the first and greatest of all *mantras*. Even OM is second to it.

Khanna: The *jiva* is said to be mind plus illumination. What is it that desires Self-realization and what is it that obstructs our path to Self-realization? It is said that the mind obstructs and the illumination helps.

Bhagavan: Although we describe the *jiva* as mind plus the reflected light of the Self, in actual practice, in life, you cannot separate the two, just as, in the illustrations we used yesterday, you can't separate cloth and whiteness in a white cloth or fire and iron in a red-hot rod. The mind can do nothing by itself. It emerges only with the illumination and can do no action, good or bad, except with the illumination. But while the illumination is always there, enabling the mind to act well or ill, the pleasure or pain resulting from such action is not felt by the illumination, just as when you hammer a red-hot rod it is not the fire but the iron that gets the hammering.

Khanna: Is there destiny? And if what is destined to happen will happen is there any use in prayer or effort or should we just remain idle?

Bhagavan: There are only two ways to conquer destiny or be independent of it. One is to enquire for whom is this destiny and discover that only the ego is bound by destiny and not the Self, and that the ego is non-existent. The other way is to kill the ego by completely surrendering to the Lord, by realizing one's helplessness and saying all the time: 'Not I but Thou, oh Lord!', and giving up all sense of 'I' and 'mine' and leaving it to the Lord to do what he likes with you. Surrender can never be regarded as complete so long as the devotee wants this or that from the Lord. True surrender is love of God for the sake of love and nothing else, not even for the sake of salvation. In other words, complete effacement of the ego is necessary to conquer destiny, whether you achieve this effacement through Self-enquiry or through *bhakti-marga*.

Khanna: Are our prayers granted?

Bhagavan: Yes, they are granted. No thought will go in vain. Every thought will produce its effect some time or other. Thought-force will never go in vain.

2-7-46

This evening after *parayana*, Venkatramaiyar came and told Bhagavan: "It seems that Mrs. Taleyarkhan and her guest, a cousin of Sir Mirza of Mysore, were sitting on the Hill, talking about Bhagavan and the Hill, and Mrs. Taleyarkhan said: 'Bhagavan is a walking God and all our prayers are answered. That is my experience. Bhagavan says this Hill is God Himself. I cannot understand all that, but Bhagavan says so, so I believe it.' Thereupon her friend replied: 'I would take it as a sign, according to our Persian beliefs, if it would rain.' Almost immediately there was a shower and they came to me drenched and told me about it."

3-7-46

A visitor said: I am told that according to your school I must find out the source of my thoughts. How am I to do it?'

Bhagavan: I have no school; however, it is true that one should trace the source of all thoughts.

Visitor: Suppose I have the thought 'horse' and try to trace its source; I find that it is due to memory and the memory in its turn is due to prior perception of the object 'horse', but that is all.

Bhagavan: Who asked you to think about all that? All those are also thoughts. What good will it do you to go on thinking about memory and perception? It will be endless, like the old dispute, which came first, the tree or the seed. Ask who has this perception and memory. That 'I' that has the perception and memory, whence does it arise? Find out that. Because perception or memory or any other experience only comes to that 'I'. You don't have such experiences during sleep, and yet you say that you existed during sleep. And you exist now too. That shows that the 'I' continues while other things come and go.

Visitor: I am asked to find out the source of 'I', and in fact that is what I want to find out, but how can I? What is the source from which I came?

Bhagavan: You came from the same source in which you were during sleep. Only during sleep you couldn't know where you entered; that is why you must make the enquiry while waking.

Some of us advised the visitor to read *Who am I?* and *Ramana Gita* and Bhagavan also told him he might do so. He did so during the day and in the evening he said to Bhagavan: "Those books prescribe Self-enquiry, but how is one to do it?"

Bhagavan: That also must be described in the books.

Visitor: Am I to concentrate on the thought 'Who am I?'

Bhagavan: It means you must concentrate to see where the I-thought arises. Instead of looking outwards, look inwards and see where the I-thought arises.

Visitor: And Bhagavan says that if I see that, I shall realise the Self?

Bhagavan: There is no such thing as realising the Self. How is one to realise or make real what is real? People all realise, or regard as real, what is unreal, and all they have to do is to give that up. When you do that you will remain as you always are and the Real will be Real. It is only to help people give up regarding the unreal as real that all the religions and the practices taught by them have come into being.

Visitor: Whence comes birth?

Bhagavan: For whom is birth?

Visitor: The *Upanishads* say "He who knows Brahman becomes Brahman."

Bhagavan: It is not a matter of becoming but being.

Visitor: Are the *siddhis* mentioned in Patanjali's *sutras* true or only his dream?

Bhagavan: He who is Brahman or the Self will not value those *siddhis.* Patanjali himself says that they are all exercised with the mind and that they impede Self-realisation.

Visitor: What about the powers of supermen?

Bhagavan: Whether powers are high or low, whether of the mind or super-mind, they exist only with reference to him who has the powers; find out who that is.

Visitor: When one attains Self-realisation, what is the guarantee that one has really attained it and is not under an illusion like the lunatic who thinks he is Napoleon or some such thing?

Bhagavan: In a sense, speaking of Self-realisation is a delusion. It is only because people have been under the delusion that the non-Self is the Self and the unreal the Real that they have to be weaned out of it by the other delusion called Self-realisation; because actually the Self always is the Self and there is no such thing as realising it. Who is to realise what, and how, when all that exists is the Self and nothing but the Self?

Visitor: Sri Aurobindo says the world is real and you and the *Vedantins* say it is unreal. How can the world be unreal?

Bhagavan: The *Vedantins* do not say the world is unreal. That is a misunderstanding. If they did, what would be the meaning of the *Vedantic* text: "All this is Brahman"? They only mean that the world is unreal as world, but it is real as Self. If you regard the world as not-Self it is not real. Everything, whether you call it world or *maya* or *lila* or *sakti*, must be within the Self and not apart from it. There can be no *sakti* apart from the *sakta.*

Visitor: Different teachers have set up different schools and proclaimed different truths and so confused people. Why?

Bhagavan: They have all taught the same truth but from different standpoints. Such differences were necessary to meet the needs of different minds differently constituted, but they all reveal the same Truth.

Visitor: Since they have recommended different paths which is one to follow?

Bhagavan: You speak of paths as if you were somewhere and the Self somewhere else and you had to go and reach it. But in fact the Self is here and now and you are that always. It is like you being here and asking people the way to Ramanasramam and complaining that each one shows a different path and asking which to follow.

Nagamma has been keeping a record of interesting events that she writes to her brother, D.S. Sastri, at Madras in the form of letters. This was placed before Bhagavan and he looked through it and suggested that she should paste a list of contents on the cover. One of the extracts referred to squirrels and this led Bhagavan to start speaking about them.

"There was once a regular war between the people here and the squirrels for a whole month. They used to build their nests over my head. Each day the people would destroy them and the next day the squirrels would have built them again. At last all the holes in the roof were stopped up and the squirrels could do nothing. At one time they used to run all over my couch and get into the sides and under the pillows and everywhere, and I had to look carefully before I sat down or leaned back. It has sometimes happened that I have accidentally leaned heavily on some small squirrel and given it *samadhi* without knowing. The same thing sometimes happened on the Hill too, at Skandasramam. There too the squirrels used to nestle in my mattress and pillows. It began even before that. Even when I was at Gurumoortham birds and squirrels used to build their nests all round me. There is a bird that builds its nest of mud. Once while I was there such a nest was built and after the birds had left it squirrels occupied it."

12-7-46

On the 8th news had come of the death of Madhava Swami and Bhagavan had spoken a good deal about it. In the evening Kunjuswami left for Kumbakonam, where the death took place, and this morning he returned. He said: "It seems that about 20 days before his death Madhava Swami left Kumbakonam saying he was coming here, but actually he took a ticket to Palni. After staying there he seems to have gone to Palghat and to his home village. Then he went to Trichy and stayed a few days with our Tirumala Chetty and from there returned to Kumbakonam about a week before his death. It seems that the whole of this week he was saying: 'Wherever I go I feel wretched. I don't feel at ease anywhere. If I go to Ramanasramam they may not allow me there, but after having had the privilege of serving Bhagavan for so long I can no longer bear the burden of this body anywhere else. I must throw it off." It seems that this thought was constantly with him and he went about moody and morose. The day before he died he was complaining of indigestion, but for a whole week his digestion had not been good."

Bhagavan asked what gave him indigestion.

Kunju Swami said, "It seems to have been due to eating a mango. They never agreed with him. At about four on Sunday afternoon, the 7th, he was offered some lunch but refused it and asked for a bottle of soda-water. Soon after that he perspired all over and left his body, sitting in the *padmasana* posture."

When the post arrived it brought a letter with news of the death of L. Sarma's first daughter-in-law. This led Bhagavan to speak of death. He said: "The dead are fortunate. It is only those who are left behind who feel miserable. It is our constant concern to bear the burden of this body and look after its needs. Day in, day out, this is our occupation — bathing, eating, massaging our legs, and so on — no end to it. When we die it takes four persons to carry this body and yet we carry it about constantly without even stopping to think that we are doing so. We can easily lift a heavy stone under water, but as soon as we take it out we find how heavy it is, and in the same way we don't feel the weight of the body as long as a *chaitanya* or life force permeates it.

"Deathlessness is our real nature, and we falsely ascribe it to the body, imagining that it will live for ever and losing sight of what is really immortal, simply because we identify ourselves with the body. It says in the *Upanishads* that the *jnani* looks forward eagerly to the time when he can throw off the body, just as a labourer carrying a heavy load looks forward to reaching his destination and laying it down."

16-7-46

Some of the Khairagarh party came and asked leave of Bhagavan to go to Skandasramam. I told Bhagavan that yesterday Venkatramaiyar and I went with the Rani and Kamakshi and when we were at Virupakshi Cave, Venkatramaiyar told us that if anyone sits there quietly by himself and listens, he hears the sound 'OM'. I asked him whether he had ever heard it and he said that he had not yet had the chance to try. So I now ask Bhagavan whether it is true.

Bhagavan only said: "They say so."

I asked: "But did Bhagavan hear it?" And then I corrected myself and added: "But it is no use asking, because Bhagavan would hear OM or the *Pranava* sound everywhere, and it would not be due to the place if Bhagavan heard it there."

Thereupon Bhagavan said: "Why don't you go and find out for yourself?"

"Yes," I said, "I want to go and see. If a dunce like me has the experience then there can be no doubt that it is due to the influence of the place."

After a while Bhagavan added, "It is generally said that not only is the cave in the shape of OM but the sound OM is heard there. Suddhananda Bharati mentions it in his *Ramana Vijayam*. He ought to know because he lived there." So saying, Bhagavan took the book and showed me the relevant passage in Chapter 24, entitled *Guhan*.

A visitor asked Bhagavan what one should do for the betterment of *atma*.

Bhagavan: What do you mean by *atma* and by betterment?

Visitor: We don't know all that; that is why we come here.

Bhagavan: The Self or *atma* is always as it is. There is no such thing as attaining it. All that is necessary is to give up regarding the not-Self as Self and the unreal as Real. When we give up identifying ourselves with the body the Self alone remains.

Visitor: But how is one to give up this identification? Will coming here and getting our doubts removed help in the process?

Bhagavan: Questions are always about things that you don't know and will be endless unless you find out who the questioner is. Though the things about which the questions are asked are unknown, there can be no doubt that a questioner exists to ask the questions, and if you ask who he is, all doubts will be set at rest.

Visitor: All that I want to know is whether *sat sang* is necessary and whether my coming here will help me or not.

Bhagavan: First you must decide what is *sat sang.* It means association with *sat* or Reality. One who knows or has realized *sat* is also regarded as *sat.* Such association with *sat* or with one who knows *sat* is absolutely necessary for all. Sankara has said (Bhagavan here quoted the Sanskrit verse) that in all the three worlds there is no boat like *sat sang* to carry one safely across the ocean of births and deaths.

17-7-46

This morning Bhagavan was speaking about a letter from Mr. Pande, Principal of a college at Khatmandu, telling about an incident that Mr. Pande has already described in the *Souvenir* volume. A.N. Rao and I wanted to see it, so Bhagavan asked for the letter to be shown to us. This is the incident: Pande went to the great temple in Tiruvannamalai on the evening of his departure. When he entered the innermost shrine the *lingam* of Arunachalam was pointed out to him, and the young man who was with him, also a devotee of Bhagavan, cried out: 'Arunachala! Arunachala!'; but Pande could not see any *lingam* but only the face of Bhagavan whichever side he turned — everywhere the face of Bhagavan!

18-7-46

This morning questions were put by a visitor, by name S.P. Tayal.

S.P. Tayal: I have been doing *sadhana* for nearly 20 years and I can see no progress. What should I do?

Bhagavan: I may be able to say something if I know what the *sadhana* is.

S.P. Tayal: From about 5 o'clock every morning I concentrate on the thought that the Self alone is real and all else unreal. Although I have been doing this for about 20 years I cannot concentrate for more than two or three minutes without my thoughts wandering.

Bhagavan: There is no other way to succeed than to draw the mind back every time it turns outwards and fix it in the Self. There is no need for meditation or *mantra* or *japa* or *dhyana* or anything of the sort, because these are our real nature. All that is needed is to give up thinking of objects other than the Self. Meditation is not so much thinking of the Self as giving up thinking of the not-Self. When you give up thinking of outward objects and prevent your mind from going outwards and turn it inward and fix it in the Self, the Self alone will remain.

S.P. Tayal: What should I do to overcome the pull of these thoughts and desires? How should I regulate my life so as to attain control over my thoughts?

Bhagavan: The more you get fixed in the Self, the more other thoughts will drop off by themselves. The mind is nothing but a bundle of thoughts, and the I-thought is the root of all of them. When you see who this 'I' is and whence it proceeds all thoughts get merged in the Self.

Regulation of life, such as getting up at a fixed hour, bathing, doing *mantra, japa,* etc., observing ritual, all this is for people who do not feel drawn to Self-enquiry or are not capable of it. But for those who can practise this method all rules and discipline are unnecessary.

At this point K.M. Jivrajani interposed, "Has one necessarily to pass through the stage of seeing occult visions before attaining Self-realization?"

Bhagavan: Why do you bother about visions and whether they come or not?

K.M. Jivrajani: I don't. I only want to know so that I shan't be disappointed if I don't have them.

Bhagavan: Visions are not a necessary stage. To some they come and to others they don't, but whether they come or not you always exist and you must stick to that.

K.M. Jivrajani: I sometimes concentrate on the brain centre and sometimes on the heart — not always on the same centre. Is that wrong?

Bhagavan: Wherever you concentrate and on whatever centre there must be a *you* to concentrate, and that is what you must concentrate on. Different people concentrate on different centres, not only the brain and the heart but also the space between the eyebrows, the tip of the nose, the tip of the tongue, the lowermost *chakra* and even external objects. Such concentration may lead to a sort of *laya* in which you will feel a certain bliss, but care must be taken not to lose the thought 'I Am' in all this. You never cease to exist in all these experiences.

K.M. Jivrajani: That is to say that I must be a witness?

Bhagavan: Talking of the 'witness' should not lead to the idea that there is a witness and something else apart from him that he is witnessing. The 'witness' really means the light that illumines the seer, the seen and the process of seeing. Before, during and after the triads of seer, seen and seeing, the illumination exists. It alone exists always.

K.M. Jivrajani: It is said in books that one should cultivate all the good or *daivic* qualities in order to prepare oneself for Self-realisation.

Bhagavan: All good or *daivic* qualities are included in *jnana* and all bad *asuric* qualities are included in *ajnana.* When *jnana* comes all *ajnana* goes and all *daivic* qualities come automatically. If a man is a *jnani* he cannot utter a lie or do anything wrong. It is, no doubt, said in some books that one should cultivate one quality after another and thus prepare for ultimate *moksha*, but for those who follow the *jnana* or *vichara marga* their *sadhana* is itself quite enough for acquiring all *daivic* qualities; they need not do anything else.

19-7-46

Again today a visitor put questions: I do not understand how to make the enquiry 'Who am I?'

Bhagavan: Find out whence the 'I' arises. Self-enquiry does not mean argument or reasoning such as goes on when you say, "I am not this body, I am not the senses," etc.: all that may also help but it is not the enquiry. Watch and find out where in the body the 'I' arises and fix your mind on that.

Visitor: Will *gayatri* help?

Bhagavan: What is *gayatri*? It really means: "Let me concentrate on that which illumines all." *Dhyana* really means only concentrating or fixing the mind on the object of *dhyana.* But meditation is our real nature. If we give up other thoughts what remains is 'I' and its nature is *dhyana* or meditation or *jnana,* whichever we choose to call it. What is at one time the means later becomes the end; unless meditation or *dhyana* were the nature of the Self it could not take you to the Self. If the means were not of the nature of the goal, it could not bring you to the goal.

20-7-46

In the afternoon Sundaresa Aiyar told Bhagavan that his daughter-in-law (Narayanaswami Aiyar's daughter) had severe labour pains and finally could bear it no longer and cried out: "Ramana! I cannot bear it!"; and immediately the delivery took place. Bhagavan merely said: "Is that so?"

21-7-46

In the afternoon the following two questions were put by Mr. Bhargava, an elderly visitor from Jhansi in U.P.:

(1) How am I to search for the 'I' from start to finish?

(2) When I meditate I reach a stage where there is a vacuum or void. How should I proceed from there?

Bhagavan: Never mind whether there are visions or sounds or anything else or whether there is a void. Are you present during all this or are you not? You must have been there even during the void to be able to say that you experienced a void. To be fixed in that 'you' is the quest for the 'I' from start to finish. In all books on *Vedanta* you will find this question of a void or of nothing being left, raised by the disciple and answered by the Guru. It is the mind that sees objects and has experiences and that finds a void when it ceases to see and experience, but that is not 'you'. You are the constant illumination that lights up both the experiences and the void. It is like the theatre light that enables you to see the theatre, the actors and the play while the play is going on but also remains alight and enables you to say that there is no play on when it is all finished. Or there is another illustration. We see objects all around us, but in complete darkness we do not see them and we say, 'I see nothing'; even then the eyes are there to say that they see nothing. In the same way, you are there even in the void you mention.

You are the witness of the three bodies: the gross, the subtle and the causal, and of the three states: waking, dream and deep sleep, and of the three times: past, present and future, and also of this void. In the story of the tenth man, when each of the ten counted and thought there were only nine, each one forgetting to count himself, there is a stage when they think one is missing and don't know who it is; and that corresponds to the void. We are so accustomed to the notion that all that we see around us is permanent and that we are this body, that when all this ceases to exist we imagine and fear that we also have ceased to exist.

Bhagavan also quoted verses 212 and 213 from *Vivekachudamani,* in which the disciple says: "After I eliminate the five sheaths as not-Self, I find that nothing at all remains", and the Guru replied that the Self or That by which all modifications (including the ego and its creatures) and their absence (that is the void) are perceived is always there.

Then Bhagavan continued speaking on the subject and said: "The nature of the Self or 'I' must be illumination. You perceive all modifications and their absence. How? To say that you get the illumination from another would raise the question how he got it and there would be no end to the chain of reasoning. So you yourself are the illumination. The usual illustration of this is the following: You make all kinds of sweets of various ingredients and in various shapes and they all taste sweet because there is sugar in all of them and sweetness is the nature of sugar. And in the same way all experiences and the absence of them contain the illumination which is the nature of the Self. Without the Self they cannot be experienced, just as without sugar not one of the articles you make can taste sweet."

A little later Bhagavan also said: "First one sees the Self as objects, then one sees the Self as void, then one sees the Self as Self, only in this last there is no seeing because seeing is being."

Mr. Bhargava also said something about sleep, and this led Bhagavan to speak about sleep as follows:

"What is required is to remain fixed in the Self always. The obstacles to that are distraction by the things of the world (including sense objects, desires and tendencies) on the one hand, and sleep on the other. Sleep is always mentioned in books as the first obstacle to *samadhi* and various methods are prescribed for overcoming it according to the stage of evolution of the person concerned. First, one is enjoined to give up all distraction by the world and its objects or by sleep. But then it is said, for instance in the *Gita*, that one need not give up sleep entirely. Too much and too little are alike undesirable. One should not sleep at all during the daytime and even during the night restrict sleep to the middle portion, from about ten to two. But another method that is prescribed is not to bother about sleep at all. When it overtakes you, you can do nothing about it, so simply remain fixed in the Self or in meditation every moment of your waking life and take up the meditation again the moment you wake, and that will be enough. Then even during sleep the same current of thought or meditation will be working. This is evident because if a man goes to sleep with any strong thought working in his mind he finds the same thought there when he wakes. It is of the man who does this with meditation that it is said that even his sleep is *samadhi*. A good way to reduce the amount of sleep needed is to take only *sattvic* food and that in moderation and to avoid work or activity of any kind."

22-7-46

This morning Vaidyanathan, the R.D.O., came into the hall and asked whether he could bring in the adviser, Ramamurti. Bhagavan gave permission and he brought in Ramamurti and his party. Ramamurti began to speak to Bhagavan in Telugu and said, "I know that Bhagavan speaks Telugu, because I came here ten years ago with Raghaviah and found that Bhagavan spoke Telugu quite well. This (pointing to the man next to him) is my brother. He has opened an Institute of Naturopathy in Bangalore. Kameswara Sarma is also working there."

Thereupon his brother said, "Bhagavan was pleased to send his blessings when the institute was opened." After that he added, "I find it difficult to believe in a personal God. In fact I find it impossible. But I can believe in an impersonal God, a Divine Force which rules and guides the world, and it would be a great help to me, even in my work of healing, if this faith were increased. May I know how to increase this faith?"

After a slight pause Bhagavan replied, "Faith is in things unknown; but the Self is self-evident. Even the greatest egoist cannot deny his own existence, that is to say, cannot deny the Self. You can call the ultimate Reality by whatever name you like and say that you have faith in it or love for it, but who is there who will not have faith in his own existence or love for himself? That is because faith and love are our real nature."

A little later Ramamurti asked, "That which rises as 'I' within us is the Self, is it not?"

Bhagavan: No; it is the ego that rises as 'I'. That from which it arises is the Self.

Ramamurti: They speak of a lower and a higher *atman.*

Bhagavan: There is no such thing as lower or higher in *atman.* Lower and higher apply to the forms, not to the Self or *atman.*

Soon after, the party took leave, declining an invitation to stay to lunch, as they had already arranged for lunch elsewhere.

In the afternoon Mr. Tayal of Calcutta spoke with Bhagavan again.

Tayal: I do not always concentrate on the same centre in the body. Sometimes I find it easier to concentrate on one centre and sometimes on another. And sometimes when I concentrate on one centre the thought of its own accord goes and fixes itself in another. Why is that?

Bhagavan: It may be because of past practices of yours. But in any case it is immaterial on which centre you concentrate since the real heart is in every centre and even outside the body. On whatever part of the body you may concentrate or on whatever external object, the heart is there.

K.M. Jivrajani, intervening, asked: Can one concentrate at one time on one centre and at another time on another or should one concentrate always consistently on the same centre?

Bhagavan: As I have just said, there can be no harm wherever you concentrate, because concentration is only a means of giving up thoughts. Whatever the centre or object on which you concentrate, he who concentrates is always the same.

24-7-46

Bhargava: What is awareness and how can one obtain and cultivate it?

Bhagavan: You are awareness. Awareness is another name for you. Since you are awareness there is no need to attain or cultivate it.

This was obviously a bit too much for Bhargava and he was wondering how it was an answer to his question, but Bhagavan came to his help by adding: All that you have to do is to give up being aware of other things, that is of the not-Self. If one gives up being aware of them then pure awareness alone remains, and that is the Self."

28-7-46 Morning

At about 10 a.m. as I entered the hall, Bhagavan was telling a visitor from Jaipur, "What is the use of coming away from your house? You have left one home. This is another home. What can the home do? Nothing. It is the mind that does everything." After saying this he continued: "Immediately the question is asked. 'Then why did you come away from home'?" I asked Bhagavan, "Why, did this man also ask that question?"

Bhagavan: No. He has not asked it. But I myself realise the inconsistency (எனக்குள்ளேயே உதைச்சிக்கிறதே).

On previous occasions, Bhagavan has answered this question in the following way, "I came away because it was my *prarabdha*, and you will also go away if it is your *prarabdha*."

In the evening, some *bairagi* from Rishikesh came and complained in Hindi before Bhagavan for a long time that some Malayali *sadhus* there were trying to wipe out the existence of Ramanasramam at Rishikesh, founded by one Govindananda 25 years ago, and that he had come here to see that the land on which the Asramam was built 25 years ago is purchased and duly registered, so that nobody can oust the present inmates of the Asramam from the place. He was told that the *Sarvadhikari* who alone could deal with such matters was absent and that Bhagavan would do nothing. The *bairagi* was greatly vexed and left the hall, even without staying for supper.

On the 29th I left for Chingleput and returned only on the night of 2-8-46.

3-8-46

I find among the arrivals here during my absence the Zamindarini of Vuyyur visiting the Asramam for the first time and another young boy of nine years, Apparao, hailing from Anakapalle. The boy is in some ways precocious and professes to be inclined towards *sannyasa* or spiritual life and is remarkably free from all fear. It seems he heard about Bhagavan first from his father who visited Bhagavan about two years ago. The boy remembers and narrates accurately some incidents in Bhagavan's life at Skandasramam and Virupakshi which he has heard from his father or others. It seems some swami visiting Anakapalle recently spoke about Bhagavan, and hearing that, the boy in a mood of enthusiasm has run away here all by himself unknown to his parents. It is said that once before he ran away to Benares and stayed there for a day and returned. When somebody asked him, "Is it proper for you to take up this sort of life so soon? Your business now is to attend school and learn," he replied, "Did not Shankara leave his home when he was only seven?" The boy is still here and our Nagamma has written to his mother about the boy's arrival.

This afternoon, at 2-30 p.m., I found Bhagavan seated on a cot in the dining hall. While I was wondering why, a party of a dozen devotees came and took their seats in front of Bhagavan. They soon started a *bhajan,* which went on till 4 p.m. and was full of devotion. The party had come from Srivilliputtur, where they belong to 'Rama Matam' which, it seems, has been in existence for more than fifty years. They not only sang, but danced and performed *kummi* and went through various movements, all reminiscent of Krishna's diversions in Brindavan.

After evening *parayana*, P.C. Desai and Viswanath were correcting in Bhagavan's presence the proofs of Kapali Sastri's Sanskrit commentary on *Ramana Gita*.

4-8-46

This morning Yogi Ramiah arrived. About 9-30 a.m. Bhagavan was looking into the Tamil paper *Hindusthan* and read out to me the following dialogue from it.

1st man: It is only if sorrows or troubles come to us that we think of God.

2nd man: Ah, you fool. If we are always thinking of God, how can any sorrows or troubles come to us?

Why Bhagavan drew my attention to this, I do not know. I wonder if it is because I generally argue with him that it should not be necessary for an all-powerful and all-loving God to make us pass through pain to turn us towards Him.

Most of the day the proof correction went on.

5-8-46

The proof-reading continued today and was finished in the evening. The boy Apparao would seem to be only a truant. His brother has written to Nagamma in reply. The Zamindarini of Vuyyur, who is leaving for Madras today, has taken the boy with her promising to send him by train to Anakapalle.

6-8-46 Morning

A visitor introduced himself to Bhagavan as one who was at Singapore for many years and who knows Mr. Narayana Iyer of

Singapore. I found later that this gentleman is Rajam Iyer from Tinnevelly.

In the afternoon, T.S. Rajagopal, while clearing and rearranging the book shelves, came across a notebook. Bhagavan said, "This is the notebook K.K. Nambiar gave me. It was a very strange thing. There used to be a number of bound notebooks like this with us then. But still, Madhavan did not give me one, though I was asking for one for two or three days. Somehow, he was indifferent and I too did not press him. On the third day, Nambiar, who was then engineer here, came and gave me this notebook and said 'Here is the notebook Bhagavan wanted'. Then it came out that he had a dream in which, it seems, I told him I wanted a notebook of such and such a kind and of such and such dimensions. He is now in America."

7-8-46 Afternoon

A notebook in which I had written down some favourite Tamil songs of mine was missing for some time and so I began copying those songs again in a fresh notebook. This was brought to Bhagavan's notice by T.S.R., and soon afterwards Mr. Somasundaram Pillai of Cuddalore came and told me that my old notebook had not been lost but was with his family. In this connection, T.S.R. told me, "Various incidents, too numerous to remember, happen like this. The moment I told Bhagavan, you got your notebook. It seems Bhagavan's mother once wanted *kadukkai* (Indian myrobolan) and soon afterwards somebody brought it. You ask Bhagavan about it." Thereupon I asked Bhagavan and he said, "It was not mother that wanted *kadukkai*. I used to have a cough and also constipation in those days. I was then in Virupakshi Cave. I used to munch *kadukkai* now and then. One day our stock of *kadukkai* had become exhausted. In those days, overseer (Sesha Iyer) used to come to me daily in the evenings, after his usual official round in the town, and he used to look after our requirements. So we told him we wanted *kadukkai*. He would generally attend promptly to any such want. But, somehow, he did not send it the next day and so I told Palaniswami, 'When you go to fetch meals from the *chattram* this noon, remind the overseer about the *kadukkai*.' But before he went, the following incident happened. One Adimulam and his friends, from a village near Chengam, used to come here once a month, to go round the Hill. They would visit me also. They came that day, stayed with me some time, took leave and departed. After going a few paces, they came back and asked if we had any possible use for *kadukkai*. We said 'Yes' and then they brought a whole bag of them and requested us to keep it. We took about two measures, selecting the best, and returned the rest to them. It seems, as they were coming, they found this *kadukkai* all along the Chengam Road and they had gathered a whole bag. Evidently, some bags, carried overnight in the bandies plying on that road, were leaking and these had spilled out. So, I asked Palaniswami to tell the overseer not to send *kadukkai* from the town."

When he was finishing the above narration, Mr. Kuppanna came and prostrated himself before Bhagavan. Bhagavan said, "Look at this. We are talking about the overseer and here is his nephew." (K. is overseer's brother's son.) Then T.S.R. put in, "Such coincidences are too numerous. Recently, we spoke about Janaki Ammal and she arrived the following day. The other day, Krishnaswami remarked to Bhagavan that Yogi Ramiah had not come here for about two years, and he arrived the following day and is with us now." Bhagavan continued, "Kuppuswami's coming reminds me of another incident. One day, for something or other, I wanted dried grapes and asked those with me whether we had any in the Asramam. They had none. And we thought no more of that. That night Kuppuswami's father arrived from Madras, and he brought with him a *viss* of good, clean dried grapes, not the sticky and dirty stuff which we generally get here. It seems he arrived in the town late in the night and wanted to buy some sweets to bring them to me. He had never before brought any such thing, but on that occasion it struck him he should buy something for me. It seems all the shops were closed. But one grocer's shop was open and he went there. He had no idea of purchasing grapes at all. But the shopkeeper volunteered the information, 'I have fresh, good dried grapes, recently arrived. They are very good. Buy some.' And he bought a viss and took it to us."

Bhagavan added, "The notebook incident is even more remarkable. Nambiar came and sat in the hall as usual. As he was leaving, he came and showed the notebook to me. I asked him what the notebook was for, and he said, 'You asked for it and so I have brought it. You came in my dream and asked for it, giving me full directions as to length, width, thickness, etc., and so I have made it accordingly and brought it.' Madhavan was not then in the hall. When he returned I called him and said, 'What have I been asking you for, these two or three days?' He replied, 'That bound notebook.' Then I asked, 'Why didn't you give it to me?' He replied, 'Somehow I forgot about it.' Then I showed him the notebook brought by Nambiar and told him, 'You would not give it and so he has brought this.' Mr. Nambiar is now in America. Mrs. Dowe has written about Nambiar and Bose. She likes Nambiar very much and says he is a quiet man, unlike Bose, who is talkative. Such happenings were very common in the case of Ayyaswami who was with me. The moment I thought of anything, the same thought would occur to him and he would do what I wanted. I used to ask him, 'Why did you do this?' and he would reply, 'I don't know. Somehow the thought came to me and so I did it'." T.S.R. said, "How is it, it is not our good fortune to have such calls made on us, as on Nambiar?" Then I told him, "Why? You were asked to get ink and you brought the same." Then Bhagavan said, "Yes. He brought a bottle of Stephens ink, saying he had a dream in which I wanted it."

When Bhagavan said, "Things like these have not been included in any book, in any of the biographies, I think." I replied, "I am noting down all such things in my diary. I shan't omit them."

This morning, T.S.R.'s son-in-law K. Sarma and his wife and child arrived here. Bhagavan made kind enquiries of them and asked Sarada if her child Lakshmi was talking now and she replied, "She talks a few words and supplements them by gestures." In the afternoon, a visitor Ramanatha Poddar, arrived from Bombay and enquired after L. Sarma and his son K. Sarma. It seems these two tried their naturopathy on R.P.'s relation about a year ago and then stayed in his house for about two months.

This morning, Yogi Ramiah brought a small notebook in which Bhagavan had long ago copied for the Yogi some of Bhagavan's works, and wanted the binding to be mended. Bhagavan gave some directions and entrusted the work to T.S.R. In the evening T.S.R. gave the notebook mended to Bhagavan and Bhagavan approved of the work and handed it to Yogi, saying, "Look at your notebook now." Yogi said, "All is Bhagavan's grace," or some such thing. Muruganar took up the notebook and, seeing only a fourth of the notebook had been written up and the rest was empty, quoted the words from the *Purusha Sukta*, and remarked, "Like a fourth only of God manifesting in the entire universe and the remaining three-fourths lying outside it unknown, this book contains only a fourth of Bhagavan" and all laughed, including Bhagavan.

8-8-46

Mr. Viswanath said, "Shroff is asking me to find out from Bhagavan why it is that in spite of his being sincerely keen on being near Bhagavan, he did not get posted to Madras or any place near Tiruvannamalai, but was sent to Bombay." Bhagavan replied, "What can we say? Things happen in a way we don't understand. Those whom one never expects suddenly come here.

Some who are here are suddenly and unexpectedly made to go away from here. What can we say about it?" About 10 a.m. Mrs. Desai read out before Bhagavan her Gujarati verse translation of Jagadisa Sastri's *Abhayashtakam*, an English translation of which was recently made by Mr. V. Iyer for inclusion in the *Golden Jubilee Souvenir* volume. Bhagavan received today the first copy of *New Times*. It seems when Mr. Tirumal Rao was here recently he took from Mr. Frydman a small article on Bhagavan for inclusion in the first issue of his paper. For the benefit of all, I read out the article in the hall. Bhagavan said, "Show it to Mr. Frydman."

Afternoon

Yogi Ramiah gave his notebook to Bhagavan and said, pointing to Muruganar, "People like him would write verses on occasions like the forthcoming Jubilee. But people like me can do no such thing. Instead, I want Bhagavan to write something in my notebook." Thereupon Bhagavan wrote on the back of the front page in the notebook, which he found blank, the Telugu version of the Tamil song which Bhagavan had composed when the late Somasundara Swami requested Bhagavan to write an 'எழுத்து' in his notebook. The Sanskrit word for எழுத்து being both a character in the alphabet and an imperishable thing, Bhagavan wrote punningly:

அக்கரம தோரெழுத் தாகுமிப் புத்தகத்தோ
ரக்கரமா மஃதெழுத வாசித்தா—யக்கரமாம்
ஓரெழுத்தென் றுந்தாளு யுள்ளத் தொளிர்வதாம்
ஆரெழுத வல்லா ரதை.

Here in this book I write
For you to read
An *akshara*,
But who can write
The *Akshara*
For ever shining in the heart?

9-8-46

In the morning *tapal* was a letter from Mr. V. P. Sastri. It was full of devotion to Bhagavan and said how Bhagavan and his teachings were unique.

Afternoon

About 3-30 p.m., Bhagavan was reading a letter going to the post. After returning it to Mauni, he said, "One says my subtle body is three miles long — three miles," and laughed. It seems Mr. G. V. S. of Nellore came across a swami, Narasimham I think by name, who said this. He also said Aurobindo's subtle body was three furlongs long. Nagamma reported this. Bhagavan laughed and said, "How long is his own subtle body?"

Bhagavan read out from a Tamil journal a passage which said, "It is false philosophy which regards the world as false or full of misery. If you learn to use the intelligence and the power which is latent within you, you can live happily in this world." After reading this out, Bhagavan said, "These people belong to the school which believes in *sakti* and *siddhis.*" He also added, "But I suppose they too will have to die."

This morning we had gruel and groundnuts for breakfast. Bhagavan told us this sort of gruel used to be given to him by the famous Keerai Patti in those days and so they thought they would try and prepare the same here today. It is made of milk and rice, with fenugreek, a little garlic, a little dried ginger, a little salt and sugar. Bhagavan said that the gruel had not come out quite well and that a little more salt and sugar should have been added.

In the evening, after *parayana*, Viswanath read out some songs from *Uma Sahasram* and also some other Sanskrit songs of Nayana on the Goddess, apparently because this is Varalakshmi *vrata* day.

10-8-46 Morning

Bhagavan came across some verses in honour of the late R. Raghava Aiyangar by his relation M. Raghava Aiyangar, in today's *Swadesamitran* and, seeing that Muruganar was not in the hall, asked Viswanath to tell him about it. Bhagavan added, "Ever since R.'s demise, in every paper, appreciations have been regularly appearing. But these are in verse and composed by his close relation. They are அத்தைப்பிள்ளை அம்மாஞ்சி (cousins). I think M. would like to see the verses." In this connection I said, "Would not Muruganar write something, seeing they were great friends?" To this Viswanath said, "Not likely, because he has taken up the stand that he should not sing the praises of any but Bhagavan." Mrs. Taleyarkhan wanted to know about R. Aiyangar and Bhagavan told her, "He was the Samasthana Vidvan of Ramnad, the Poet Laureate, you may call it, of that State." Then, we fell to talking about the small patronage, poets as a class have had in our country, and remarked that things were getting better, with such events in our days as the poet Ramalingam of Namakkal being presented with a purse of Rs.10,000. Muruganar's vow also reminded me of the famous Telugu poet, Pothana, declining to dedicate his *Bhagavatam* to his king, in spite of the earnest entreaties of his brother-in-law Srinatha, the court poet, and the commands of the king. This story was then related to Mrs. Taleyarkhan by Mr. G.V. Subba Rao.

The post brought a letter from Chinnaswami. Bhagavan said, on perusing it, "It seems they have gone to Madras and will meet the Raja of Ramnad there. They seem to have effected a little alteration in the Madura house, renovating the two rooms in front, making the whole thing one hall and having the street entrance in the middle of the house instead of on one side as before." Bhagavan asked the note to be shown to Mrs. T., as it contained the information that some contribution made by her had been utilised for this purpose, though originally it was thought the sum could be spent on the forthcoming Jubilee. The letter was accordingly shown to her by Viswanath.

Afternoon

As soon as Muruganar came, Bhagavan told him about the article in *Swadesamitran* and also about another in the Tamil *Hindustan* on R.R. Aiyangar, and gave the two papers to him. He also added, "The latter article concludes by saying that R.R. and the late Rt. Hon. V.S.S. Sastri were great friends and, except for the fact they employed different languages, they were equally great speakers."

Bhagavan gave Nagamma some instruction as to where and how she might begin the portion in the life of Jnaneswar which she is translating into Telugu — the portion where Jnaneswar goes to the forest, argues with his father and brings him back to the city and family. In this connection, Bhagavan wanted to see where and how we began when we translated the above portion for Manu Subedar's benefit, and so I took out Manu Subedar's 1945 edition of *Gita Explained* (*Jnaneswari*) in which the above translation is given as an appendix. Bhagavan perused it and said, "We shall begin the Telugu translation in some such way."

After evening *parayana*, Desai began reading some verses in Sanskrit and translating them into English. After a few minutes, I asked Bhagavan what it was all about, and then he said, "Just now they have found that there is some space available in the Jubilee volume and think that the same could be filled up by a few verses which are really *stotras* from the Sanskrit Biography written by Viswanatha Sastri. So Desai is translating them. Viswanath is probably already translating them into Tamil or English without telling these people." Then Bhagavan told Desai, "You had better write your translation in English. We shall all go through it then and see."

11-8-46

This morning, the young man Natarajan of Tanjore arrived. He brought from Janaki Ammal a walking stick with a silver knob and a pair of wooden slippers with silver gilt for Bhagavan. Bhagavan said, "I shall touch them and give them back. Let her have them in her puja." So saying, he inspected them and gave them back to the attendant. Later, I asked N. and found out that the allusion in the seventh stanza of his *Vetkai* (வேட்கை) is to the following incident: It seems one morning during his last visit he came into the dining hall late for his lunch, and that all except Bhagavan had risen. It seems then Bhagavan also rose and came and stood by N.'s side and when he tried to get up Bhagavan told him 'வந்த வேலையைப் பார்' (attend to the business for which you have come) and walked on. N. now read out before Bhagavan his poem 'குயிலொடு கூறல்' which he had not read out on his previous visit.

Afternoon

Bhagavan looked into the Tamil *Bhakta Vijayam* and told Nagamma, "You may begin by saying that when the Brahmins complained to the king against Jnaneswar's grandfather, that he was spoiling the Brahmin caste, etc., Jnaneswar went to the king and argued with him so ably on behalf of his grandfather, that the king was greatly struck by the boy's genius and wanted to see what sort of man was the father who gave birth to such a child, and sent Jnaneswar with his own retinue to go to the forest and fetch his father." Bhagavan also asked me to show Mr. D.S. Sastri (Nagamma's brother), who arrived this morning, the appendix to Manu Subedar's *Gita* (*Jnaneswari*). Later the talk turned to the proposed journal for our Asramam, on which Mr. D.S. Sastri has been very keen. D.S. Sastri said that the Calcutta gentleman who was equally keen, met him at Madras and talked to him about it. D.S.S. said, "But it won't do to edit it from Calcutta. There must be someone here who would show everything to Bhagavan and get his approval before it is sent to the press." I suggested Dr. Anantanarayana Rao's name, as I felt unequal for any such responsible work. Bhagavan said, "Even today we received a letter from somebody who asks if there is not some journal — some organ of the Asramam."

Later, on a visitor's request, Bhagavan said, "Concentrating one's thoughts solely on the Self will lead to happiness or bliss. Drawing in the thoughts, restraining them and preventing them from going outwards is called *vairagya*. Fixing them in the Self is *sadhana* or *abhyasa*. Concentrating on the Heart is the same as concentrating on the Self. The Heart is another name for the Self."

This afternoon, I was reading the current *Vedanta Kesari* which begins with some conversation of Latu Maharaj (Adbhutananda). Then I told Bhagavan that Adbhutananda was Latu, who was wholly illiterate; that such a man was later able to hold such conversations as are recorded in this article was regarded a miracle and so Latu was named Adbhutananda. Bhagavan said, "Is it so?"

12-8-46

This morning, Bhagavan was perusing a letter from Madhavi Amma (K.K. Nambiar's sister) and told us, "She says: 'If I were a man, would I allow anybody else to massage Bhagavan's legs?' She says this in connection with Madhavan and his death. She massaged my legs once. She gave hot fomentation. She is expert at that. The cloth would hardly touch my limbs. She would apply just the hot vapour alone to the legs."

Natarajan read out today his *Vetkai*, consisting of ten songs. I had asked him to read this yesterday. But he read first his 'குயிலொடு கூறல்' (*Kuyilodu Kooral*) and in the singing so lost himself that he forgot all about my request. So he read out *Vetkai* today. He also read out another song composed by him today in which he has embodied Janaki Ammal's request sent through him to Bhagavan. He told Bhagavan, "I have already shown it to Muruganar." Bhagavan perused it and made one small correction.

In the evening Desai and Viswanath read out their English translation of the eight or nine verses of *stotra* extracted from V. Sastri's Sanskrit life of Bhagavan.

13-8-46

In the afternoon Mr. T.K. Doraiswami Iyer told Bhagavan of Prof. Swaminathan and others in Madras suggesting that on the Jubilee Day we might have here some music performance and speeches in different languages from eminent persons. Bhagavan did not seem to be much in favour of it. He said, "What is this, sending for such people from such long distance? After all, each of them can speak only a few minutes as there are to be so many. And what expense!" Then I told Bhagavan, "This is all for our benefit. These people who will be coming here will be coming not simply to lecture. They will be coming primarily for Bhagavan's *darshan* and we are going to ask them to speak too. That is all."

14-8-46

This morning Mrs. Taleyarkhan told Bhagavan, "Bhagavan, I have got a letter from Shanta (the Maharani of Baroda). Bhagavan has performed a miracle and she is writing about it. It seems she went out in a car and on the way the car broke down and the driver could do nothing about it. So, it seems, he took the Rani's permission and went to phone for another car. Meanwhile, it seems a striking-looking and mild *sadhu* suddenly appeared on the scene and touched the car and said, 'You can go on now.' The driver returned and when he started the engine, the car moved on without any trouble. The Rani thinks it was all Bhagavan's grace. She is writing, expressing regret for her inability to be present at the Jubilee." So saying Mrs. T. showed the letter and Bhagavan perused it. He came across "Roman Emperor" in the letter and asked, "Who is the Roman Emperor?" I told Bhagavan that by that they mean our *Sarvadhikari*, and Mrs. T. added "Yes. We call him that".

Soon afterwards, as directed by Bhagavan, I read out a long letter from a devotee of Calcutta who was here two or three years ago for five or six days, it seems. In that letter he relates how, after he thought that Bhagavan was not showing him any grace, suddenly on the fifth day of his stay, he got, by no effort of his own, experience of a state in which consciousness of body, world and all, totally left him and he was pure consciousness and nothing else.

Afternoon

The *Sarvadhikari*, Mr. T.K.D., and Ranganatha Iyer have all fixed up a programme for the speeches and the music performance on 1-9-46, and they sent me to Bhagavan with it for getting his approval for the same. He declined to give any opinion and said, "Let them fix it up as they like. Don't ask me anything about it." When I pleaded for his approval, he remarked, "Why should they consult me about this now? Did they consult me before deciding to have these speeches and music, that they should consult me now about the time?" Thereupon I said, "True, at Madras, on the suggestion of Mr. Swaminathan and others, they had decided on having all these things. But even now, if Bhagavan does not like all this, we can stop it, what is there?" Thereupon he relented and said, "You may tell them I have no objection. But I must be left off at my usual hours." I at once replied, "Of course, that will be done" and we so ordered the programme that Bhagavan could rise at 4-45 p.m. as usual, after all the speeches, and could come back about 5-00 p.m. to start the music by Musiri.

In the evening, Muruganar brought a few verses composed by him at our request for the Golden Jubilee. Bhagavan at once went through them and made one or two corrections and kept them aside saying, "Tomorrow we shall do the rest, deciding what heading we shall give them."

17-8-46

This morning, a number of Gujerati visitors arrived here, evidently returning from Pondicherry, after *darshan* there on the 15th. One of them asked Bhagavan, "What is meant by Self-realisation? Materialists say there is no such thing as God or Self." Bhagavan said, "Never mind what the materialists or others say; and don't bother about Self or God. Do *you* exist or not? What is your idea of yourself? What do you mean by 'I'?" The visitor said he did not understand by 'I' his body, but something within his body. Thereupon, Bhagavan continued, "You concede 'I' is not the body but something within it. See then from whence the 'I' arises within the body. See whether it arises and disappears, or is always present. You will admit there is an 'I' which emerges as soon as you wake up, sees the body, the world and all else, and ceases to exist when you sleep; and that there is another 'I' which exists apart from the body, independently of it, and which alone is with you when the body and the world do not exist for you, as for instance in sleep. Then ask yourself if you are not the same 'I' during sleep and during the other states. Are there two 'I's? You are the same one person always. Now, which can be real, the 'I' which comes and goes, or the 'I' which always abides? Then you will know that you are the Self. This is called Self-realisation. Self-realisation is not however a state which is foreign to you, which is far from you, and which has to be reached by you. You are always in that state. You forget it, and identify yourself with the mind and its creation. To cease to identify yourself with the mind is all that is required. We have so long identified ourselves with the not-Self that we find it difficult to regard ourselves as the Self. Giving up this identification with the not-Self is all that is meant by Self-realisation. How to realise, *i.e.*, make real, the Self? We have realised, *i.e.*, regarded as real, what is unreal, the not-Self. To give up such false realisation is Self-realisation."

In the evening, after *parayana*, a visitor asked Bhagavan, "How to control the wandering mind?" He prefaced the question with the remark, "I want to ask Bhagavan a question which is troubling me." Bhagavan replied, after laughing, "This is nothing peculiar to you. This is the question which is always asked by everybody and which is dealt with in all the books like the *Gita*. What way is there, except to draw in the mind as often as it strays or goes outward, and to fix it in the Self, as the *Gita* advises? Of course, it won't be easy to do it. It will come only with practice or *sadhana*." The visitor said, "The mind goes after only what it desires and won't get fixed on the object we set before it." Bhagavan said, "Everybody will go after only what gives happiness to him. Thinking that happiness comes from some object or other, you go after it. See from whence all happiness, including the happiness you regard as coming from sense objects, really comes. You will understand all happiness comes only from the Self, and then you will always abide in the Self."

21-8-46 Afternoon

A visitor from Bengal asked Bhagavan, "Shankara says we are all free, not bound, and that we shall all go back to God from whom we have come as sparks from fire. Then, why should we not commit all sorts of sins?"

Bhagavan: It is true we are not bound, *i.e.*, the real Self has no bondage. It is true you will eventually go back to your source. But meanwhile, if you commit sins, as you call them, you have to face the consequences of such sins. You cannot escape their consequences. If a man beats you, then, can you say, 'I am free, I am not bound by these beatings and I don't feel any pain. Let him beat on?' If you can feel like that, you can go on doing what you like. What is the use of merely saying with your lips 'I am free?'

The visitor also asked, "The books mention several methods for Self-realisation. Which is the easiest and best?"

Bhagavan: Several methods are mentioned to suit several minds. They are all good. You can choose whatever method appeals to you best.

Later, Lakshmi (Sambasiva Rao's sister) read before Bhagavan a few Telugu songs composed by her for Bhagavan's Golden Jubilee. Bhagavan came here fifty years ago on *Navami tithi* following *Gokulashtami* and, as this is *Navami*, the Golden Jubilee of his arrival according to *tithi* will be today, and hence she thought her songs could most appropriately be sung today. She began, however, reading in such a low key that after a few minutes Bhagavan asked her, "Are you able to hear it yourself?" Somebody suggested Nagamma might read the verses instead and so N. read them out aloud.

This morning, Mr. Somasundaram Pillai brought his wife's verses and mine, which he got printed at Conjeevaram and showed to Bhagavan a copy of each set. Bhagavan perused them and said, "The paper is thick and good." Then I explained, "These are the copies to be laid at Bhagavan's feet. The other copies are printed on slightly inferior paper."

On 23-8-46 morning I left for Madras to attend the marriage of my daughter's son on the 28th inst. and returned on the 30th evening.

30-8-46

On the 30th evening, when I arrived, the Asramam was already crowded with devotees who had come from various parts to attend the Jubilee on 1st September. The new (thatched) shed, built contiguous with Bhagavan's hall on its northern side, had been already completed with the floor also fully cemented, and the old ugly parapet wall of the well had been removed and in its place a fine looking parapet wall erected. The steps leading from the eastern verandah of Bhagavan's hall to the quadrangle and the new shed on the north have been considerably improved and beautified. Further, a temporary shed, contiguous with the new northern shed, has also been put up to provide sitting accommodation to the crowds that are expected on the 1st. I found Bhagavan seated at the western end of the new shed, on a stone platform. Mr. C. Madhavaraya Mudaliar (my brother-in-law) and myself prostrated ourselves. Bhagavan asked, "You have just come? How did you come; and who else?" I replied, "I came by train up to Katpadi, arriving there about 12 noon. From thence I went to Vellore and took the bus and have arrived here just now. There was no difficulty at all about travelling. I and my brother-in-law alone have come now. But Kotiswaran and his wife will come tomorrow evening."

31-8-46 Morning

An address in Malayalam, composed by Narain Pisharoti (our compounder) was read out by him. Then an address in Tamil composed by Uma (*i.e.*, Mrs. Somasundaram Pillai) was read out by her husband.

Most of the morning, the blind Brahmin girl, Janaki Ammal of Conjeevaram, entertained Bhagavan with her music on the Veena.

Afternoon

Mr. Siva Mohan Lal of Hyderabad read out an address in Hindi. We asked him to translate the same into English for the benefit of those who did not know Hindi. But as he could not easily translate it extempore, we asked him to write out the translation and to read the same before Bhagavan later. Then Ramachandra Rao began to read out an address in Canarese. But soon he began delivering a speech with the writing in his hand only as notes for his speech. Bhagavan also remarked, "He is not simply reading an address. With the address in his hand, he is firing away as he pleases (கையிலே Notes வச்சுண்டு அவர் பாட்டுக்கு அடிக்கிறார்)."

He has also composed two songs in Canarese and he finished by saying that those songs would be sung by Chandramma.

Somasundaram Pillai next read out a message from one Angayarkkanni in Tamil. Next Chandramma read out the Canarese songs of R. Rao.

Finally Balaram read out the Telugu message sent by G.V.Subbaramayya, which was short and sweet. It said in effect, "May the Golden Jubilee of the day which joined Ramana to Arunachala — (that Ramana who is always shedding compassion and grace) — be a grand success!"

1-9-46

This is the Golden Jubilee of Bhagavan's arrival at Tiruvannamalai. I went to the hall about 5-30 a.m. hoping to see Bhagavan there, to fall at his feet, and to offer some fruits and two bath towels. But I found that today the *parayana* was started about 4 a.m. and closed at 5 a.m. and that Bhagavan went to the bathroom as early as 5 a.m.

After Bhagavan had his breakfast and returned from his stroll, a number of married women (*sumangalis*) headed by Uma came from the Temple in a procession, doing *bhajan* and carrying a milk-pot, and Uma and her daughter sang a Tamil song and offered milk to Bhagavan. He took a spoon of the milk and the rest was distributed among the devotees. Then I read out Colombo Ramachandra's *Ramanashtakam*, in Tamil, and also my five stanzas composed for the Jubilee. Then Uma read out her *Muthumalai* composed for the occasion. Printed copies of all the three compositions were then distributed to the devotees. Printed copies of tributes by Turiyananda in Tamil, K.Vaidyanatha Aiyar of Vellore in English verse, T.K. Sundaresa Iyer in Tamil verse, and K.R. Seshagiri Aiyar in English were also read out and distributed. One Mr. Bhatt also read out his Canarese songs. Then a gentleman introduced by Dr. T.N.K. gave a performance on *gottu vadyam*. Mr. Chellam Iyer, of *Kalaimagal* office, read out Muruganar's poems composed for the occasion, including one which he composed at the moment.

After lunch Bhagavan would not allow himself even his usual rest, but insisted on being available for devotees who had come from far and near and so, soon after his return from the after-lunch stroll, various addresses in different languages were read out. One of them was from the Hindi Prachar Sabha. Another was Dr. Siva Rao's tribute in English which was read out and also translated into Tamil by Mr. T.K.D. Iyer. Mr. Siva Mohan Lal also read out the English translation of the Hindi address he read to Bhagavan yesterday. Dr. Siva Rao's address in effect said, "I have been trying my humble best to cure Bhagavan of various bodily ailments of his. But all my efforts have proved vain, except to give some temporary relief. I believe this is due to my ego having presumed that it can cure Bhagavan. All people today are offering various things to Bhagavan — fruits, flowers, clothes, books, etc. I have decided to offer my ego. I place it at Bhagavan's feet and beg him to accept it."

About 2-30 p.m., the programme already planned and published for the Jubilee was begun with Mr. Justice Kuppuswamy Aiyer as President. He made a few introductory remarks in English. Then Mr. T.K.D. read out Sir S. Radhakrishnan's article, intended for inclusion in the *Souvenir* Volume, but which, though posted in Calcutta on 7th August, was received here only on the 30th. Then the following spoke: Swami Rajeswarananda and Prof. T.M.P. Mahadevan of the Madras University, in English,

Justice Chandrasekara Iyer in Telugu, Chellam Iyer of *Kalaimagal* office and Omandur Ramaswami Reddiar in Tamil, Mr. S.R. Venkatarama Sastri (of Vivekananda College) in Sanskrit, and Mr. Airavatam Aiyer, in Malayalam. After the speeches, Viswanatha Sastri recited a few Sanskrit songs, and Kunjuswami a few Tamil songs of Bhagavan and of one Venkatarama Iyer (author of *Ramana Stuti Panchakam*). Bhagavan then rose at 4-45 p.m. as usual. After he returned about 5 p.m., Mr. Annamalai Pillai, the local Congress leader, made a speech in Tamil, on behalf of the citizens of Tiruvannamalai, expressing joy and gratitude on Bhagavan's completing fifty years' stay here. Then Musiri Subramania Iyer gave a very moving and devotional musical performance till about 6-45. For the speeches and music excellent loudspeaker arrangements had been made by the local Municipal Chairman and it was a great convenience for the crowds who had gathered. Finally *Veda parayana* brought the day's function to a close.

2-9-46

Early in the morning, old Mr. Ranganatha Iyer told Bhagavan, "We have had a very good shower of rain last night. It is fortunate that it did not interfere with our celebrations yesterday, but came on only in the night after everything was over." Bhagavan said, "I remember the same thing happened on the night of 1-9-1896, when I arrived here. It seems they had no rains for a long time then. But on that night there was a heavy downpour. I was then staying at the *mantapam* in front of the Big Temple. Only that morning for the first time I had discarded all my clothes, except a cod-piece and, on account of the rains beating in, and the cold winds blowing about, I found the cold unbearable, and so I ran from there and took shelter on the pial of a house nearby. About midnight some inmates of the house came out opening the street door and I ran into the Big Temple. For some days after that too, it rained!"

After Bhagavan's morning stroll, various articles about Bhagavan were read out in the hall, two from the *Sunday Times*, one from *Free India* and one from *Bombay Samachar* (in Gujerati). In the afternoon Nagamma read out her Telugu poem on *Ramana Swarna Utsava Vaibhavam*. Only today Bhagavan had time to look at the *Souvenir* Volume, which was presented to him on the Jubilee Day. He had been given a volume bound in silk and with gold-washed front and back pages. The deluxe edition had a gold-washed front page. The library in the hall had been given one ordinary copy and one deluxe edition. The *Sarvadhikari* came and saw these, as also a specially bound volume of V. Sastri's Sanskrit *Life of Bhagavan* and instructed T.S.R. that the specially bound volumes of the *Souvenir* and V. Sastri's book should not be given to anybody. After *Sarvadhikari* left, Bhagavan asked T.S.R., laughing, "He has told you these volumes should not be given to anybody. May I read them?" T.S.R. said, "He only meant I should not give these to anybody except Bhagavan."

In the evening Mr. Desai read out an English translation of Ganga Ben Patel's Gujerati article in the *Bombay Samachar*. There was a reference in the article to the cow Lakshmi; and Rani Mazumdar who was listening to the article from the verandah close to the eastern window of the hall asked me to put the following question to Bhagavan and get his reply.

Question: It is said that the old lady Keerai Patti was born as Lakshmi. How can one, who had the unique good fortune of serving Bhagavan well and lovingly, have to be born again at all, and even if she had to be born, how could she be born as a cow? Is it not said in all our books that birth as a human being is the best birth one can have?

Bhagavan: I never said Keerai Patti had been born as a cow.

I said, "I have already told Rani so. But she says, 'It has been said and also written down in so many books and articles and Bhagavan has not denied it. So we can take it as the truth'." I added, "But she puts the question on the assumption that the cow is the old woman reborn, whether Bhagavan has said so or not, and she desires an answer." Thereupon Bhagavan said, "It is not true that birth as a man is necessarily the highest, and that one must attain realisation only from being a man. Even an animal can attain Self-realisation."

In the conversation that followed on this, Bhagavan said, "Even as a calf only some days old, Lakshmi behaved in an extraordinary way. She would daily come to me and place her head at my feet. On the day the foundation was laid for the *goshala* (cow-shed), she was so jubilant and came and took me for the function. Again on the day of *grahapravesam* she came straight to me at the time appointed and took me. In so many ways and on so many occasions, she behaved in such a sensible and extremely intelligent way that one cannot but regard it as an extraordinary cow. What are we to say about it?"

This night Mr. Framji Dorabji, ably helped by Mrs. Taleyarkhan, showed Bhagavan the film 'Nandanar' in Tamil in our dining hall.

3-9-46 Afternoon

Nagamma read out Nellore Narasinga Rao's poem on Bhagavan for the Jubilee. Bhagavan suggested that the *Souvenir* be read out, adding, "I don't know what it contains. I have not looked into the articles so far." Thereupon I read out a few pages. In the night the film 'Tukaram' in Marathi was shown to Bhagavan.

4-9-46 Morning

About 10 a.m. I continued reading the *Souvenir*. In the afternoon again, I read out the Souvenir and then Viswanath and also Balaram.

This night another film, 'Bhartruhari' in Hindi, was shown to Bhagavan.

5-9-46

Reading out the *Souvenir* was continued by me, V. and B. in the afternoon.

The whole day Bhagavan was trying to find out the true history of King Bhartruhari and looked into a number of books, giving various versions of the famous King's life. The first account Bhagavan looked into was Banky Bihari's introduction to his English translation of Bhartruhari's poems. Finally Bhagavan said, "No version agrees with another, and there are four or five of them. But all agree that the immortality-yielding object was given by the King to his queen and by the queen to someone else and that the King renounced all because of his sudden discovery that his queen was not true to him. In that, last night's film also did not err from the original."

6 to 9-9-46

Reading of the *Souvenir* was continued and the same ended on the last date.

11-9-46

It seems today Rangaswami (an attendant) was trying to coax Bhagavan into eating an orange about noon and, when he told Bhagavan, "These oranges and other fruits are all brought in by devotees only so that Bhagavan may use them. So, why should not Bhagavan use them?" It seems Bhagavan replied, "Why should you think that I eat only when I eat with this mouth? I eat through a thousand mouths." R. told me of this.

Today Mr. T.P. Ramachandra Aiyer arrived from Madras. Bhagavan said on seeing him, "What, you have gone down very much. You look a different man." T.P.R. said, "My foot became swollen. The doctors couldn't diagnose it properly; besides, I have had a lot of strain (அலைச்சல்)." Bhagavan is criticised by some as being so impersonal and abstracted that he cannot appeal to most people. I record this instance to refute such criticism. That one remark of Bhagavan must have meant so much to T.P.R. Many others, including myself, have had such proofs of love and attention from Bhagavan. This reminds me that just a few days ago, S. Doraiswamy Iyer came here one afternoon with four or five of his friends, and Bhagavan remarked as soon as S.D. entered the hall, "Very unexpected", and thereupon S.D. explained, "These friends suddenly proposed about 10 a.m. today that we should come here, have *darshan* of Bhagavan, visit the temple and go back, and that is how I came."

12-9-46

Casually going through T.P.R.'s notebook I came across an entry there — *Mithya=Jagat; Brahma bhavam=Satyam.*

As I remembered Bhagavan occasionally saying *mithya* means *satyam*, but did not quite grasp its significance, I asked Bhagavan about it. He said, "Yes. I say that now and then. What do you mean by real or *satyam*? Which do you call real?" I answered, "According to Vedanta, that which is permanent and unchanging, that alone is real. That of course is the definition of Reality." Then, Bhagavan said, "These names and forms which constitute the world always change and perish. Hence they are called *mithya*. To limit the Self and regard it as these names and form is *mithya*. To regard all as Self is the Reality. The *Advaitin* says *jagat* is *mithya*, but he also says 'All this is Brahman'. So it is clear that what he condemns is regarding the world as such to be real, not regarding the world as Brahman. He who sees the Self, sees only the Self in the world also. To the *jnani* it is immaterial whether the world appears or not. Whether it appears or not, his attention is always on the Self. It is like the letters and the paper on which the letters are printed.

You are wholly engrossed with the letters and have no attention left for the paper. But the *jnani* thinks only of the paper as the real substratum, whether the letters appear on it or not."

13-9-46

Today, one Mrs. Barwell (whose husband, it is said, is a barrister now staying at Almora), accompanied by the principal of the Women's Christian College at Madras, visited the Asramam. The former comes introduced by Miss Merston and has already written to the Asramam for accommodation. The Asramam has not been able to find accommodation for her. But today, Mr. McIver has promised to find accommodation for her in his compound and so she is planning to go and come back here with her things in a week's time. Her friend also goes back with her and intends to spend the forthcoming *dasara* holidays here with some of her students. This lady (the principal) seems to have already met some well-known disciples of Bhagavan, such as Grant Duff.

14-9-46

This morning Mr. Naganariya came and prostrated himself before Bhagavan, placing a manuscript and some fruits at his feet. Bhagavan asked him when he came, and he replied, "I came last night itself." Then Bhagavan looked into the Ms., for a few minutes and returned it. It is *Trisulapura Mahatmyam* in Telugu verse.

Afternoon

When I went into the hall, Bhagavan was reading an article in the Tamil paper *Hindusthan* by K.R.R. Sastri, who has, it seems, just returned from a trip to England and America. In the article, he mentions he visited Ramana Asramam before he made this foreign tour. Then Bhagavan said, "I believe he has sent some poem in Tamil or English for the Jubilee." I replied that I had seen the poem and that it was in English. But I was not sure whether I read the thing in the *Souvenir* Volume or elsewhere. Not finding it in its contents, I took up the file of cuttings, etc., relating to the Jubilee and as I opened it, it opened, strange to say, exactly at the page where a typed copy of this poem of K.R.R. was found pasted. I showed the same to Bhagavan, and he said, "That is the poem I meant."

Nagamma read out the dedication to *Trisulapura Mahatmyam* of Naganariya, saying, "I find this dedication is a Jubilee tribute to Bhagavan." At the head of each chapter too, N. had a stanza in praise of Bhagavan. So we asked her to read those stanzas also. As the dedication seemed good, I requested G. Subba Rao to give us a free translation in English and he said he would write down one.

My brother has written in a letter to me that Krishna and Nammalvar have said that God will come to us in whatever form we worship Him; I wrote to my brother in my reply, "A *jnani* is the highest manifestation of God on earth, next perhaps only to an *avatar*." In connection with this sentence, I wanted to have my doubt cleared about the relative position of a *jnani* and an *avatar*. Then Bhagavan was pleased to tell me that, according to the books, the *jnani* was higher than the *avatar*. But when I corrected my letter accordingly, he said, "Why do you correct it? Let it go as it is."

A little later, R. Narayana Iyer came and Bhagavan asked him, "You have come by the 3 p.m. train, have you?" He said, "Yes", and added, "The present timings are convenient for me. On Saturday, I can arrive here earlier, and on Mondays I can leave here later than under the old timings."

Then somebody said, "Kalyanarama Aiyer is also now in Tirukoilur" and I asked about his exact relationship to the late Echamma. I was told he was her brother's son. In this connection, his sister, Chellammal, brought up by Echamma was mentioned, and Mr. Viswanath said, "It was for her that Bhagavan wrote the three songs in Tamil on *sat sang*". Then I said, "I thought it was for Rajammal that Bhagavan wrote them." Then Bhagavan related, "One day I was going out from Skandasramam. In those days Chellamma, Rajamma and others used to go to me on Saturdays and Sundays when they had no school. They would go by themselves to me, whether they had any escort or not. That day I found Chellammal had some bit of a journal or newspaper in her hand and was getting by heart a song from *Yoga Vasishtam* in praise of the benefits of *sat sang:*

அறக்குறைவை நிறைவாக்குஞ் சம்பத்தாக்கு
    மாபத்தைச் சுபமாக்கு மசுபந் தன்னைச்
சிறக்குமுயர்ந் தவர்கூட்ட மெனுங் கங்கைச்
    சீதநீ ராடினர்க்குச் செந்தீ வேள்வி
யிறக்கரிய தவந்தானந் தீர்த்தம் வேண்டா
    மிடர்பந்த மறுத்தெவர்க்கு மினியோராகிப்
பிறப்பெனும்வே லைப்புணையா முணர்வு சான்ற
    பெரியோரை யெவ்வகையும் பேணல்வேண்டும்

(The imperfect will become perfect, danger good luck, the inauspicious auspicious, by association with holy men. For those who have bathed in the Ganges of fellowship with such realized souls, *homa* (offering, oblations in fire), *yagna*, penance, alms-giving, bathing in sacred rivers, are all unnecessary. Seek, therefore, by all means the company of the good and wise, which is a boat to carry one across the ocean of birth and death).

"When I found the girl so keen on the matter I composed those three songs on *sat sang* which are a translation of the Sanskrit songs, with which by that time I had become quite familiar, because they had been so often recited before me by various devotees who visited me. At that time, I did not know that any of those Sanskrit songs had been translated by anybody in Tamil. But some years afterwards, when Rajammal delivered a lecture on *sat sang* she quoted a Tamil stanza which was a Tamil translation of one of those three songs." Then I said, "I also remember that lecture of hers. It was at Villupuram. They sent me a copy of that lecture."

Bhagavan related how Echamma, after she lost her own daughter, brought up her brother's daughter, this Chellammal, and added, "Chellammal used often to go to me as a school girl. Afterwards too, she always thought of me. In every letter of hers, she would refer to me both in the beginning and the end. She died soon after she gave birth to Ramanan, the boy who is now in Bombay. They brought the boy here, (it was soon after we came here and we had only a small thatched room in which the tomb was located and I was also staying). On seeing the babe, I could not help thinking of its mother and I wept for her." (Bhagavan was moved even now after several years when recounting the event to me).

In the evening, after *parayana*, Balaram read out an article in English in the *Sunday Leader* of Allahabad, on Bhagavan and his teachings.

15-9-46

This afternoon, Nagamma read out an account in Telugu of all that took place on the Jubilee Day. I found from what Bhagavan and T.S.R. said that, in addition to what I have noted on the first of September, two other addresses were also read, one from the Arya Vaisya Samajam and another from the firm of Messrs. Munuswami Chetti & Brothers, and that at about 11 a.m. that day, the priests from the Big Temple came with Arunachaleswarar's *prasad* to Bhagavan. Later, Nagamma also read out a portion of Naganariya's Ms. as desired by the author.

17-9-46

This night about 9-15 p.m., T.S.R.'s child Ramana was bitten by something near the well in their compound. After a few minutes, the child was suffering very much, vomiting and perspiring profusely. They consulted Dr. Siva Rao living next door and he gave something which he said was a general antidote for all poisons. In a few minutes he felt the child's pulse and advised them it would be better to take the child to Bhagavan. They accordingly brought the child and when they entered the Asramam compound the child was in a state almost of collapse, the body having become chill and the breath almost ceasing. They entered the hall, and told Bhagavan, and he touched the child, passing his hand all over the child's body as if soothing the child, and said, "It is nothing. He will be all right." It was only after that, the parents had some hope that the child would survive. When they came out of the hall, they came across our Ramaswami Pillai, and he showed them another visitor who had come to the Asramam only this afternoon, who was an expert in saving people from snake-bites, etc. and pronounced some *mantras* on the child and declared the poison had been got rid of by his *mantras*. The child recovered gradually, and the parents have told me that it was saved only through Bhagavan's grace. Another thing which may also be mentioned here is that the child himself, as soon as he felt pain, cried out, "Let us go to Bhagavan. The pain will go if we go there", though on some occasions he would even refuse to be taken to Bhagavan when the parents proposed to take him there.

This evening at about 6 p.m. Mr. Colombo Ramachandra's letter to Bhagavan with seven copies of his *Ashtakam* was received and Bhagavan gave one to me and one to Somasundaram Pillai as desired by R. in his letter. Bhagavan found the order of the stanzas was not as printed under Bhagavan's directions here. Bhagavan said, "He had stuck to his order". Thereupon I said, "These leaflets must have been printed before R. received our leaflet and the letter accompanying it."

18-9-46

This morning, when I left my room about 9-30 a.m., for the hall, it struck me I might read out the *Ashtakam* of Colombo Ramachandra, of which Bhagavan gave me a copy last evening. As I went and prostrated myself before Bhagavan, he was telling T.S.R. with the *Ashtakam* in his hand, "Should we not have it read out here, as it arrived only last evening?" and. T.S.R. said, "Here Mr. Mudaliar has also come. We will ask him to read it out." Accordingly I read out the same, telling Bhagavan, "Somehow, I too thought of reading this today here and have brought the leaflet with me. Here it is." I had read out the *Ashtakam* before Bhagavan even as it was being composed in parts, and once after all the eight were finished during Ramachandra's illness here; and again I had read it out on Jubilee Day. But it is strange that I should have thought of doing the same today also and that Bhagavan too should have thought of it at the same time.

20-9-46

This afternoon, from a book that Anandammal brought, Bhagavan was able to find out the story of how Goraknath killed his Master Maschendra's child, etc., which Bhagavan was trying to trace on the 5th instant after having seen the film "Bhartruhari" the previous night. In this story it is said that Chandu Nath wanted to write to Goraknath, but not being sure how to address him, in a patronising manner as a superior, or as a junior writing to a senior, finally sent a blank piece of paper. In this connection, Bhagavan said, "This reminds me of an incident in my boyhood. I was quite young and did not know much about letter-writing and I wrote to my aunt's son (father's sister's son) *aneka asirvadam* (*i.e.*, many blessings, in the manner of an elder giving his blessings). When he came, he ridiculed me for having sent blessings to him (who was about 10 years older than myself). But I did not know then who should bless whom. I only knew that whenever my father wrote to him, he used to write 'My blessings to Ramu', and so I thought that was the way a letter ought to be written. That to some, blessings had to be given and to others salutations — I did not know then."

Mr. Daniel Thomas, minister, visited Bhagavan today about 4 p.m. He stayed in Bhagavan's presence for about 15 minutes and then left. He was presiding over a function in the town in connection with the Golden Jubilee of this Municipality. I was in Tinnevelly for one and a half years in 1910 to 1912, when this gentleman also joined the bar. He put no questions to Bhagavan. The press representative Mr. Tilak was here and apparently took a snap of the minister.

21-9-46

This morning, as directed by Bhagavan, a letter received by me from K. Ramachandra of Colombo and another received by Uma were read out in the hall. The letters described how the Jubilee was celebrated in Mr. Ramachandra's house with about 250 devotees (of different castes), each one of whom placed flowers at Bhagavan's feet and worshipped him, and how all left with the feeling that Bhagavan was present in their midst that day. The letter to Uma quoted two stanzas from *Subrahmanya Bhujangam* as very aptly describing Bhagavan and also said that R.'s *Ashtakam* was really composed by Bhagavan who inspired the lines. Otherwise R. cannot explain why, when the children sing the *Ashtakam* at prayer time, he goes into ecstasy and forgets himself.

In the afternoon, Nagamma read out her revised account of the Jubilee celebrations. It is very well written and full of *bhakti rasa*. It will soon appear in print. When R.'s letter was read out and the two stanzas therein from *Subrahmanya Bhujangam* were quoted, Bhagavan said that it was Mr. K.V.R. Iyer (deceased brother of our Ramanatha Iyer) who first published from here the above work, though subsequently other editions and some translations in Tamil also have come out.

One Mr. V.P. Sarathi from Masulipatnam had sent a volume of typed poems in English entitled *Nivedana* to Bhagavan. It seems he offered them at Bhagavan's feet in celebration, in his house, on Bhagavan's Jubilee on 1-9-46. They were received at the Asramam recently and T.P.R. read the poems out in the hall. The poems were good and well worth hearing.

22-9-46

Today about 4 p.m. the Minister, Mrs. Rukmini Lakshmipati and Mr. Sivashanmugam (Speaker of the Legislative Assembly) visited the Asramam. They were escorted by local Congress leader Mr. Annamalai Pillai and the Deputy Collector, Mr. Vaidyanatha Aiyar. They sat in the hall for some time and then left.

1-10-46

Dilip Kumar Roy of Aurobindo's Ashram came here last night, and this morning he sang a few songs before Bhagavan. Later when Bhagavan was perusing *The New Times* of today, he read out to us that at Mount Abu, two serpents fought each other, that one vanquished the other which became unconscious and at that stage a boy who came across the scene did some first aid to the defeated serpent and put a cold bandage over it, that the injured serpent slowly revived, that seeing all this, the victor serpent was enraged and bit the boy, that the vanquished snake, which had by now recovered and revived under the boy's treatment, ran to the boy, sucked out the other serpent's poison and saved the boy. When Bhagavan read all this out to us, I said, "It looks incredible." Mrs. T. to whom T.P.R. recounted the story also remarked, "Is this a story or what?" Then Dilip asked Bhagavan whether all this was possible. Bhagavan said, "Why not? Quite possible." Roy even asked, "How could the vanquished snake know and do all this?" Bhagavan said, "Why? It was watching what the boy did to it, what the other snake did to the boy and so it ran and sucked out the poison. Snakes see and observe and can do such things. Many stories like this have been told of serpents."

2-10-46

This morning again Dilip sang a few songs before Bhagavan.

4-10-46

In the afternoon Nagamma asked that a copy of her letter to her brother, describing the first visit to Bhagavan of Princess Prabhavati with her husband after their marriage might be shown to Madhavi Amma (K.K. Nambiar's sister) now here. Thereupon, Bhagavan asked, "What is that letter? Have I heard it?" Nagamma said, "No". I said, "Then, why not read it now? We are all here (I meant Professors G.V. Subbaramayya, D.S. Sarma, K. Swaminathan) and we can all hear it." Thereupon she read out the letter. Later Bhagavan asked G.V.S. if he had seen Nagamma's song and Chinta Dikshitulu's *Nivedana* which were printed about Jubilee time. He said 'No' and thereupon Bhagavan asked T.S.R. to show him the above two pamphlets. He also asked T.S.R. to show G.V.S. the Telugu rendering of Bhagavan's four songs in connection with his mother's serious fever, made by Mr. Narasinga Rao of Nellore. G.V.S. saw the same and said, "They have not so far been translated into Telugu." In explaining the first of these Tamil songs, Bhagavan told us that in the Tamil அலையாய் வருபிறவி அத்தனையுமாற்ற மலையாய் etc., we can have either மாற்ற or ஆற்ற as we like when splitting the *sandhi*. If we take it as மாற்ற, it would mean "To change the countless waves of births and deaths, Arunachala rises as a mountain in the middle of the waves". If we take it as ஆற்ற, it would mean "To cure or heal the disease of countless births, the Arunachala Hill has risen as a medicine."

In the evening after *parayana*, Dilip again sang a few songs from Ganapati Sastri's *Forty Verses on Bhagavan*. About seven, he stopped singing. Mrs. T. told Bhagavan, "He has composed three songs on Bhagavan's smile. They are very good," and requested D. to sing them. But he excused himself, saying, "They are in Bengali". A few minutes later, I went and told him, "We generally have Tamil *parayana* between seven and seven-thirty. Today, we have cancelled that item and made that interval available for your songs. So, unless you find it inconvenient for you to sing any more, please sing one or two songs more." D. said "Is that so?" and then gave us two more songs, one on Devi and one on Siva. He told Bhagavan he was leaving the next morning and that he had great peace during his stay here.

This evening, D.S. Sarma, asked Bhagavan: "In Western mysticism three definite stages are often spoken of — *viz.*, Purgation, illumination and union. Was there any such stage as purgation — corresponding to what we call *sadhana* — in Bhagavan's life?" Bhagavan replied, "I have never done any *sadhana*. I did not even know what *sadhana* was. Only long afterwards I came to know what *sadhana* was and how many different kinds of it there were. It is only if there was any object or anything different from me that I could think of it. Only if there was a goal to attain, I should have made *sadhana* to attain that goal. There was nothing which I wanted to obtain. I am now sitting with my eyes open. I was then sitting with my eyes closed. That was all the difference. I was not doing any *sadhana* even then. As I sat with my eyes closed, people said I was in *samadhi*. As I was not talking, they said I was in *mauna*. The fact is, I did nothing. Some Higher Power took hold of me and I was entirely in Its hand." Bhagavan further added, "The books no doubt speak of *sravana, manana, nididhyasana, samadhi* and *sakshatkara*. We are always *sakshat* and what is there for one to attain *karam* of that? We call this world *sakshat* or *pratyaksha*. What is changing, what appears and disappears, what is not *sakshat*, we regard as *sakshat*. We are always and nothing can be more directly present *pratyaksha* than we, and about that we say we have to attain *sakshatkaram* after all these *sadhanas*. Nothing can be more strange than this. The Self is not attained by doing anything, but remaining still and being as we are."

5-10-46

This morning a person came and prostrated himself before Bhagavan at the dining hall. He almost touched him, and as I was wondering who it could be, the person announced himself to Bhagavan as Vasu and Bhagavan said, "Is it you? If you had not said it, I should never have recognised you. You have gone down so much." The visitor replied, "I find I must say the same about Bhagavan." To this Bhagavan said, "Why, what is the matter with me? Probably because you are reduced, your eyesight has also become reduced and I appear reduced to you!" Later, in the hall, Bhagavan introduced this gentleman to all present and said, "This is the Vasu who caught hold of me when returning from an oil bath one hot day to Skandasramam and I had that experience of what seemed like utter collapse with even the heartbeat stopping." Then Vasudeva Sastri said, "I was then too young. I did not even know that it was death. But because Palaniswami started crying, I thought it was death and I caught hold of Bhagavan and I was trembling with grief." Bhagavan said here, "I could even in that state clearly see his trembling and emotion." V. added that, after Bhagavan recovered, he told V. and Palani, "What? You thought I died? Did you believe I would die even without telling you?"

Bhagavan also said, "We were in Virupakshi Cave and when a tiger came that way one night, this is the person who hastily ran into the cave leaving us in the verandah, shut the door and then cried to the tiger, 'Come on now. What can you do?'" V. said, "Once Bhagavan and I went round the Hill during the Skandasramam days. When we reached near Easanya Mutt about

8-30 a.m., Bhagavan sat on a rock and said with tears in his eyes he would never again come to the Asramam and would go where he pleased and live in the forests or caves away from all men. I would not leave him and he would not come. It became very late. We went there about 8 or 8-30 a.m. and even when it became 1 p.m. we were still in this deadlock. Bhagavan asked me to go into the town and eat my food and then come back if I wanted. But I was afraid that if I went Bhagavan would go away somewhere. Meanwhile, the Swami of Easanya Mutt very unexpectedly came that way. Ordinarily it could not be expected he would have come there at that time at all. But strange to say, he came that way and he persuaded Bhagavan to go with him to Easanya Mutt. I left Bhagavan there and ran up to the town for my food and came back swiftly, fearing that Bhagavan might have left. But I found him there and we both came to Skandasramam afterwards."

When this was mentioned, Bhagavan said, "Another time too I wanted to run away from all this crowd and live somewhere unknown, freely as I liked. That was when I was in Virupakshi Cave. I felt my being there was an inconvenience and hardship to Jadaswami and some other swamis there. But on that occasion my plans were frustrated by Yogananda Swami. I tried to be free on a third occasion also. That was after mother's passing away. I did not want to have even an Asramam like Skandasramam and the people that were coming there then. But the result has been this Asramam and all the crowd here. Thus all my three attempts failed."

In another connection also Bhagavan mentioned this Vasudeva Sastri today. Mr. G.V.S. read out a Telugu stanza composed by him on celebration of birthdays (yesterday was G.V.S.'s birthday, it seems). When this was read out, Bhagavan said, "It is this Vasu and others that wanted to celebrate my birthday first in 1912. I was quite opposed to it. But Vasu pleaded with me: 'It is for us and so Bhagavan should not object' and they celebrated it that year for the first time."

In the afternoon, Sundaresa Iyer's grandson (about a month old) was brought by Mr. Narayanaswami Aiyar into the hall to Bhagavan, his daughter following behind. Bhagavan took the child into his hands, when it was offered by N. Aiyar and said, "I was wondering whether you were bringing some doll. He is looking at me and smiling." After holding the child, Bhagavan was about to return him to N. Aiyar, when his daughter ran up to Bhagavan and, showing a red mark on the child's abdomen, said, "There is this red mark on the child. Further he had *Brahma mudi* (literally, knot of Brahma) at the time of his birth." Bhagavan looked at the birthmark and then returned the child. The girl continued and said, "We don't know whether this mark and that knot are good. Mother asked me to ask Bhagavan. Are they good?" Bhagavan was pleased to say, "All is only good" (எல்லாம் நல்லது தான்). I consider these people extremely lucky and I believe all will be well with this child in his life. Bhagavan further remarked, after the child was returned and was seated on his grandmother's lap, "It is to attain the state of this babe that all *yoga* is performed. This babe, what thoughts has it now. It does not even blink its eyes." Then the child's mother began singing M.V.R.'s *Saranagati* song. Bhagavan turning to G.V.S. said, "Do you know what happened to this girl? She was living at Cawnpore on the second or third floor and, though there was a tap, it seems water would not flow up there. But she turned the tap and sang this song and then water flowed, it seems. That is a *siddhi*. When the father went to her, she said, 'I will show you a miracle' and repeated the performance before him."

When the birthmark was shown and there was talk about it, Bhagavan said, "I too have a red mark on the sole of my right foot. But the mark on this child's abdomen is big." Then T.S.R. said, "Mr. Ramaswamy Iyer has sung that Bhagavan's feet had become red on account of the burning tears shed at His feet by devotees and another writer has described the red mark as the anklet (*pada chilambu*) mark of Nataraja."

Vasudeva Sastri recounted another incident, which he had seen:

"One day, when we were at Skandasramam, I was aghast to find a scorpion climbing up over Bhagavan's body in the front and another at the same time climbing down his back. I was terrified and wanted to do something. But Bhagavan remained calm, as if nothing happened, and the two scorpions, after crawling over his body as if over a wall, eventually left him. After they left, Bhagavan explained to us, 'They crawl over you just as they would crawl on the floor or a wall or tree. Do they crawl over these, stinging as they go? It is only because you fear them and do something that they fear you and do something in return'."

6-10-46

This afternoon Bhagavan spoke of his days at Pachaiamman Koil, when he had to remind the office to send a reply to a relation of Rangachari (who used to go to Bhagavan daily in those days, and remained with him, during the plague scare, at the above Pachaiamman Koil). Bhagavan said, "On account of plague, the whole town was completely evacuated for six months. There was a staff of about two hundred people who went on daily disinfecting house after house and they lived in two camps, one of about one hundred and fifty near Chetti Kolam Koil and another of fifty at the other end of the town. I stayed at Pachaiamman Koil, with two or three others. The disinfecting staff used to go to me frequently. They said they were going to organise a *bhajana* at the end of their stay and that I should attend it. I did not say I would not go, thinking their proposed *bhajana* might not come off at all. But one night, suddenly, a party of thirty or forty people with torches in their hands came up to us, after we had gone to sleep, and woke us up. I asked, 'What is the matter?' Then they revealed that the *bhajana* had been arranged, that everything was ready and that I should go with them. I could not say 'No' when so many of them came like that, and so I went. They had made elaborate arrangements. So many lights, so many eatables, so many garlands and musicians of repute sent for from various places. They had arranged a seat for me and another platform for those who were to do *bhajana*. They garlanded me. All the people in the town were there. All the benches and chairs also were there. Several of the people assembled there were also drunk and so they were all in high spirits. I remained with them for some time and then took leave and came away. Some of them again came back with me with their torches and left me at Pachaiamman Koil and returned."

T.S.R. then asked, "It seems Bhagavan once had a dream and saw so many *siddhas* assembled before him, that they looked all familiar to him and that he sat there on a dais with *chinmudra*." Bhagavan replied, "Is that the only thing? I have seen several such visions. What am I to say?" He continued, "Once I came across a *sunai* (spring in a cave); I went towards it. As I approached, it was getting wider, and there were trees on either side. It became broader and broader. There was good light and the passage led to a big tank. In the middle of the tank was a temple." I asked, "This was not a dream?" Bhagavan said, "Whether it was a dream or *jagrat* (waking), call it what you like." (Somasundaram Pillai says the words Bhagavan used were கனவோ, காட்சியோ). Bhagavan also recounted that after he came here, within the last six years or so, he saw huge streets, lined with imposing houses on either side leading to the Asramam; that Chadwick and others were following him in that dream, and Bhagavan asked Chadwick, "Can anyone call all this a dream?" and that Chadwick replied, "Which fool will call all this a dream?" At that stage, he woke up. When Bhagavan distinctly calls this a dream and the previous experience he leaves to others to call, dream or waking, I am led to believe that the other vision of the tank and temple was in the waking or some other stage, which was not dream.

Mr. T.V. Krishnaswami Aiyer asked, "Were Bhagavan's brother and others aware of Bhagavan's absorption in the Self and indifference to external things?" Bhagavan said, "Yes. They could not but be aware. For though I tried my best to appear as if I was attending to external affairs, I could not succeed fully in the attempt. I would sit down to read like others, open a book, pretend to read it and after some time turn the page. Similarly, after some time I would take up another book. But all knew that my attitude had changed. They used to make fun of me for this abstraction of mine. I never took offence, as I was totally indifferent to their taunts. This encouraged them to go on with their mockery. If I was so minded, I could have silenced them all with one blow. But I did not care at all. After the 'death' experience I was living in a different world. How could I turn my attention to books? Before that, I would at least attend to what the other boys repeated and repeat the same myself. But afterwards, I could not do even that. At school, my mind would not dwell on study at all. I would be imagining and expecting God would suddenly drop down from Heaven before me."

Someone asked Bhagavan whether he deliberately went in for a study of *Periapuranam*. Thereupon Bhagavan said, "No. No. It was a mere accident. A relation of mine, my uncle, was given the book by a swami who was living near our house and was advised to read it. Thus the book happened to be in our house and, coming across it, I looked into it first out of curiosity and then, becoming interested, read the whole book. It made a great impression on me. Before that, the sixty-three images of the Nayanars in the temple were mere images and no more. But afterwards, they gained new significance for me. I used to go and weep before those images and before Nataraja that God should give me the same grace He gave to those saints. But this was after the 'death' experience. Before that, the *bhakti* for the sixty-three saints lay dormant, as it were." Mr. Somasundaram Pillai asked Bhagavan, "With what *bhava* did

Bhagavan cry before those images? Did Bhagavan pray he should have no further birth, or what?" Bhagavan replied, "What *bhava*? I only wanted the same grace as was shown to those saints. I prayed I should have the same *bhakti* that they had. I knew nothing of freedom from births or bondage."

8-10-46

This afternoon, a visitor asked Bhagavan, "No doubt the method taught by Bhagavan is direct. But it is so difficult. We do not know how to begin it. If we go on asking, 'Who am I?' 'Who am I?' like a *japa*, with 'Who am I?' for *mantra*, it becomes dull. In other methods, there is something preliminary and positive with which one can begin and then go step by step. But in Bhagavan's method, there is no such thing, and to seek the Self at once, though direct, is difficult."

Bhagavan: You yourself concede, it is the direct method. It is the direct and easy method. When going after other things, alien to us, is so easy, how can it be difficult for one to go to one's own Self? You talk of 'Where to begin'. There is no beginning and no end. You are yourself the beginning and the end. If you are here and the Self somewhere else, and you have to reach that Self, you may be told how to start, how to travel and then how to reach. Suppose you who are now in Ramana Asramam ask, 'I want to go to Ramana Asramam. How shall I start and how to reach it?', what is one to say? A man's search for the Self is like that. He is always the Self and nothing else. You say 'Who am I?' becomes a *japa*. It is not meant that you should go on asking 'Who am I?' In that case, thought will not so easily die. All *japas* are intended, by the use of one thought, the *mantra*, to exclude all other thoughts. This, *japa* eventually does for a man. All other thoughts, except the thought of the *mantra*, gradually die and then even that one thought dies. Our Self is of the nature of *japa*. *Japa* is always going on there. If we give up all thoughts, we shall find *japa* is always there without any effort on our part. In the direct method, as you call it, by saying ask yourself 'Who am I?' you are told to concentrate within yourself where the I-thought (the root of all other thoughts) arises. As the Self is not outside but inside you, you are asked to dive within, instead of going without, and what can be more easy than going to yourself? But the fact remains that to some this method will seem difficult and will not appeal. That is why so many different methods have been taught. Each of them will appeal to some as the best and easiest. That is according to their *pakva* or fitness. But to some, nothing except the *vichara marga* will appeal. They will ask, 'You want me to know or to see this or that. But who is the knower, the seer?' Whatever other method may be chosen, there will be always a doer. That cannot be escaped. Who is that doer must be found out. Till that, the *sadhana* cannot be ended. So eventually, all must come to find out 'Who am I?'. You complain that there is nothing preliminary or positive to start with. You have the 'I' to start with. You know you exist always, whereas the body does not exist always, *e.g.*, in sleep. Sleep reveals that you exist even without a body. We identify the 'I' with a body, we regard the Self as having a body, and as having limits, and hence all our trouble. All that we have to do is to give up identifying our Self with the body, with forms and limits, and then we shall know ourselves as the Self that we always are.

The visitor further asked, "May I believe that there is nothing more to be known now, so far as the technique of *sadhana* is concerned, than that which has been written in your books from time to time? This question arises from the fact that, in all other systems of *sadhana*, the *sadguru* unfolds some secret technique of meditation to his disciple at the time of initiation or *diksha*, as it is called."

Bhagavan: There is nothing more to be known than what you find in books. No secret technique. It is all an open secret, in this system.

Visitor: If, even after God-realisation, one has to pay attention to his bodily needs such as hunger, sleep, rest, heat and cold, of what use is Self-realisation? This state is something, which cannot be called completeness.

Bhagavan: What will be the state after Self-realisation? Why should you bother about it now? Attain Self-realisation, and then see for yourself. But why go to the state of Self-realisation? Even now, are you without Self? And are all these things, eating, sleeping, etc., without or apart from the Self?

9-10-46

This morning, Nagamma read out her Telugu account of the Jubilee celebrations which appeared in the journal *Navodaya*. Last evening a European lady and gentleman arrived here, with an introduction to Bhagavan from Mr. D.S. Sastri. About 2-30 p.m. today, the lady came and sat in the hall along with other ladies and had her legs stretched out in front of her and opposite Bhagavan. T.S.R. went to her and quietly told her that it was not quite good form here to sit like that before Bhagavan; and she folded her legs. Bhagavan was greatly annoyed at this and rebuked T.S.R. saying, "Why this mischief (சேஷ்டை)? It is difficult for them to squat at all on the floor like us. Why should you make it more difficult by imposing further restrictions?" After saying this, Bhagavan added, "Now, my conscience pricks me that I am having my legs stretched out in front of all." So saying, he drew in his legs, folded them and kept on like that till 4-45, when he rose as usual.

10-10-46

This morning, after his usual stroll, Bhagavan arrived in the hall about 7-35 and, sitting on the couch, stretched out his legs. But immediately, he drew them back and folded them saying, "I am forgetting", recounted yesterday's incident, and ended, "My conscience pricks me. I cannot keep my legs stretched out in front of all." Still he kept his legs folded. In the afternoon too, he had not forgotten this and was trying to keep to this new resolve of his. But before the evening he relaxed a bit, as all of us entreated him that it should be given up.

This afternoon, Mr. Subba Rao said that some incidents in Bhagavan's life had not at all been recorded in any book so far; for instance, he said, nobody knew that Bhagavan was for some time nude, but he found out by reading Bhagavan's horoscope that he must have been nude for some time. It was then discovered in the Telugu biography the above fact about Bhagavan was mentioned. This led Bhagavan to say, "It is true I was nude for some time in the early days, when I was under the *illuppai* tree in the Temple compound. It was not because I had a *vairagya* that I should have no clothing of any sort. The cod-piece I was wearing used to bring on sores where it touched the skin. When the sore became bad, I threw away the cod-piece. That is all. There used to be an old Gurukkal who for the first time arranged for some regular food for me either by supplying some from his house or by sending the *abhisheka* milk from the temple to me. After I had been nude for about a month, this old Gurukkal told me one day, 'Boy, the Kartigai Deepam is approaching. People from all the 24 districts will be flocking here. Police from all the districts will also be here. They will arrest you and put you into jail if you are nude like this. So you must have a cod-piece.' So saying, he got a new piece of cloth, made four people lift me up and tied a cod-piece round me."

Bhagavan also related today that on the morning of the day after his arrival he had his first meal at Tiruvannamalai. Apparently, he ate nothing at all on the first day. He said, "The next day I was walking up and down in the sixteen-pillared *mantapam* in front of the Temple. Then a Mauni Swami who used to be living in the old days in the Kambathu Ilaiyanar Temple came there from the

Temple. Another Palni Swami, a well-built man with long matted hair who used to do a lot of service, by clearing and cleaning the Temple precincts with the help of a band of *sannyasis*, also came to the sixteen-pillared *mantapam* from the town. Then the Mauni looking at me, a stranger here, being in a hungry and exhausted condition, made signs to the above Palaniswami that I should be given some food. Thereupon the above Palaniswami went and brought some cold rice in a tin vessel which was all black, with a little salt strewn on top of the rice. That was the first *bhiksha* which Arunachaleswara gave me!"

11-10-46

This afternoon, I made Nagamma read out to us all in the hall her account of what Bhagavan had said in reply to Prof. D.S. Sarma's questions on 4-10-46. Mr. Sarma had also sent an account himself of his talk with Bhagavan. We had that also read out. On comparison, I found that what I had already recorded in these pages needed few alterations. Nagamma has recorded all that took place then, including questions which others besides Mr. Sarma put and the answers Bhagavan gave them. In this connection, Bhagavan recollected that he had in answering Sarma quoted "*abhyasakale sahajam sthitim prahurupasanam*" (*Ramana Gita*). (What is *sahaja* state is known as *upasana* during practice). Bhagavan again repeated much of what he told Prof. Sarma and said, "What is obvious, self-evident and most immediate to us, the Self, we say we are not able to see. On the other hand, we say that what we see with these eyes alone is *pratyaksha* (direct perception). There must first be the seer before anything could be seen. You are yourself the eye that sees. Yet, you say you don't know the eye that sees, but know only the things seen. But for the Self, the Infinite Eye (அந்தமிலாக்கண்), referred to in the stanza in *Ulladu Narpadu* (*Reality in Forty Verses*), what can be seen? You want *sakshatkaram*. You are now doing *karam* of all these things, *i.e.*, real-ising these things, regarding as real all these things, making real what is not real. If this *karam* is given up out of your present *sakshatkaram* of the unreal, then what will remain is that which is real or *sakshat*."

This evening, the Polish lady, Uma Devi, arrived with a party of 25 Polish people, mostly girls, from the Kolhapur State, where there is a refugee camp of about 5,000 Poles.

12-10-46

This afternoon the Polish party entertained Bhagavan with their folk-songs and folk dances.

14-10-46

This morning I told Bhagavan, "Last night, as desired by Uma Devi, I took some of the Polish party round the Hill and on the way explained to them the tradition about the Hill and the various gods of our religion. They said 'How many gods? How can there be so many gods?' Though I explained to them that the same God is worshipped in various aspects, etc., they said they could not understand it all." Thereupon, Bhagavan suggested that they should peruse the book *All is One* which had been translated into English and asked me to find out if typed copies of the English translation were available for being given to them. I brought three copies from the Mauni. Bhagavan gave one to Uma Devi, one to the girls of the party and had the third in his hands. Meanwhile Mr. T.K.S. came there and asked for the third copy and Bhagavan gave it to him. Uma Devi said that she had finished her Polish translation of the *Gita* and that only her introduction and Sir Radhakrishnan's foreword had to be written before the book could be sent to the press.

15-10-46

This morning the Polish party left. This evening Dr. B.K. Roy who has been staying in Ramana Nagar for about a month or more and visiting the Asramam, told Bhagavan that, as desired, he had gone through Zimmer's book, and found that the translation the Asramam had already of a portion of the book was quite good and that he could not improve it, and that the rest of the book contained nothing original of Zimmer but was only a translation of Bhagavan's works. (This Dr. Roy seems to be a Bengali writer, well-read in English and other languages. He is a Doctor of Philosophy who has stayed long in Germany, Switzerland and other places).

16-10-46

This night, the above Dr. Roy took leave of Bhagavan, saying he was leaving the following morning. Mrs. Taleyarkhan also told Bhagavan that one Miss Boman, a Swiss lady who has been here for the last three days, would be leaving tomorrow, and Miss B. made her *namaskarams* and left. (This Miss B., it seems, has been in India for about eight years, at the head of the Baroda palace staff of servants. It seems she does not believe in God, but believes in social service. She has come here having heard of Bhagavan from Mrs. T. when the Maharani of Baroda was staying at Ooty last summer and Miss B. was in the Rani's party. Before coming here she wrote to Mrs. T. "I am coming to see your God and hope I can make him mine too", (or words to that effect).

This night, another Dr. Roy, a blind gentleman, arrived here from Sri Aurobindo Ashram, where it seems Dilip Kumar Roy advised him to come here. It seems he went blind in his seventh year, but has managed, in spite of it, to educate himself so well that till recently he was a lecturer in Calcutta University and is now a lecturer in the Tata Sociological Institute at Bombay. He has married an American wife and, from the picture he has been kind enough to show me and some others here, she is a beautiful woman. He is a very remarkable person. He has travelled all alone from Bombay now. But this is nothing. He has travelled to America,

Japan and other places all alone. When we complimented him on all he has been able to achieve, he says it is nothing compared to what Helen Keller, who lost all her senses at 18 months, has been able to achieve for herself.

This gentleman had a private talk with Bhagavan after 8 p.m. today, when he narrated his eye-trouble and prayed for Bhagavan's mercy.

17-10-46

This morning Dr. Roy showed before Bhagavan how he writes, reads, reads his watch, etc. I have learnt he is a M.A., B.L., of Calcutta University and afterwards became a Ph.D. of an American University. In the afternoon, when I entered the hall about 3 p.m., Dr. Roy was asking Bhagavan, "In the case of persons who are not capable of long meditation, will it not be enough if they engage themselves in doing good to others?" Bhagavan replied, "Yes, it will do. The idea of good will be at their heart. That is enough. Good, God, Love, are all the same thing. If the person keeps continuously thinking of anyone of these, it will be enough. All meditation is for the purpose of keeping out all other thoughts." After some pause, Bhagavan said, "When one realises the Truth and knows that there is neither the seer nor the seen, but only the Self that transcends both, that the Self alone is the screen or the substratum on which the shadow both of the ego and all that it sees, come and go, the feeling that one has not got eyesight, and that therefore one misses the sight of various things, will vanish. The realised being, though he has normal eyesight, does not see all these things." (He sees only the Self and nothing but the Self).

After further discussion with Dr. Roy, Bhagavan added, "There is nothing wrong in seeing anything, this body or the world. The mistake lies in thinking you are the body. There is no harm in thinking the body is in you. The body, world, all must be in the Self; or rather nothing can exist apart from the Self, as no pictures can be seen without the screen on which the shadows can be cast." In answer to a question as to what is the best way to the goal, Bhagavan said, "There is no goal to be reached. There is nothing to be attained. You are the Self. You exist always. Nothing more can be predicated of the Self than that it exists. Seeing God or the Self is only being the Self or yourself. Seeing is being. You, being the Self, want to know how to attain the Self. It is something like a man being at Ramanasramam asking how many ways are there to reach Ramanasramam and which is the best way for him. All that is required of you is to give up the thought that you are this body and to give up all thoughts of the external things or the not-Self. As often as the mind goes out towards outward objects, prevent it and fix it in the Self or 'I'. That is all the effort required on your part. The different methods prescribed by different thinkers are all agreed on this. The *Advaita, Dvaita, Visishtadvaita* schools and other schools all agree that the mind must give up thinking of external things and must think of the Self, or God as they may call it. That is called meditation. But meditation being our nature, you will find when you realise the Self that what was once the means is now the goal, that while once you had to make an effort, now you cannot get away from the Self even if you want."

18-10-46

This afternoon a visitor from Shimoga asked Bhagavan, "How to still the tossing mind?" Bhagavan replied, "Who asks this question? Is it the mind or you?" The visitor said, "The mind."

Bhagavan: If you see what this mind is, it will be stilled.

Visitor: How to see what the mind is?

Bhagavan: What is your idea of the mind?

Visitor: My idea is, it is thought.

Bhagavan: The mind is a bundle of thoughts. But the source of all thoughts is the I-thought. So if you try to find out who this 'I' is, the mind will disappear. The mind will exist only so long as you think of external things. But when you draw it from external things and make it think of the mind or 'I' — in other words introvert it — it ceases to exist.

25-10-46

For the last three or four days, Mr. Subba Rao has been reading out in the hall his *Life of Bhagavan* in Telugu. He has mentioned various new things in this book. One is, that the mongoose which came to Bhagavan when he was on the Hill was golden-coloured. S. also says that Nayana had told him that the mongoose was none other than God Arunachala come to see Bhagavan. Another thing I have not recorded before is found in this *Life* by S. It seems Nayana used to say that dogs cannot long survive contact with a person like Bhagavan whose *granthi* (knot) has been sundered; and that he used to drive away all dogs. In this connection, Bhagavan said, "Yes, he used to drive the dogs away. But there was an exception. It was a dog we used to call Neela. She used to come and always sit on my lap. But she would not allow any other dog, even her own mother or sisters and brothers, to pass beyond the gate of the Skandasramam. Nayana used to say, 'This has been born a dog by mistake'."

S. has also recorded that whatever Nayana said always came true, and cited an event in his own life to prove this.

26-10-46

The morning *tapal* had brought a letter signed Kannan. Bhagavan read the letter but was not sure who wrote it. In the afternoon, he sent for the cover in which it came and from various facts made sure the writer was Mr. Krishnamurti of Madura College, son of Mr. Ranganatha Aiyer. At Bhagavan's suggestion, Viswanath added to a letter that was being sent today to Mr. Ranganatha Iyer, "Tell Mr. Krishnamurti that the 'Kannan' who escaped detection this morning when the *tapals* were read was discovered this evening and brought into publicity."

The following is the English translation of Kannan's letter as made by Mr. T.P.R, and myself the next day:

"Oh Emperor Supreme, Ramana, who rules the world under the canopy of universal sovereignty, seated on the throne of the Heart! That day you graciously said: 'Oh child, you being our beloved son, we bestow kingship on you. Assuming this sovereignty, be you happy!'

"I am seated in the audience hall. There have gathered the Prime Minister, mind, the assistant ministers, *viz.*, the five sense organs, and the heads of executive authority, *viz.*, five organs of action. Before me, they are making noise as they please. They daringly defy my authority. Often and suddenly, they darken the audience hall. If I say, 'Enough. Leave me alone, all of you, and get away', they are indulging in obstructive tactics and say that they will not go. I am having endless trouble. Enough for me, this kingship devoid of power. I have surrendered this kingship unto the Lotus Feet of Ramana who is my father and Master.

"Bhagavan should release me and give his gracious protection or else teach me the secret of sovereignty, granting the necessary power.

"Oh King, Refuge, Refuge, Refuge I-crave.

Kannan.

"You gave me refuge, saying, 'Child, when the bell of extroversion rings, the assembly will gather. In the audience hall, be ever raising the incense of *vichara* or enquiry. Mind, the minister, is a drunkard. Confusing himself with the intoxication of thought, he will keep confusing the assembly as well. This incense of *vichara* will clear the intoxication of thought. The assembly will function in order. As this incense of *vichara* increases more and more, those assembled will take leave. When the bell of 'abidance' rings, mind will finally disappear. All that incense of *vichara* transformed into light, you will abide as yourself, alone and blessed.

" 'Therefore, you should not give up even for a moment this 'Self-Enquiry' of 'Who am I?' With the progressive increase of *vichara, jagrat* and *swapna* will merge in *sahaja nirvikalpa samadhi*. All sleep will become *kevala nirvikalpa samadhi*. The *vichara* will merge in *swarupa*.' "

Prayer

"Ramana, my mother and father, you gave me the sword of *jnana*, termed *vichara*. Grant to this humble self, that has sought refuge at your feet, the necessary desirelessness to lay low and destroy the demon of 'thought' as and when it arises, with determination, and without any pity or compassion.

"Lord, I surrender myself.

Kannan."

Mr. Thiagaraja Iyer, Official Receiver of Madras, who was in the hall, asked Bhagavan, "Is this all imagination, the creation of the writer's fancy, or real?" Bhagavan replied, "We don't know. How can we say anything?" Next Bhagavan asked me to read out an article entitled *Ramana's Grace* which was not in the first edition of the *Souvenir* Volume, but has been included in the second Edition, which arrived here yesterday or so. I read it out accordingly. There, the writer mentions how Bhagavan's grace made him have direct realisation and experience of the Self or the awareness of 'I', in

Bhagavan's hall for some little time, and describes it vividly and in detail. After I finished reading the article, Bhagavan remarked in answer to Mr. T. Iyer's original question, "Now, what are we to say about this? Was it all real or fancy?"

In the evening, after *parayana*, Alamelu Ammal got up and told Bhagavan that she was present at Seshadri Swami's *samadhi*, this morning when the following incident took place. She said, "The party from Coimbatore including the man who says Seshadri Swami is speaking and writing through him on a planchette came to the *samadhi* and found the place locked. They went round the *samadhi* shrine three times and meanwhile Thiruvengadam Pillai, the retired Police constable who is in charge of the shrine, came and opened the temple. Then the Coimbatore party proceeded to say that Seshadri Swami was writing on the planchette which also they had brought with them. There was some writing produced by the planchette. But T. Pillai asked the party, 'Now, tell me what S. Swami told me one day soon after he had a shave and was sitting on the pial of Gurukkal's house.' The party gave some answer. Mr. T. put another question, which was also answered. Thereupon T. remarked both the answers were wrong and that there was no necessity to ask further questions and that he could not believe S. Swami was speaking through them. The party then broke up in disorder."

Bhagavan and the Asramam had been already informed of the intended visit of this Coimbatore party. The party in fact wanted to have our Asramam as their headquarters and carry on their activities from this centre. But the Asramam had declined to allow any such thing. When originally Bhagavan heard from this party that S. Swami was speaking through them, he humorously remarked, "It seems S. Swami is speaking to them. He was well known to us and moved with us all closely. It is a pity he does not come and speak to us."

29-10-46

This morning a letter was received by Bhagavan from Mrs. Noye, Bettie and Mr. K.K. Nambiar, in which Mrs. Noye expressed joy and gratitude for K.K.N. having met her and Bettie at the suggestion of the Asramam, and described how she felt as if Bhagavan was present with her.

About 2-30 p.m. when I went near Bhagavan's hall, T.P.R was outside at the entrance, and told me Bhagavan was being given hot fomentation for some pain on his right hip and that therefore people were not allowed to go in just then. So I waited and went in along with others at about 2-55 p.m. Bhagavan felt that he had caused great inconvenience to the devotees by his attendants having kept visitors out for a few minutes and he remarked, "All these people were kept waiting for half an hour." Bhagavan occasionally gets these pains. Today, it was obvious, the pain was severe. But he made light of it and would not allow anything else to be done for it. He himself took some liniment and was occasionally rubbing it on his right hip. Seeing this, I suggested to friends that we could all clear out of the hall and leave Bhagavan to lie down if he felt like that. But Bhagavan would not allow it. A little later, Dr. Anantanarayana Rao came into the hall, and he offered to massage the part and give some relief. Bhagavan however would not have it and humorously remarked, "It is enough the matter has reached your ears. Your hands need not be employed. I am already feeling better." (This was in reference to our common belief that if we have any trouble it is enough if our complaint reaches Bhagavan's ears). Bhagavan continued to have this pain at intervals till we left the hall at 7-30 p.m.

Alamelu Ammal reported to Bhagavan that the Coimbatore party told her various people spoke to them through the planchette, including our Bhagavan, and that one Kolandai Swami of Madura, deceased, spoke through the planchette and wrote a song on

Bhagavan. So saying, she produced the song and Bhagavan perused it and gave it to T. S. R., saying, "You are the custodian of these songs. Do what you like with this."

Bhagavan remarked, "These *siddhis* won't come to us. No swami comes and speaks to us." When Alamelu Ammal said the party claimed that Bhagavan also spoke through their planchette, Bhagavan said, "Ah, is it so?"

Bhagavan showed Muruganar a cutting from some Tamil paper in which an account had been given of the celebration of Golden Jubilee at Golden Rock on 1-10-46, instead of 1-9-46 owing to the South Indian Railway strike.

30-10-46

This morning Dr. S. Rao, Anantachari and Balaram returned from their trip to Madura and Tiruchuzhi. Dr. Rao had brought with him *dosai prasad* from Alagar Koil near Madura. Bhagavan had several times told us of this *dosai.* That is why Dr. Rao was so particular about bringing it. Bhagavan partook of it with relish and spoke of the days when he used to eat it frequently. Bhagavan was kind enough to make enquiries about Karpoora Bhattar and was glad to hear that K.'s wife in full pregnancy, attended to our party's comforts, etc., and was confined just the day before Balaram left Tiruchuzhi. Balaram said the labour was easy and the child was a female one; and that the lady's mother arrived just in time to assist at the confinement. The morning *tapal* brought a letter from Victoria Doe, saying that she had met Swami Siddheswarananda in London. Curiously, the same post brought a letter from Swami S. saying that he had arrived in India and was in his native place.

1-11-46

Mrs. Taleyarkhan took a lot of pains and arranged for 'Harischandra' a Tamil film to be shown to Bhagavan in the dining hall this night. The show could not be started before 9-30 p.m. and so Bhagavan had to keep awake till 12-30. But Bhagavan sat through it all and I believe he enjoyed it.

2-11-46

Bhagavan looked up Harischandra's story in Tamil and said, "They had abridged the story very much at one place. They did not show how Chandramathi was suspected of having killed the king's son and was sentenced to death for that supposed murder of hers." In the afternoon, Bhagavan was looking into the life of Pundarika in *Bhakta Vijayam*; the Tamil film 'Bhakta Pundarika' was going to be shown this night to him. There is a lot of difference between the story in the book and the film version.

3-11-46

This afternoon, I read out in the hall a letter received from Mr. K.K. Nambiar. Besides describing the air journey which was made at a great height with snow-capped mountains beneath them in the flight, the letter described his meeting Mrs. E. Noye and her sister, how Mrs. E.N. was greatly moved by K.K.N.'s presence, how they all meditated for a while on Bhagavan and how Mrs. E.N. shed copious tears. She was trying her best to come here again.

This night Bhagavan was shown a Hindi film 'Karna'.

4-11-46

Today a letter was received from Mrs. E. Noye, about Mr. K.K.N.'s visit to her and her sister and how they all felt that Bhagavan was actually present with them.

5-11-46

This night the film 'Mira Bai' was shown to Bhagavan.

6-11-46

As it was proposed that tonight the film 'Sivakavi' should be shown, Bhagavan took up *Pulavar Puranam* (Story of the Poets), and read out portions to us. When he came to the stanza in which it is said that the poet fell repenting at Subramanya's Feet and said, "I would not care for you. Still such was your grace that you of your own accord appeared before me, set me right and took me into your grace. How can I thank you for your mercy?" Bhagavan could hardly restrain his tears. He was choked with emotion. I have often observed how such things move him deeply.

Bhagavan is having a very bad cold. When somebody said, "Probably sitting late last night to see the film has affected Bhagavan's health," he said. "No. No. I sat there as I sit here. Part of the time, I was sleeping there. Further, they themselves give so many intervals. Whenever the reel was not moving, I closed my eyes. That gives me sufficient rest. Even if I sit for the whole night like that, it would make no difference to me."

7 to 13-11-46

Bhagavan has been having a bad cold, slight cough and fever for two or three days.

18-11-46

The following was supplied to me by Mr. G.V. Subba Rao. A visitor introduced by T.S.R. asked Bhagavan whether by doing annual ceremonies, etc., to the dead, we can confer any benefit on them. To this Bhagavan replied, "Yes. It all depends on one's belief."

Mr. Somasundaram Pillai's version of the above question and answer is given below:

Question: If such rites as the annual ceremony performed by descendants are able to do away with the karma of the dead, it seems to strike at the root of the theory of karma. For then a man may escape the evil consequences of his bad acts through the help of the rites performed by his sons, etc.

Answer: Such rites only help the deceased to a small extent. It is on the same principle that *prayaschittam* and good deeds are said to mitigate the evil consequences of one's bad actions.

After the visitor went away I asked Bhagavan, "Till three years ago, I was under the impression that doing annual ceremonies to the dead would confer benefit on them so long as they are not reborn." Bhagavan intervened with the remark, "They will receive benefit though they are reborn several times and there is an agency to look after all this. Of course, *Jnana marga* does not say all this." After a while I said, "Bhagavan used to say that if one believes in the existence of this world, one should also believe in the existence of other worlds." Bhagavan said that it was so. I asked, "The *jnani* transcends all stages and he is not bound by any karma (*vidhi* or *nisheda*). The *ajnani* should do his own *dharma* prescribed by *sastras* till he gets *jnana*. But while he is attempting to reach *jnana*, will he be held responsible for the consequences of not doing the ordinary karma or will he be presumed to have done all this karma, just as a person reading in a higher class is presumed to have finished the lower classes?" Bhagavan said, "It depends on the superiority of the path one pursues. Unless a person has finished (in this or previous births) the other paths, he will not pursue the *jnana* path; and he need not bother himself that he has not done the various karmas prescribed by *sastras*. But he should not wilfully transgress the *sastraic* injunctions by doing things prohibited by them."

19-11-46

About 10-30 a.m. today a visitor asked Bhagavan, "The realised man has no further karma. He is not bound by his karma.

Why should he still remain with his body?" Bhagavan replied, "Who asks this question? Is it the realised man or the *ajnani*? Why should you bother what the *jnani* does or why he does anything? You look after yourself." A little later he added, "You are under the impression you are the body. So you think the *jnani* also has a body. Does the *jnani* say he has a body? He may look to you as having a body and doing things with the body, as others do. The burnt rope still looks like a rope, but it can't serve as a rope if you try to bind anything with it. So long as one identifies oneself with the body, all this is difficult to understand. That is why it is sometimes said in reply to such questions, 'The body of the *jnani* will continue till the force of *prarabdha* works itself out, and after the *prarabdha* is exhausted it will drop off. An illustration made use of in this connection is that of an arrow already discharged which will continue to advance and strike its target. But the truth is the *jnani* has transcended all karmas, including the *prarabdha* karma, and he is not bound by the body or its karmas."

The visitor also asked, "When a man realises the Self, what will he see?" Bhagavan replied, "There is no seeing. Seeing is only Being. The state of Self-realisation, as we call it, is not attaining something new or reaching some goal which is far away, but simply being that which you always are and which you always have been. All that is needed is that you give up your realisation of the not-true as true. All of us are realising, *i.e.*, regarding as real, that which is not real. We have only to give up this practice on our part. Then we shall realise the Self as the Self, or in other words, 'Be the Self'. At one stage one would laugh at oneself that one tried to discover the Self which is so self-evident. So, what can we say to this question?

"That stage transcends the seer and the seen. There is no seer there to see anything. The seer who is seeing all this now ceases to exist and the Self alone remains."

23-11-46

A letter was received from Dr. Mees in which he has described all his doings and experiences at Madura and Tiruchuzhi. He says there, besides other things, "I went from the place where the river has joined the ocean (Tiruvannamalai), to the source of the river (Tiruchuzhi), past the place where the river came down as a waterfall to the level of the ocean (Madura)."

24-11-46

Mrs. Chenoy (from Bombay) asked Bhagavan this evening (after reading *Who am I?*) whether it was the proper thing to do if she asked herself "Who am I?" and told herself she was not this body but a spirit, a spark from the divine flame. Bhagavan first said, "Yes, you might do that or whatever appeals to you. It will come right in the end." But, after a little while, he told her: "There is a stage in the beginning, when you identify yourself with the body, when you are still having the body-consciousness. At that stage, you have the feeling you are different from the reality or God, and then it is, you think of yourself as a devotee of God or as a servant or lover of God. This is the first stage. The second stage is when you think of yourself as a spark of the divine fire or a ray from the divine Sun. Even then there is still that sense of difference and the body-consciousness. The third stage will come when all such difference ceases to exist, and you realise that the Self alone exists. There is an 'I' which comes and goes, and another 'I' which always exists and abides. So long as the first 'I' exists, the body-consciousness and the sense of diversity or *bheda buddhi* will persist. Only when that 'I' dies, the reality will reveal itself. For instance, in sleep, the first 'I' does not exist. You are not then conscious of a body or the world. Only when that 'I' again comes up, as soon as you get out of sleep, do you become conscious of the body and this world. But in sleep you alone existed. For, when you wake up, you are able to say 'I slept soundly.' You, that wake up and say so, are the same that existed during sleep. You don't say that the 'I' which persisted during sleep was a different 'I' from the 'I' present in the waking state. That 'I' which persists always and does not come and go is the reality. The other 'I' which disappears in sleep is not real. One should try and realise in the waking state that state which unconsciously everyone attains in sleep, the state where the small 'I' disappears and the real 'I' alone is." At this stage, Mrs. C. Asked, "But how is it to be done?" Bhagavan replied, "By enquiring from whence and how does this small 'I' arise. The root of all *bheda buddhi* is this 'I'. It is at the root of all thoughts. If you enquire wherefrom it arises, it disappears."

Mrs. C. then asked, "Am I not then to say (in answer to my own question 'Who am I?') 'I am not this body but a spirit etc.'?" Bhagavan then said, "No. The enquiry 'Who am I?' means really the enquiry within oneself as to wherefrom within the body the 'I'-thought arises. If you concentrate your attention on such an enquiry, the 'I'-thought being the root of all other thoughts, all thoughts will be destroyed and then the Self or the Big 'I' alone will remain as ever. You do not get anything new, or reach somewhere where you were not before. When all other thoughts which were hiding the Self are removed, the Self shines by itself."

Mrs. C. then referred to the portion in the book (*Who am I ?*) where it is said, "Even if you keep on saying 'I', 'I', it will take you to the Self or reality" and asked whether that was not the proper thing to be done. I explained, "The book says one must try and follow the enquiry method which consists in turning one's thoughts inwards and trying to find out wherefrom the 'I', which is the root of all thoughts, arises. If one finds one is not able to do it, one may simply go on repeating 'I', 'I', as if it were a *mantram* like 'Krishna' or 'Rama' which people use in their *japa*. The idea is to concentrate on one thought to exclude all other thoughts and then eventually even the one thought will die." On this, Mrs. C. asked me, "Will it be of any use if one simply repeats 'I',

'I' mechanically?" I replied, "When one uses 'I' or other words like 'Krishna', one surely has in one's own mind some idea of the God one calls by the name 'I' or anything else. When a man goes on repeating 'Rama' or 'Krishna', he can't be thinking of a tree as the meaning behind it." After all this, Bhagavan said, "Now you consider you are making an effort and uttering 'I', 'I' or other *mantrams* and making meditation. But when you reach the final stage, meditation will go on without any effort on your part. You can't get away from it or stop it, for meditation, *japa*, or whatever else you call it, is your real nature."

27-11-46

In the afternoon, when I entered the hall, Nagamma has just finished reading a Telugu article entitled *Vinnappalu* (Submissions) written by Mr. Venkatachalam (father of Souris), appearing in the Telugu journal *Andhra Silpi*. I requested Mr. G.V.S. to translate it. The gist of it was a complaint that Bhagavan, after enabling Venkatachalam to have a few experiences in the beginning, seems to have grown utterly indifferent and to have completely neglected and ignored him since. The article goes on like a loving child quarrelling with its beloved father or master, and in one portion says, "Do you think I am not aware how necessary I am for you? If I don't have you, I have all this world and its enjoyments with which I could occupy and console myself. But what can you do without the love of your devotees, as you depend solely on such love and devotion?" Some people, including Nagamma, did not like this way of writing. Mrs. Chenoy, for instance, asked, "But, why are you all making so much fuss about this silly letter?" I explained to her that others did not think the letter so silly, that, so far as I could judge, even Bhagavan did not think so, and that other devotees, long before Venkatachalam, have sometimes quarrelled with God, and even abused him for what seemed utter indifference to their urgent supplications, that it was a passing phase in the devotee's life, who would feel remorse at the very next moment, and feel grateful to God for various mercies he has had, and so on. Bhagavan said, "It seems Venkatachalam has written another article in this vein and that Nagamma has seen it. But she has not shown it to me." He asked Nagamma, "Where is that article?" She replied, "I don't know where it is. I have thrown it away." She added that she had shown it to Mauni and that he also disapproved of it. It looks as though Nagamma and Mauni, having gone through the article, decided it was not fit to be taken to the hall for Bhagavan's perusal. But so far as I could judge, Bhagavan wants to see it.

28-11-46

This evening just before *parayana*, a Telugu gentleman wrote a few questions and presented them to Bhagavan. Bhagavan replied to him. The questions in effect were: "They say that *jivanmuktas* are always having *brahmakara vritti*. Would they be having it during sleep? If they have it, then who is it that sleeps in their case?"

Answer: "Of course, the *jivanmuktas* are having *brahmakara vritti* always, even during sleep. The real answer to the last question and the whole set of questions is that the *jnani* has neither the waking, dreaming, or sleeping *avasthas*, but only the *turiya* state. It is the *jnani* that sleeps. But he sleeps without sleeping or is awake while sleeping."

8-12-46

A French official from Pondicherry has been here for two days, and he told Bhagavan that he intended giving up his job and doing some *sadhana* in the spiritual line. As usual, Bhagavan told him it was not necessary to give up one's job or renounce the world or go to a forest, etc., to do any *sadhana*; and that, wherever one might be, and whatever duties one might be discharging in one's office or family, one could still practise *sadhana*. (I was not present at the above conversation. But Mrs. Osborne told me about it).

25-12-46

I was away at Madras from the 13th and returned last night. This evening at about 6-30, our Framji's brother's son, who has been staying here for about a month with his wife and child, came with his party to take leave of Bhagavan, as they intended leaving for Bombay the next morning. Mother and son stood near Bhagavan's feet, and T. S. R. told Bhagavan that the party had come to take leave. The child about three years old went up to Bhagavan, and stood near him close to the grating. Bhagavan graciously took hold of the boy's right arm and shook it and let him go. He went back to his mother and, as they were prostrating, said something to her in Gujarati. Bhagavan asked what it was all about. The mother said, "He is saying Bhagavan did not place his hands on his head and bless him." Bhagavan was surprised at this remark of the child. The mother took advantage of the situation, and told her son to go near Bhagavan. Bhagavan began saying, "I have touched his arm. It is enough." But the child had come up to him and put his head across the grating. Bhagavan touched his head and remarked, "I thought he would be satisfied with my having touched and fondled him. But he persists and wants this."

26-12-46

This afternoon, Colombo Ramachandra put into my hands an article in English, which he had been preparing for the last two or three days, as suggested by our Mauni, to be sent in response to a request for an article from the assistant editor, *Hindu Organ* (English) and *Indu Sadhanam* (Tamil) and asked me to show it to Bhagavan for approval. I showed the article to Bhagavan. But as I found he was not inclined to go through the long article, I offered to read it out to him, and he heartily approved of the idea, saying,

"Yes. Others also can hear it then." Thereupon I read it out. As requested by R., I also gave for Bhagavan's perusal the above letter from the assistant editor, as it contained some personal matter meant apparently for Bhagavan's notice and seeking relief through Bhagavan's grace. I also told Bhagavan that, while the above article was to be sent to the *Hindu Organ*, Uma's Tamil article on Bhagavan written at the time of the Golden Jubilee in September this year, but so far not published, was going to be sent by R. to the *Indu Sadhanam*. Uma has written a new poem for the *Jayanti* on the 7th January and this is also going to be sent to *Indu Sadhanam*.

27-12-46

This night, a gentleman quoting a few stanzas from Tamil works like *Thiruppugazh,* and those of Thayumanavar and Manikkavachakar, wanted to know, whether, as he had been told by a certain teacher of his in interpreting these passages, the proper way to attain salvation was to see to it that the body did not die, drop off from the 'உயிர்' (life) and get destroyed, but that it gradually became less and less and finally vanished merging into the Supreme. The gentleman prefaced his remarks with the submission that he was without eye, *i.e.*, understanding "நயனங்களற்றதோர் ஊர் ஏறுபோலவே" (*i.e.*, like a bull roaming about without eyes) and that he prayed for enlightenment.

Bhagavan asked him, "Have you not got eyes?" He replied, "I want the eye which would enable me to see what is the body and what is the soul."

Bhagavan: You say this. You have a body and you say 'my body', etc. How do you see all this?

Visitor: With the fleshy eye (*oonakkan*). I lead the life of egoism.

Bhagavan: Exactly. So, to see wherefrom this *ahamkara* rises and to go back to its source is the only way. You wanted the way.

This is the only way, to go back by the same way by which you came. You said பெரியோர் போனவழி (the way which the great ones of old trod). They all used only this way. Because you asked 'Which way?', I replied 'The way by which you came'.

The visitor still pointed out that his teacher, basing himself on various texts from the above authors, had taught him that the proper yoga is to see that the body does not die.

Bhagavan: People put various interpretations on the same texts, according to their pet theories. You quote for instance from Manikkavachakar and say he used the way advocated by your teacher, the way in which the soul உயிர் is to be made to leave the body by the tenth gate (and not by the nine gates). Can you point out a single line in that saint's works where the phrase (tenth gate) occurs? You said the great ones used this yoga. What is the *viyoga* (separation) from? Who got that *viyoga*, and who wants to achieve yoga (union) again? That must first be known.

The visitor also asked in the course of his long talk: "How else is the *jiva* (individual soul) to join *sivam* (God), how is the *jivatman* to become one with the *Paramatman*?" Bhagavan said, "We do not know anything about Siva or the *Paramatman*. We know the *jiva*. Or, rather, we know we exist. 'I am' is the only thing that always abides, even when the body does not exist for us, as for instance, when we are asleep. Let us take hold of this, and see wherefrom the 'I' sense or *ahamkara*, as you put it, arises."

The visitor asked Bhagavan, "I am asked to go the way by which I came. Then what will happen?" Bhagavan replied, "If you go, you go away. That is all. There is nothing more. You won't come back. Because you asked 'which way?', I said 'The way you came'. But who are you? Where are you now and where do you want to go, that one may show the way? All these questions will have to be first answered. So the most important thing is to find out who you are. Then all else will be solved."

Mr. T.S.R. found in the visitor's hands a book by his master Thirunagalinga Swami, entitled 'ஆத்ம ரக்ஷாமிர்த ஆதாரக் கட்டளை' and having looked at it for a minute, passed it on to Bhagavan. Bhagavan glanced at its contents for a few minutes, and then returned it. He said, "There has been a school like that which went about saying that he who left his body behind could not be a *jnani* or a perfected being. But all those who said so have also left their body behind at death." The visitor, however, still said, "I prefer to believe literally what is said of a saint like Sundaramurti, that he did not leave his body behind but went on the white elephant sent from heaven for taking him there."

The above is only a poor attempt to give the gist of a long talk between the visitor and Bhagavan.

This evening, another visitor, a young and bright-looking man, Girish Ganapat, read out a long prayer to Bhagavan, which he had composed in English, consisting of about twenty stanzas, and then gave it to Bhagavan. Bhagavan received the same very graciously, after listening to it with appreciative smiles all along. I extract below five out of the above stanzas.

"In search of Truth I wandered;
But found nothing but confusion,
With hopeful eyes, I arrived here,
Expecting light, to avoid illusion.

"Came I and sat at your feet,
Peace and calmness captured self.
In an unseen way, O Lord,
You helped me in your wondrous silence.

"Light of hope cheered me,
I saw my dream succeed,
Oh, see with the sword of stillness
Are cut the veils of darkness.

"Yet, O Lord, my sinful soul
Is not free from old habits.
Hence the help from you, Guru.
Begging I am with eager eyes.

"So will you not help me, O Lord?
Will my childish prayer reach
Thy ear, O merciful Ramana?
And will my veils mysterious drop
By your single ray serene?"

The above young man took a copy of Colombo Ramachandra's article (see under date 26-12-46) and said he was going to make a translation of it into Gujerati and get it published in a Gujerati paper.

31-12-46

A visitor asked Bhagavan, "What is the right conception of life?"

Bhagavan: If you know who wants to have this cleared, *i.e.*, who puts this question, then all will be solved. What is meant by life, by right conception, and who are you?

Visitor: I am a man. I want to know what is the right conception of life so that I may live accordingly.

Bhagavan: Life of man is what is. That which is, is. All the trouble arises by having a conception of it. Mind comes in. It has a conception. All trouble follows. If you are as you are, without a mind and its conceptions about various things, all will be well with you. If you seek the source of the mind, then alone all questions will be solved.

Another visitor asked Bhagavan, "Will not right conduct be enough to secure salvation?"

Bhagavan: Salvation for whom? Who wants salvation? And what is right conduct? What is conduct? And what is right? Who is to judge what is right and what is wrong? According to previous *samskaras*, each one regards something or other as right. It is only when the reality is known, what is right can be known. The best course is to find out who wants this salvation, and in tracing this 'who' or ego to its original source consists all right conduct.

This answer did not satisfy the visitor, and he kept on asking whether doing *nitya karmas* and *sat karmas* will not lead to salvation, as mentioned in books. Thereupon Bhagavan said, "It is said so in books. Who denies that good conduct is good or that it will eventually lead you to the goal? Good conduct or *sat karma* purifies the *chitta* or mind and gives you *chitta suddhi*. The pure mind attains *jnana*, which is what is meant by salvation. So, eventually *jnana* must be reached, *i.e.*, the ego must be traced to its source. But to those to whom this does not appeal, we have to say *sat karmas* lead to *chitta suddhi*, and *chitta suddhi* will lead to right knowledge or *jnana*, and that in its turn gives salvation."

1-1-47

An old lady, a Brahmin widow, was talking to Bhagavan in the hall, recollecting various incidents connected with her family and Bhagavan, during Bhagavan's stay in Virupakshi Cave and Skandasramam. Thereupon I asked T.S.R. who the lady was. He said she was the widow of one Mr. Venkatramier of Madura who stayed with Bhagavan for a long time and was greatly attached to Bhagavan. Thereupon Bhagavan asked me, "Haven't you met him? His photo must be in our groups in the *Life*." I said "No". Then Bhagavan asked T.S.R. to get a copy of the first edition of *Self-Realisation* by B.V.N., took out a group photo (second *Jayanti*) and showed us the above Mr. V. Iyer in that group.

The lady began singing some Tamil songs. Among them were *Ramana Stuti Panchakam* songs. In this connection T.S.R. asked Bhagavan how many times the author of those songs had visited Bhagavan, and where he was now. Bhagavan replied, "He came only once when we were at the Virupakshi Cave. The first four songs, he wrote while he was here, one each day of his stay, and the fifth, the *sadguru* song, he sent after going to his place. He never again came here and we know nothing more about him. The day that he wrote the *kummi* song, Mr. M.V.Ramaswami Aiyar, probably Ramanatha Dikshitar, and others — all crazy chaps (பைத்தியங்க) — joined together at night and sang this song and did *kummi*."

Afterwards the lady began singing a few extracts from Bharati's 'Kannan' song. She began 'பிழைக்கும் வழி சொல்ல வேண்டுமென்றால்'. At once, Bhagavan asked the lady, "Do you know Alamelu? She used to sing this song." The lady replied, "Yes. I know. It is through her I got acquainted with this song", and continued her song.

I was going through a book on Ma Ananda Mayi, recently received by the Asramam. On pages 127-129 of the book the question is put as to whether she is to be deemed to be in the super-conscious state, knowing all, when she speaks in the ordinary way of the world, asking her disciples when they came, whether they have had their food, or how their family was, etc. She replied that in that super-conscious state there could be no conversation and no duality in fact; and that when she converses, she does so like other persons, and not with all knowledge. But she added, "There is another state when whatever I tell any particular person will be true." I asked Bhagavan what was this state and what was its name. Bhagavan said, "I don't know what they mean by it. Some are able to see what is hidden by time or space. But that is among the *siddhis* so called, and nothing to do with *jnana* or Liberation of the Perfected Being."

4-1-47

This afternoon T.S.R. was pasting, in the file opened for 1947, a copy of Uma's song printed for the coming *Jayanti*, with

Colombo K. Ramachandra's song at the top. Nagamma asked Bhagavan, "Has the song been printed? How has it been done, on a single sheet or as a folder?" Bhagavan replied, "It has been done as a small folder with K.R.'s song on top," and asked T.S.R. to show it to N. In this connection, Bhagavan told T.S.R., "K.R. has not put his signature to the song, but has subscribed himself as 'A devotee'. You may perhaps note down there 'K.Ramachandra' to indicate who the author was for any reference in the future."

Later, Bhagavan told me, "R.'s article has appeared in *The Sunday Times.*" Bhagavan asked me to read it out for the benefit of all. R. had referred to *siddhis* as 'sub-normal powers'. With Bhagavan's approval, I corrected it into 'supra-normal powers'.

GLOSSARY

Abhaya : State of fearlessness; offering shelter to one who seeks refuge.

Abheda : Without difference.

Abheda buddhi : Concept free from ideas of difference.

Abhishekam : The sacred bath of water, milk, curd, etc., given to a deity.

Abhyasa : Practice.

Abhavam : Non-existence; absence.

Adhama : Inferior.

Adi : Beginning.

Advaita : Non-duality; no-otherness.

Advaitic : Pertaining to advaita.

Advaitin : One who believes in non-duality.

Aham : I; the ego.

Ahamkaram : Ego-sense.

Aham vritti : The 'I' thought.

Ajnana : Ignorance; nescience.

Akasa : Space; ether; sky; Brahman.

Ananda : Bliss.

Ananya bhakti : Whole-hearted devotion.

Angushtha-pramana: Of the size of the thumb.

Anta : The end.

Antaryami : The controller within us. God.

Anugraha : Blessing; grace.

Anupallavi : Sub-refrain of a song.

Apachara : Sacrilege.

Arati : The waving of lights before a sacred image.

Archana : Offering flowers to a sacred image.

Arupa manas : Mind which has no form or concept.

Asariri : Without body; a celestial voice.

Asat : Non-existence.

Ashta Dik Palakas: Protectors of eight quarters.

Ashta lingam : Eight lingams.

Ashta Vasus : Celestial beings who are eight in number.

Asti : Exists.

Asuric : Demoniac.

Atma : Self.

Atma-sakshatkaram: Perceiving (realizing) the Self directly.

Avadhuta : An ascetic who has given up everything including his clothes.

Avastha : State, especially the state of waking or dream or sleep.

Avatar : Incarnation; descent of God in a worldly form.

Avidya : Ignorance; nescience.

Aviyal : A South Indian preparation in which several kinds of vegetables are used.

Avyabhicharini bhakti: Bhakti which does not change from one object to another.

Bhagavat-Bhakta: One who is devoted to Bhagavan (Vishnu).

Bhajan : Singing devotional songs in chorus.

Bhakti : Devotion to a personal God.

Bhakti marga : The spiritual path of devotion to a personal God.

Bhakti rasa : The joy of bhakti.

Bhati : Shines, manifests, is aware.

Bhava : Feeling ; emotion.

Bheda bhava : A sense of separateness.

Bhiksha : *lit.* The food offered to begging ascetics in charity; a feast given to ascetics and other religious persons.

Bhoga Kshetra : A place of enjoyment.

Bhu : A sacred and symbolic syllable called a *vyahriti*.

Bhuvar : A sacred and symbolic syllable called a *vyahriti*.

Bindu : A dot; in yoga the dot over OM.
Brahmacharya : The first stage of life, the stage of the student.
Brahmajnana : Realization of Brahman.
Brahmakara vritti: Concept of the form of Brahman.
Buddhi : Intellect.
Chaitanya : Consciousness; sentience.
Chakora : A mythical bird which is to feed only on rain water.
Chakra : A yogic centre in the body.
Chalana : Movement.
Charanam : The body of a song.
Charya : Regular observance of rites.
Chattram : A place of free lodging for pilgrims and travellers. Sometimes food is also provided free.
Cheetah : A small leopard.
Chembu : A small round water pot made of brass or copper.
Chidabhasa : The reflected consciousness; the jiva.
Chidakasa : The akasa or ether or space in the heart; Brahman.
Chinmudra : The hand-pose indicating illumination.
Chiranjivi : One who lives for ever.
Chit : Consciousness.
Chit-Jada-granthi: The knot which ties the sentient (Self) and the inert (the body).
Chitta suddhi : Purity of mind.
Daharakasa : The tiny akasa; A term applied to the Self which is realized in the Heart.
Daivic : Godly; divine.
Darshan(a) : Seeing a holy person or image.
Dasara holidays : The ten days devoted to the worship of the Universal Mother.
Deham : Body.
Dehatma buddhi: The idea that the body is the Self.

Deva : A celestial being.
Dhoti : A long piece of cloth tied round the waist.
Dhyana : Meditation; contemplation.
Diksha (deeksha): Formal initiation of a disciple by the Guru.
Dosai prasad : Prasad (Offering to God) consisting of *dosai*, a pancake made out of rice and blackgram.
Drishti srishti : Perception followed by creation.
Dvaita : Duality.
Dvaitic : Pertaining to dvaita.
Dvaitin : One who believes in duality.
Eka chintana : Concentrated thinking.
Ekagra bhakti : Complete devotion to one.
Ganjira : A tabor-like musical instrument.
Gayatri : A well-known Vedic mantra.
Giri Pradakshina: Going round the Hill.
Gokulashtami : The eighth lunar day on which Sri Krishna was born.
Gos(h)ala : A place where the cows are kept.
Gottuvadyam : A stringed musical instrument.
Grihapravesam : House warming.
Grihasta : One who is in the second stage of life, that of a householder.
Guna : Quality; mode.
Guru stuti : Praise of the Guru; verses in praise of the Guru.
Harikatha : A religious discourse interspersed with devotional songs.
Hasta diksha : Spiritual initiation in which the Guru places his hand on the head of the disciple.
Hastamalaka(m): An amalaka fruit in the hand.
Hatha yoga : A form of yoga involving difficult bodily postures.
Homa : Sacrifice offered in the sacred fire.

Idam : This, usually applied in Vedanta to the world.

Ishta devata : The deity whom one desires to worship or contemplate.

Isvara : God.

Isvara maya : The maya (delusion) produced by God.

Isvaravadi : One who expounds the doctrine of a personal God.

Jada : The inert.

Jagrat : The waking state.

Japa : Repetition of a sacred word or syllable or the name of God.

Jada : Matted hair.

Jayanti : The birthday of a God or a holy person.

Jibba : A long, loose shirt without collar and cuffs.

Jiva : The individual.

Jivanmukta : One who is Liberated while alive.

Jivatman : The individual self.

Jnana : Knowledge; Wisdom; Enlightenment.

Jnanottara Bhakti: Bhakti which follows Jnana.

Jutka : A carriage on two wheels drawn by a pony.

Jyoti : Effulgence.

Jyoti maya : Full of effulgence.

Kainkaryam : Service rendered to God, the Guru, etc.

Kalakshepam : A religious discourse interspersed with songs.

Kali yuga : The last of the four yugas (aeons).

Kamandala(m) : A receptacle for holding water used by ascetics and generally made out of the shell of a large coconut.

Kanji : Gruel.

Kashaya : Taint; impurity.

Kattalai : Offerings made to a temple at regular times by a devotee.

Kayakalpa	:	A medicinal preparation for longevity.
Kirtan	:	A devotional song.
Koham	:	Who am I?
Kripa	:	Mercy.
Kripa drishti	:	Look of mercy or grace.
Kriya	:	An act.
Kshetra	:	A field; a place; the body.
Kshira sagara	:	The ocean of milk in which Vishnu lies on a serpent with a thousand hoods.
Kummi	:	A song which accompanies a kind of rustic dance.
Kumkum(am)	:	Vermilion applied to the forehead, generally by women.
Kundalini	:	The mystic circle of three and a half coils situated in the umbilical region. The yogic principle of Serpent power. The Primordial Maya.
Kuvalaya	:	The lotus.
Laya	:	Dissolution; absorption.
Lila	:	Sport.
Lingam	:	Symbol; the symbol of Siva.
Lingamaya	:	Full of lingas.
Madhu	:	Honey; enjoyment.
Madhu Vidya	:	The name of a spiritual and esoteric practice.
Madhwada	:	One who enjoys the good and bad things in the world; the jiva.
Madhyama	:	Middling.
Maha Prana	:	The important life-force.
Manana	:	Reflection on what has been heard.
Manas	:	Mind.
Manasa japam	:	Japam done mentally.
Mangalam	:	Auspicious.
Manigar	:	The person in charge of an institution.

Mano nasa	:	The extinction of the mind.
Mantapam	:	A raised platform of stone covered over with an ornamental roof supported by pillars.
Manthi	:	A grown up male monkey.
Mantra	:	A sacred word or words supposed to have spiritual potency.
Mantra japam	:	Repetition of mantra.
Mantramaya	:	Full of mantra.
Marundu	:	Medicinal preparation.
Mattu Pongal day	:	The day on which the cows are venerated.
Mauna (mowna)	:	Silence.
Mayavadi	:	One who expounds the doctrine of maya.
Megha	:	Cloud.
Megha mandala	:	A bank of clouds.
Mithya	:	Unreal; false.
Moham	:	Delusion.
Moharrum	:	A Muslim festival.
Moksha	:	Liberation.
Mridangam	:	A small drum which is struck with the fingers of both the hands and used in South Indian Musical Concerts.
Mudra	:	Pose of the hands.
Mukta	:	One who is liberated.
Mukti	:	Liberation.
Muladhara	:	The name of the lowest Yogic chakra or centre.
Mumukshu	:	One who desires to be Liberated.
Nada	:	Sound; in yoga the sound represented by OM.
Nadi	:	River.
Nadi	:	Yogic nerve.
Nadi horoscope	:	A system of astrology.
Naham	:	I am not the body.
Naivedya(m)	:	Food offered to a God at the time of worship.

Nakshatra : A star; an asterism.

Nama : Name.

Nama smarana : Repetition of the name of God.

Navami : The ninth lunar day.

Nididhyasana : Uninterrupted contemplation.

Nirvikalpa samadhi: Samadhi in which all differences between the individual self and Brahman cease to exist.

Nishkama karma: Action done without a selfish motive.

Nitya karma : The daily rites which are obligatory.

Niyati : Law; rule; established order.

Om(kar) : The sacred syllable which represents Brahman.

Padaiveedu : A temple or shrine built on the site of a battle fought by gods with demons.

Padmasanam : The lotus-posture of sitting for meditation.

Pakva : Fit; proper; mature.

Pallavi : Refrain in a piece of music.

Paramatma(n) : The Supreme Self; Brahman.

Parayana : The chanting of the Vedas.

Pathasala : A school, especially one in which boys are taught to chant the Vedas.

Pipal : A sacred tree; the *ficus religiosa*.

Poli : A North Indian preparation made of wheat flour fried in ghee.

Pongal : A South Indian preparation made of rice, pulses, nuts, ghee, etc.

Pongal Prasadam: Pongal offered to God.

Pooran poli : A North Indian sweet preparation.

Pradakshina : Going round a sacred object or person.

Prakara : The paved yard surrounding the shrine in a temple.

Prakriti : Nature; compound of the three gunas, satva, rajas and tamas.

Prana : Life-force; the vital airs, breath.

Pranayama : Regulation or control of breath.

Prarabdha : That part of one's karma which has to be worked out in this life.

Prasad(am) : Food distributed to devotees after it is offered to God, the Guru, etc.

Pratyaksha : Direct; immediate.

Pravritti : Activity.

Prayaschittam : An expiatory act.

Priyam : Bliss.

Puja : Ceremonial worship with flowers, water, etc.

Punarvasu : The name of an asterism.

Punya : Merit; the result of a good deed.

Puranas : Ancient poems containing mythological stories, legends, etc.

Purusha : Man; the Self.

Purushottama : The best of men; an epithet of God.

Ramamaya : Full of Rama.

Sadhana : Spiritual practice.

Sadhu : An ascetic; a sannyasin.

Sadguru : The Self-realized Guru.

Sahaja samadhi : Samadhi which is natural and constant.

Sahaja sthiti : Natural state.

Sadhak(a) : An aspirant; one who follows a spiritual discipline.

Sahasrara : The lotus of the thousand petals; the topmost yogic centre situated in the head.

Sakshat(kara) : Direct perception.

Sakti : Power; Energy.

Samasanam : *See* Sama asraya.

Sama asraya(m) : Vaishnava method of initiation.

Samkalpa : Idea, concept; imagination.

Samsara : Cycle of births and deaths.

Samskara	:	impression.
Samudra(m)	:	Ocean.
Sanchitakarma	:	Karma which has been accumulated in former lives and which has not yet taken effect.
Sandal	:	A fragrant paste made by rubbing a piece of sandalwood on a rough and moist stone.
Sandhi	:	Conjunction, especially of syllables and words.
Sannyasa	:	Asceticism; the fourth stage of life.
S(h)anti	:	Peace; tranquillity.
Sastra	:	Scripture; a science.
Sannyasi	:	An ascetic; a person belonging to the fourth stage of life.
Sariram	:	Body.
Sat	:	Existence; being.
Satavadhana	:	Attending to various things at one and the same time.
Sat Karma	:	Good or meritorious acts.
Sat sang	:	Contact with good or pious persons.
Satakam	:	A poem of one hundred stanzas.
Satvic	:	Good; wholesome; possessing the quality of satva.
Satya yuga	:	The first of the four yugas (aeons).
Siddhi	:	Supernatural attainment.
Siva lingam	:	The symbol of Siva which is an object of worship.
Sivanamavali	:	Repetition of the names of Siva.
Sloka	:	A stanza in Sanskrit poetry.
Soham	:	I am He.
Sphurana	:	Manifestation.
Sravana	:	Hearing, especially the sacred truth.
Srishti	:	Creation.
Srishti drishti	:	Creation followed by perception.
Sruti	:	That which is heard or revealed; inspired words, generally applied to the Vedas.

Sthalapurana : The legend of a sacred place.

Sthapati : An architect of temples and other sacred structures.

Sthitaprajna : One who is stable in intelligence; a Self-realized Sage.

Stotram : A hymn of praise.

Suddha manas : Pure mind; mind without concepts.

Sukshma : Subtle.

Sukshma sarira : The subtle body.

Sushumna nadi : A yogic nerve.

Sushupti : The state of deep and dreamless sleep.

Sushupti ananda : The bliss experienced in sushupti

Sutra : Aphoristic words or phrases.

Suvar : A sacred syllable known as a vyahriti.

Svabhavasthiti : Natural state.

Svanubhava : One's own experience.

Svarga loka : The world of the Personal God.

Swarupa : Nature; form; Self.

Taila : Medicated oil.

Tapal(s) : Mail; the post.

Tapam : Heat.

Tapas : Austerities; severe spiritual discipline.

Tapasvi : One who performs tapas.

Tapasya : *See* Tapas.

Tat : That; Brahman.

Tattwa : Truth; significance.

Thai : The name of a Tamil month corresponding to the middle of January to the middle of February.

Thai poosam : The day on which the moon is in conjunction with the asterism Pushya in the Tamil month of Thai.

Thengalai : A sect among the Vishnu Worshippers.

Thevaram : Songs composed by important Tamil Saints which are venerated like Vedas.

Tithi : A lunar day.

Tope : A grove of trees.

Triputi : A triad like knower, known and knowledge.

Tulsi : A sacred plant.

Turiya : The fourth state which is beyond the three states of waking, dream and dreamless sleep.

Turiya ananda : Bliss experienced in the state of turiya, the fourth state, Brahman.

Turiyatita : Beyond turiya, the fourth state beyond waking, dream and dreamless sleep.

Upades(h) : Spiritual instruction.

Upadhi : An adjunct.

Upadhi ananda : Bliss which is caused by an adjunct.

Upasana : Contemplation of a deity or word or syllable like Om.

Uppuma : A South Indian preparation made of semolina or broken rice.

Uttama : Superior; the best.

Vadai : A South Indian preparation of blackgram dough which is fried in oil.

Vaikasi : The name of a Tamil month corresponding to the middle of May to the middle of June.

Vairagya : Dispassion.

Varnasrama (dharma): The order of castes and stages of life; the duties pertaining to the several castes and order of life.

Vasana : Inherent tendency.

Vibhuti : Sacred ashes.

Vichara : Enquiry.

Vichara marga : The path of enquiry.

Videha mukti	:	Liberation after death.
Vidya	:	A spiritual and esoteric discipline.
Vikalpa	:	Doubt; wrong concept.
Vikshepa	:	Tossing to and fro.
Vimanam	:	The upper portion of the tower of a temple; a celestial car.
Viparita	:	Contrary.
Viparita buddhi	:	A wrong conception.
Visishtadvaita	:	Advaita in a modified form.
Viyoga	:	Separation.
Vrata	:	A rite; an observance.
Vritti	:	An idea, a thought.
Yajna	:	Ritualistic sacrifice.
Yama	:	Control.
Yama	:	the god of death.
Yathartham	:	Truth; a thing as such.
Yoga nidra	:	Yogic sleep.
Yuga	:	A long period of time consisting of thousands of years (aeons).

INDEX

THE LIFE OF SRI BHAGAVAN

THE TEACHINGS OF SRI BHAGAVAN

A

C

D

E

F

G

K

L

M

N

O

P

Q

R

S

V

W

Y

THE WORKS OF SRI BHAGAVAN

WORKS ON SRI BHAGAVAN AND HIS TEACHINGS

OTHER SCRIPTURES, BOOKS AND MAGAZINES

ANCIENT SAINTS AND SAGES

DEVOTEES AND VISITORS

A

S

T

U

V

W, Y, Z

OTHER PEOPLE

STORIES

SIMILES AND PARABLES

MISCELLANEOUS